CONTENTS

PREFACE

Recently, tech leaders Apple and Google passed Coca-Cola as possessing the most well-known and second most well-known trademarks in the world.[1] Information technology (IT) companies' shares now represent 16 percent of the total capitalization of shares on U.S. securities markets and in that, as well as in other respects such as employment, are growing.[2] In rough terms, IT's market capitalization is equivalent to 16 percent of 127.2 percent of $18.86 trillion (estimated 2016 U.S. gross domestic product), or $3.84 trillion.[3] That valuation, for one industry alone, exceeds the total gross domestic products of France ($2.59 trillion) and the United Kingdom ($2.65 trillion), and rivals Germany's. U.S. IT's market capitalization trails only Japan's and China's GDPs.[4] Information technology deems itself "the emerging center of the world," and rightly so.[5]

Yet tech is the most backward of major industries in promoting women to leadership positions or positioning them for future ascension into executive positions. Even lower down in the ranks, the number of women tech companies employ has declined from 37 percent of employees in 1995 to 24 percent today (2016), with prognostications that the number will decline further, to 22 percent or lower in the next decade.[6]

Higher up, in leadership ranks, as revealed in compensation tables that companies file with the Securities and Exchange Commission (SEC), women account for only 5 percent of the most highly paid tech company executives (see chapter 1). The underrepresentation of women—and the lack of diversity overall—is stark and noteworthy.

Furthermore, despite awareness of the issues involved within the industry, the situation does not improve. Jodi Kantor of the *New York Times* titled her 2014 in-depth study "A Brand New World in Which Men Ruled: Instead of Narrowing Gender Gaps, the Technology Industry Created Vast New Ones."[7]

By way of comparison, women constitute 19.2 percent of directorships in large corporations generally, 19 percent of Congress, 21 percent of

Fortune 500 general counsels, and 26.4 percent of college and university presidents.[8]

In information technology, of those women in executive positions, a supermajority of them have law degrees (JDs) or master's degrees in business administration (MBAs), leading one to question the headlong push for STEM (science, technology, engineering, and mathematics) education for women. Or, at least, educators should consider modifying the STEM emphasis in ways more conducive to assumption of leadership roles.

I had originally planned to title this book *The Boo List and the Paradox*, referring to what had attracted me to the subject in the first place, namely, that while only 5 percent of senior executives in tech are female (the "boo list"), compared with 25 percent for U.S. public companies generally, twelve large IT corporations have had female CEOs (the paradox). But the present title helps in better answering the question early reviewers posed: "Who is the audience?" Throughout, the book emphasizes that the audience is the industry and companies within it. In contrast, the books on the market today, especially emerging over the last two decades, are all first and foremost advice and "how-to" books for aspiring women. A recent leader in that regard, featured on the cover of *Time* no less, was Sheryl Sandberg's *Lean In* (2013).[9] Chapter 8 lists many of those "how-to" and advice books for women.

A second set of books on diversity in information technology aims at educators and academic institutions, telling them what they should do to encourage and train girls and young women. Chapter 6 reviews certain of those.

But few authors—maybe none—have written extensively about a third subject, what the industry and individual companies within it might do.[10] Those who do write about the area have given the industry a free pass. It's high time for observers, pundits, and scholars to turn the spotlight on the corporations themselves. With the illumination so provided, finger pointing—indeed, a significant amount of finger pointing—is in order. What can and should the industry and companies within it be considering, evaluating, and possibly adopting to solve this social and economic problem, one with significant ramifications for tech businesses and their shareholders?

A question that seemingly always arises is, Why women? Betty Friedan's *The Feminine Mystique* appeared in 1963.[11] Germaine Greer published *The Female Eunuch* in 1970.[12] Bella Abzug, "Battling Bella," reached the House of Representatives in 1970.[13] Soon after, once the women's movement had taken root, leaders of business and corporate boards made statements and promises on the equality of women in their organizations, promises that nearly fifty years after have only partially been fulfilled in some instances, and not at all in others. The issue has been with us for a half century, but another group of leaders and spokesmen, uniformly men, continue to ask the "Why women" question, over and over again.

Although not a primary subject for this book, there are a number of reasons to encourage diligent efforts to include more females on promotion ladders and in senior positions:

> *Role Models within Organizations.* Women as directors and senior managers serve as important role models to the manifold numbers of women lower down in today's workforces, including 50 percent of the middle managers who today are female.

> *Avoidance of Excessive Risk.* The near-death economic experience of 2008-2009 taught the perils of excessive risk and the disregard of sustainability considerations. Women are more aware of and in tune with risk. They are better judges of risk. Christine LaGarde, managing director of the International Monetary Fund, said it well, remarking that "if Lehman Brothers had been Lehman Sisters," the august financial firm would still exist.[14]

> *Role Models in Broader Contexts.* Today, in stark contrast to forty years ago, young women play sports of all kinds, attend university, go on to graduate and professional schools, become physicians, scientists, accountants, and lawyers (50 percent of the students in U.S. law schools are women), and obtain MBAs (40 percent of the students in graduate schools of business are women). Women who reach the highest levels in business are important role models for our daughters and for succeeding generations of women.

> *Avoidance of Groupthink.* A cast of managers, all or mostly all male, who share common backgrounds, is less likely than a diverse one to ask probing questions or raise objections. The social data support the proposition that the presence of gender diversity is a safeguard against groupthink and its perils.[15]

> *Economic Common Sense.* Global theorists contrast those nations in
which women do not work, say Pakistan, with similar countries in which
women work, achieve, and reach positions of influence and power,
say, India. Adjusting for differences in countries' respective sizes, the
gross domestic product of the latter greatly exceeds the gross domestic
product of the former, its neighbor. Theorists go on to attribute much
of the difference to the inclusion of women in the labor force and in
leadership.[16]

There are many more reasons given for increasing the number of
women on boards of directors, in the C-suite, and in senior management.[17] One reason that is unquantifiable but ubiquitous is the promise
that boards of directors and corporations have held out to women for a
larger and more meaningful role in corporate affairs, promises they have
made but not always fulfilled for decades now. As Eleanor Roosevelt
said years ago, "A woman is like a tea bag, you never know how strong
it is until it's in hot water." It's time corporations, especially in the tech
industry, live up to the promises they have made and to find out just how
right Mrs. Roosevelt was.

A further question is, Why women? in the sense of a field for study.
Twenty years ago, when I began studies on diversity in corporate governance and management, I intended to explore multiple aspects of the
diversity question: nomination, election, and appointment of African
Americans and Latinos, as well as of women. I sent a phalanx of law students out to research aspects of SEC filings, including proxy statements
and compensation tables. The students found the task difficult, if not impossible. They could not, for instance, readily identify who was African
American from either first names or surnames, while they could identify
females from their first names. I then truncated the diversity studies to
the subject of women as corporate directors or senior managers. Later,
students in my diversity seminar such as Dan Garcia have researched the
subject of Latino directors of public companies. By and large, though,
while recognizing the immense importance of the subject, I leave it for
another day.

I wrote the first treatise in the United States about legal and business aspects of corporate leadership, *Corporate Governance* (1993).[18] I
have authored several other law/business books about corporate gov-

ernance.[19] For a number of years, I co-taught the corporate governance offering at the University of Melbourne School of Law in Australia as well as from time to time here at the University of Pittsburgh. As a consultant, I have conducted a number of daylong governance workshops for boards of publicly held companies. On the subject of women's role in corporate governance, I have authored two of the best-known books: *No Seat at the Table: How Governance and Law Keep Women Out of the Boardroom* (2007),[20] and *The Last Male Bastion: Gender and the CEO Suite in America's Public Companies* (2010).[21]

Women on corporate boards and in executive positions have become front-burner issues in many countries on the Pacific Rim. The issue has acquired much currency in Europe since Norway adopted a 40 percent quota law in 2003.

The book is an attempt to marry extensive scholarly and hands-on involvement with corporate governance with what I know or can learn about one particularly pressing problem, namely, the dearth of women in leadership roles in an important industry, information technology. The focus is on what companies could do. That is the audience, as opposed to women themselves, or educators and educational institutions, or academics who regard themselves as experts in the field.

Reviewers, especially academic ones, wish to see tome-like treatises, laden with statistics, studies, critiques of other studies, and long narratives based upon interviews. Those were the books of the 1980s and 1990s. They were by academics at leading institutions such as Harvard, Carnegie Mellon, MIT, or the University of Minnesota, to name a few. Laudatory as they may be, those books have not moved the needle. The number of women in tech and in leadership roles in information technology companies has not advanced. Indeed, as journalist Jodi Kantor of the *New York Times* has pointed out, evidence exists to maintain that the number is declining. Most of all, though, 200,000- and 300,000-word treatments have become obsolete. The Internet has rendered them so. Any deeper one wishes to go, or any ammunition one wishes to gather for counterargument, is available with a few keystrokes. It's "in the cloud," accessible via the Internet.

In her latest book, Stanford professor Deborah Rhode chronicles the progress that corporations have made on the diversity front, noting that we now "confront second generation problems of equality that involve not deliberate discrimination but unconscious bias, in-group favoritism, and inhospitable work-family structures."[22] Information technology, however, remains largely mired in first-generation problems, those of the pinups on the firehouse wall era. Rampant objectification of women, inhospitable and hostile environments, inequalities in pay for comparable work, tokenism, imposition of stereotypes, and other evils of the past still bedevil information technology companies.

I wish to thank my assistant, Patty Blake, for her help in getting the manuscript to the publisher. I also wish to thank Eric Lowe, University of Pittsburgh, JD 2013; Katie Hopkins, JD 2014; Chad Ostrosky, JD 2016; and Michael Roche, JD 2017, for research assistance in preparation of the book. Above all, I wish to thank Linda Tashbook, a reference and international law librarian here at the University of Pittsburgh, for her help and support along the way. Many individuals at New York University Press lent a hand in preparing the manuscript for publication, including Clara Platter, Amy Klopfenstein, Betsy Steve, Ciara O'Connor, and Dorothea Stillman Halliday.

Pittsburgh, Pennsylvania, January 5, 2018

PART I

THE CONUNDRUM

1

INDUSTRIES THAT DO NOT HIRE OR PROMOTE

There are many reasons why the information technology industry belongs at the top of a list of industries that do not promote and, in many instances, do not hire women for important jobs. I denominate as "the boo list" a ranking of industries and of companies within those industries according to the extent to which they do not hire and do not promote women. Among major industries, information technology is last at integrating women into leadership roles, senior management, and even middle management positions. Information technology, then, represents the perfect storm of gender imbalance.

Externally, telltale signs of information technology's less than lackluster performance include the following:

> In this day and age, a high-profile information technology company, Facebook, went public in a long-awaited public offering. Among the controversies surrounding the offering was that Facebook went public without a single woman on its board of directors.[1] Only two of Facebook's first fifty employees were women, and women remained exceedingly scarce as the company matured.[2] When asked why his board had no women, Facebook's Mark Zuckerberg shot back, "I'm going to find people who are helpful, and I don't particularly care what gender they are."[3]

> A short while later, another high-profile information technology company, Twitter, went public with no women board members, having learned nothing from its predecessor's ham-fisted misstep.[4] A business journalist pointed out that women and men use Twitter almost equally.[5]

> Then the CEO of IT giant Microsoft, Satya Nadella, belittled women employees in tech and "set off a storm about the wage gap" between women and men.[6] When asked why tech companies pay women 10 to 25 percent less for comparable work, Mr. Nadella replied, "It's not really about asking for a raise but knowing and having faith that the system

will reward you the right raises as you go along." "It's not good karma" for women to ask for raises.[7] In other words, in Mr. Nadella's opinion, there is no wage gap. Women employees make less because they contribute less: if their contributions were equal, his and other companies would have recognized that in pay envelopes (does anyone receive their pay in an envelope anymore?).

> Early in 2017, the Department of Labor (DOL) sued both Oracle and Google over perceived payment disparities between men and women employees. The DOL's initial reviews "found systematic compensation disparities against women, pretty much across the board," at both IT companies.[8]

Not only IT leaders have tin ears on the subject of diversity. Widely acclaimed, even worshipped, CEO Warren Buffett has caused his company, Berkshire Hathaway, to proclaim, "Our nominating committee does not seek diversity, no matter how defined."[9] At a more mature Facebook, with a market capitalization of $300 billion, only one of the fifty highest-paid executives, as opposed to the first fifty employees in earlier years, is female. That executive, chief operating officer Sheryl Sandberg, author of *Lean In*, is famous in her own right (see chapter 8).

Overall, Catalyst, the advocacy group for women in business, reports that women hold 20.2 percent of the seats on large cap (Fortune 500) companies' boards of directors, up from 9.6 percent in 1997, 15.7 percent in 2010, and 16.6 percent in 2012.[10] Catalyst further reports that women hold 23 percent of senior-level manager positions and 39.2 percent of management positions overall at S&P 500 corporations.[11] By contrast, the Forte Foundation, a Texas-based consortium of corporations and business schools that encourage women to enter business careers, pegs the first number at 14 percent.[12]

Whatever statistic the reader finds credible, the 2015 Lean In and McKinsey & Company's *Women in the Workplace* "concluded that we were 100 years away from gender equality in the c-suite."[13] In information technology, the outlook is not so good—and in fact is much more daunting.

To complete the summary, and by way of further contrast, women occupy 45 percent of the board seats in the not-for-profit sector, a significantly higher number. At the largest not-for profits, including health care providers, United Way organizations, museum complexes, arts groups, and other large organizations, women occupy 37 percent of the board seats, more than double the proportion in business corporations.[14]

The Landscape

Those overall percentages are aggregate figures. If we look at specific industries we find that, at least several years ago, near the bottom in terms of numbers of female directors was the retail drug industry, a grouping of companies "in the business of large-box (or medium-box) retailing in which many items (not just drugs) are sold and a majority of the shoppers are women."[15] CVS, Walgreen's, Rite Aid, and Long's Drugs all had but a single woman on their boards of directors.[16] Near the bottom also was the airline industry, "a consumer-oriented industry with a large female employee group." Media corporations, financial services companies, and, surprisingly, grocery store chains performed very poorly in naming women to their boards of directors.[17]

In 2017, however, the worst industry in its treatment of women, at least in recruitment and retention of them as directors, was information technology, including development and sale of computer hardware and software:

> Nine [information technology] corporations [in the Fortune 500] had six women directors out of seventy-eight. . . . Four large publicly held corporations [had] no women directors at all. Apple Computer and Steve Jobs [sold] iPods and computers for purchase by women and mothers but [had] no women on their board.[18]

That was the negative picture at the top, with the inescapable message to women lower down in those organizations that, at least at the apex of the pyramid, "good ole boys" were still in control.

A Changing Landscape

But there is a more encouraging picture, one that has changed over time. Twenty-five or thirty years ago the prevailing advice to women aspiring to careers in business was to avoid altogether certain predominantly male industries, say, electric utility companies, oil and gas ventures, or paint and chemical entities. Engineers and cost accountants were thought to rule the roost in those quarters. Further, the standard view was that those in power (the engineers and the accountants) would not be receptive at all, either not hiring women or being hesitant in the extreme about giving women added responsibilities or promoting them. All that seems to be changing. Many industries and corporations once thought to be inhospitable to women now seem to excel in offering opportunities for female hiring and advancement. Thus, although the advice might not be for everyone, women with certain backgrounds (science, engineering, finance, accounting) and a bit of moxie may discover the fastest track to be the one only recently thought to be a dead end, including obscure and remote postings.[19]

A number of women who have reached the top, becoming chief executive officers (CEOs) of Fortune 500 companies, have followed this pattern:

> Paula Rosput Reynolds, CEO of Safeco Insurance, after a career spent in public utilities.
> Lynn Good, CEO of a public utility holding company, Duke Energy.
> Kimberly Lubel, CEO of another utility company, Sempra Energy.
> Ellen Kullman, CEO of a paint and chemicals company, Dupont de Nemours, capping a career at that company.
> Susan Ivey, who had a successful career at the helm of a tobacco company, Reynolds American.
> Her successor as CEO of Reynolds (now to be acquired by British Tobacco), Susan Cameron.
> Patricia Woertz, an executive with Gulf Oil and then Chevron, and still later with Texaco, who became CEO of Archer Daniels Midland, our largest agribusiness corporation.
> Mary T. Barra, CEO of automotive giant General Motors.
> Marillyn Hewson, CEO of defense and aerospace corporation Lockheed.
> Phebe Novakovic, CEO of another defense firm, General Dynamics.
> Lynn Elsenhans, CEO at Sunoco, a leading East Coast refiner and retailer of petroleum products.
> Kathleen Mazzarella, CEO of electrical products and supply firm Graybar Electric.[20]

Reaching beyond industries in which women have had some success—that is, marketing, retailing, or food products—we see that women have achieved success in places where they would not have gone thirty years ago. Other women have counterprogrammed in other ways. "The times, they are changing."

Dreary, Unchanging Landscapes

But not everywhere. And certainly not in information technology.

The financial services sector shows little change. Only 12.5 percent of executives at banks and other publicly held financial services entities are women, compared with the Catalyst finding of 23 percent in the Fortune 500 overall. "Finance has long been dominated by (white) men, whose testosterone flows freely and machismo is never more than two or three cubicles away."[21] Much worse is the transportation sector. Securities and Exchange Commission (SEC) Regulation S-K, Item 502 provides that companies reporting to the SEC must include in proxy statements and annual reports filed with the SEC (10-Ks) a compensation table. The table must show the total compensation (salary, bonuses, present value of stock options, other cash benefits, etc.) of the five highest-paid executive officers in the organization. Reviewing the compensation tables of seventeen publicly held transportation companies reveals that only 7.1 percent of the listed most highly compensated executives (six of eighty-five) are women.[22] Changing the experimental group slightly, the Dow Jones Transportation Index basket of twenty companies is nearly the same: 7 percent, that is, only seven of the hundred highest-paid executives are women.[23]

The transportation sector, however, does not top the list. The industry that tops that list and whose record in hiring and promoting women is truly deficient, and that regards itself as a cutting-edge industry, at the very center of the twenty-first century, is information technology.

A Census

Appendix A contains a list of 127 information technology companies whose shares are publicly traded and information is therefore available. Of the entities on the list, 110 are domiciled in the United States.

Examination of the compensation tables of those 110 companies shows that, excluding the women CEOs, 30 women, out of a total of 550 executives, or 5.5 percent, number among the highest-paid officers and executives in the sector.[24]

If the array of companies surveyed is broadened to include the sample's 17 foreign IT companies that have a U.S. presence (a stock exchange share listing: China, with five, and Bermuda, Canada, England, France, Germany, India, Ireland, Israel, Netherlands, Taiwan, and Singapore, with one each), the numbers increase to 36 women and 635 potential positions. The percentage of women in executive positions increases slightly, from 5.5 percent to 5.66 percent.[25]

Other statistics are available, for example, from the Clayman Institute for Gender Research at Stanford University or in the National Academy Reports of the National Science Foundation.[26] Those statistics, though, focus on the industry's employment of women overall. They do not attempt to derive a snapshot of women in leadership roles.[27]

The information technology sector ranks last as well in the percentage of its directors who are female: "just 8.4% of Silicon Valley companies have women directors, one of the lowest averages," compared with the Catalyst finding of 20.2 percent overall.[28] So the information technology industry waddles onward, not at all improved from its earliest days, at least in terms of promoting women to senior executive positions and to board of directors' seats. Information technology is through and through a male-dominated industry. You would think it would be different.

Venture Capital and Sand Hill Road

Much of the foregoing moved to a central place on the national stage with a legal case involving not an information technology company but a close relative. That relative was a leader of the venture capital industry, housed figuratively if not literally a stone's throw from Silicon Valley, on Sand Hill Road in Palo Alto, California. On Sand Hill Road sits the headquarters of the king, and the platonic form as well, of venture capital firms, Kleiner Perkins Caufield & Byers. There, Kleiner Perkins reigns, the monarch among a strip of other West Coast venture capital firms that populate the Sand Hill Road neighborhood. Kleiner Perkins provided much-needed startup capital to (and shared greatly in the outsized success of) Amazon, Google, Yahoo!, Netscape, and others.[29] By virtue of the appreciation in the value of the firm's investments, a partnership in the Kleiner firm has been the pathway to fantastic riches. Kleiner is the best-known, preeminent VC partnership.

Historically, however, women have found venture capital firms as chauvinistic as companies in the tech industry itself. One early female staffer at Facebook penned a note of her impressions: "[The VCs] had an obvious predilection for boys who looked like younger versions of themselves. I could see that as a woman, I would automatically appear alien."[30]

Despite that alleged mindset, Kleiner hired Ellen Pao in 2005, putting her on the partnership track by naming her a junior partner. Accomplished to a degree seldom seen, Ms. Pao had obtained a bachelor's degree in electrical engineering from Princeton University, followed by both MBA and law degrees from Harvard University. Ultimately, however, Kleiner never admitted Ms. Pao to partnership. Further, in 2012, the firm dismissed her after she filed suit against Kleiner for denial of partner status, alleging sexual discrimination and a hostile work environment. She brought a suit in the California Superior Court asking for $16 million in damages.

As the case proceeded toward the trial phase, Ms. Pao's lawsuit received daily news coverage, along with editorial commentary, in the national press. The case brought to the forefront "long-simmering concerns about the treatment of women in Silicon Valley."[31] The case "launched a wide-ranging discussion about how women are treated in Silicon Valley." Even though Ms. Pao eventually lost her court case, "some said that the trial remains a rebuke to Silicon Valley's male-dominated culture and a warning sign to other technology firms."[32] Disgruntled female employees filed similar suits against Facebook and Twitter, among others.

The Evidence

Testimony revealed that Ms. Pao had an affair with a male Kleiner partner, Ajit Nazre. After Ms. Pao ended the affair, Mr. Nazre retaliated by dropping Ms. Pao from lists for critical meetings, also seeing that email chains generally dropped Ms. Pao's name from the address list. Ms.

Pao also had persuaded Kleiner's partners to invest in a startup, RPX, for which, as part of her job, she had been the point person. In such a scenario, the Sand Hill Road and venture capital tradition is that the point person receives a seat on the startup's board of directors, where the VC representative acts as the eyes and ears of the VC partnership.[33] Kleiner, though, nominated a male partner, Randy Komisar, to the RPX board instead of Ms. Pao, later justifying its choice on grounds that Mr. Komisar "needed a win."[34] The firm denied that the firm's nomination of Mr. Komisar rather than Ms. Pao evinced discrimination on the basis of sex.

There were other allegations in Ms. Pao's case, coupled with proof to back them up. Evidence included a male manager's gift to Ms. Pao of a book of erotic poetry (*The Book of Longing*), male partners' discussion of porn stars in Ms. Pao's presence, and all-male ski trips from which the males excluded Ms. Pao. The sum total was to shine a harsh light on the "boys' club" and fraternity row antics that women in technology have complained about for years.

Despite the damaging reputation that venture capital had mistreated women for years, the firms took no corrective action. The representation of women in venture capital firms had not gone up; instead, the percentage of women in the industry actually had declined, from 10 percent in 1999 to a meager 6 percent in 2010. Against that background, and with proof of actual discrimination and a hostile environment, Ms. Pao nevertheless lost her case against Kleiner Perkins.[35]

Fallout

Broader lessons were learned from the *Pao* litigation, though, or so interested observers thought:

> "Ellen's experiences rang true. They struck a chord" (Freada Klein, chair, Kapor Center for Social Impact).
> "The order she has shaken up concerns the Valley itself and the clubby way of doing things in a place that fancies itself as the center of the world" (Farhad Manjoo, *New York Times*).
> "'It would be crazy' for anyone to think that performance was determinative of promotion and pay. The standard at Kleiner was conveniently

fuzzier and subjective: the ability to fit into 'Team KP' and provide thought leadership" (Margaret Carlson, Bloomberg News).[36]

> The venture capital industry seemed to have learned nothing. A 2016 survey of seventy-one venture capital firms found that only 8.2 percent of the firms had female investment managers. Many firms had none at all.[37]

> On the receiving end of VC activity, women do poorly as well. They receive "hardly any" venture capital investment. Women-led firms contribute to "fewer than 1.2 percent of the IT patents and 1.2 of open source software programs."[38]

Of course, there were naysayers. In the *Wall Street Journal*, guest columnist Heather MacDonald characterized Ms. Pao's suit as a "feminist vendetta against Silicon Valley." To Ms. Macdonald, information technology is "America's most vibrant economic sector ... [with a] ruthlessly meritocratic culture. Ms. Pao had a female chip on her shoulder"; the jury's verdict against her was "a triumph of common sense."[39]

Predicting the Future

What is the takeaway from *Ellen Pao v. Kleiner Perkins Caufield*? One prediction is that the case will not have the effect advocates for women once predicted. Some believe that a supermajority of Silicon Valley males, including those who hold the reins of power, share Heather MacDonald's views. "Many men in the Valley genuinely believe that their company is a meritocracy. They think that the gender problem is something that happens somewhere else."[40]

As an industry, information technology also continues its efforts to make an end run around any deficiencies in hiring, training, or promoting women. Instead, in order to remedy the anemic state of the information technology workforce, the industry and its lobbyists seek to drastically expand the H-1B visa program (see chapter 15). Under their vision of the future, the industry must have the ability to bring into the United States 180,000 software engineers, computer science specialists, programmers, and system planners yearly. The industry would recruit and hire, mostly from India, and all or mostly all of the hires would be male, emigrating here for three-year initial tours, which more often than not stretch toward permanence. The industry gives little or no thought to hiring and training women, who after all are already here in the United States, in order to fill the gaps at many companies and throughout the industry.[41]

In its 1970 biennial conference, the American Civil Liberties Union (ACLU) took particular note of the need to increase gender diversity in our society. The ACLU must, the conference recommended, "take affirmative and vigorous action . . . to increase significantly the representation of women on all policy making bodies and committees," both internal and external to the ACLU. The ACLU itself "had underutilized the potentialities and talents of women."[42] The ACLU as well as numerous other organizations, industries, and corporations recognized that imperative a half century ago. Apparently, the information technology industry has not.

2

THE PARADOX

Actually, a close examination of the information technology field reveals that there are several paradoxes:

> A cutting-edge industry, information technology "fancies itself the emerging center of the world,"[1] America's most vibrant economic sector. Together, information and U.S. ingenuity "made the modern world."[2] Yet, as an industry, information technology is the caboose in hiring women. Information technology also is the caboose in promoting women to senior management positions. And information technology is the caboose in appointing women to positions on corporate boards of directors.

> Who would have thought that a West Coast–based conglomeration of computer software, computer hardware, and venture capital firms, in the main based in California, where attitudes are enlightened and inclusiveness the order of the day, would have such a poor record on diversity issues?[3] The claim that "American culture starts in California and moves east" does not hold true for information technology, at least in terms of the hiring and promotion of women.[4]

> Yet another paradox is that information technology, while comprising enterprises that universally exhibit an informal, relaxed, nonconformist attitude toward dress, work habits, and other characteristics, has such a poor record and seeming bias toward women in the workplace. "You might think that at a place where [employees] bring their dogs to work, wear jeans, and play football, there would be little tolerance for man-terrupting, all-male social events, or telling women to take the notes at a meeting." But those and similar signs of a lack of socialization predominate, as they do in "boys' clubs" or college fraternities, generally indifferent or inhospitable to women.

Some of the Silicon bravado is over-the-top. As one entrepreneur and board director described it,

Silicon Valley is entrepreneurship on steroids. Companies scale here like nowhere else. . . . Everything is magnified. . . . Many personalities (on boards and in the C-suite) are bigger than life. . . . In Silicon Valley, people are encouraged to swing for the fences and to "dent the universe," as Steve Jobs used to say.[5]

The most intriguing paradox of all, though, may jump out at you. No fewer than twelve large cap, prominent information technology companies have or have had female CEOs:

> Carleton Fiorina, CEO at Hewlett-Packard.[6]
> Anne Mulcahy, CEO at Xerox.
> Patricia Russo, CEO at Lucent Technologies (later Alcatel).
> Meg (Margaret) Whitman, CEO at eBay.
> Ursula Burns, Anne Mulcahy's successor as CEO of Xerox.
> Virginia Rometty, CEO at International Business Machines (IBM).
> Lisa T. Su, CEO at Advanced Micro Devices (AMD).
> Carol Bartz, CEO at Autodesk.
> Meg Whitman, CEO at Hewlett-Packard.
> Carol Bartz, CEO at Yahoo!.com.
> Safra Catz, co-CEO at Oracle.
> Marissa Mayer, CEO at Yahoo!.

A Benefit of Women at the Top: The Trickle-Down Theory

With women in the ascendancy, the pathways for women to board positions and upper management should multiply, the theory goes. Commentators refer to this as the "trickle-down effect" or the "talent rationale."[7] Many feel that "female CEOs . . . will be particularly sensitive to women's concerns."[8] A 2015 Pew Research Center survey found that 71 percent of women "believed that having more women in leadership positions in business . . . would improve the quality of life for all women."[9] Having a woman at the top should correlate well with an increase in women directors and managers. The theory has intuitive appeal. Former secretary of state Madeleine Albright supported the theory with the much-acclaimed statement, "There's a special place in hell for women who don't help other women."[10]

Although the sample is small, the overall record of women as CEOs of large companies (not in information technology) confirms the theory. The evidence in support of the trickle-down theory, across a spectrum of companies and industries, seems robust:

> At Avon Products, [with] Andrea Jung as CEO, four women were directors. The same was true at Sara Lee, with Brenda Barnes as CEO and three women directors. . . . PepsiCo, with Indra Nooyi as CEO, had three women among ten directors. Marion Sandler, as CEO of Golden West Financial, presided over a board with four women directors.[11]

And the trickle-down trend continues. Thanks to its CEO Sheri McCoy (now departed), Avon Products now has seven women on an eleven-person board. With women CEOs, the following corporations have three or more female directors on their boards: General Motors, DuPont, International Business Machines, PepsiCo, Xerox, Hewlett-Packard (before the split), Frontier Communications, and International Game Technology.[12]

The further case is that a trickle down would replicate itself among the executive ranks, and not only in boardroom seats, should a woman become the CEO of a corporation.[13] Anecdotal evidence supports this claim as well. "For example, since Susan Ivey became CEO at tobacco company Reynolds American [RAI], the company has appointed 19 women to officer positions and four of the top seven corporate officials [were] women. Four of the seven highest officials at the company are women."[14] Moreover, Ms. Ivey's successor as RAI CEO, who also is a woman, Susan Cameron, has followed in Ms. Ivey's footsteps.[15]

The Trickle-Down Effect in Tech

In information technology, the evidence, such as it is, is mixed. A tendency exists for some women in leadership roles not to give a leg up, or a hand, to other women lower down in the organization, believing that subordinates should "do it themselves." Moreover, certain of the female senior managers have been outspoken about beliefs of the latter sort. For example, on one hand, while Patricia Russo was CEO of Alcatel-Lucent, she saw to it that three other women joined her on the board of directors. In stark contrast, Carleton Fiorina, for six years CEO of tech giant Hewlett-Packard, took no interest in advancing the careers of female subordinates, making a point of publicly proclaiming her stance.

On the *Today Show*, Ms. Fiorina proclaimed to the interviewer and the audience that her gender had never held her back. "I have spent a lifetime believing that the most important thing is to focus on what's inside the package."[16] Ms. Fiorina vehemently denied the existence of any such thing as a glass ceiling, stressing that "a competitive industry cannot afford sexism." Ms. Fiorina flatly refused the title "role model for women."[17] She told a *New York Times* reporter, "I hope that we are at the point that everyone has figured out that there is not a glass ceiling."[18] Confirming the views that she expressed, there is no evidence of any trickle down whatsoever during Ms. Fiorina's six years at the helm of HP.[19] "Few women broke into the management ranks under [Carleton Fiorina]: no trickle down occurred."

Yahoo! under CEO Marissa Mayer seemed to have resembled HP under CEO Carly Fiorina. Shortly before taking the Yahoo! position, while Ms. Mayer was the highest-ranking woman at Google, she openly proclaimed, "I'm not a girl at Google, I'm a geek at Google."[20] Then at Yahoo!, when she had become CEO, Ms. Mayer ended work-at-home and telecommuting arrangements that women employees found to be especially valuable when they had child-rearing responsibilities. At nearly the same time, Ms. Mayer had built a childcare center for her own child adjacent to her office. Commentators labeled it "one of the most tone-deaf decisions in recent memory."[21]

In contrast, at Reynolds American under CEO Susan Ivey, a trickle down (a robust trickle down at that) took place. The difference is not due to any specific factor (increased mentoring, elimination of information asymmetries). The difference is due to tone at the top.[22]

Hypothetically at least, then, with women at the helm of a number of information technology corporations, females should have an average or above average representation in management and on boards of directors. They most decidedly do not.

Why not? Is it because, as many in the industry maintain, that as a group women lack the educational background and aptitude to enter the industry in the first place, and thereafter to climb upward through the ranks? Is the underrepresentation of women because, perceiving themselves as "masters of the universe," those in charge of Silicon Valley and Silicon Valley institutions believe themselves too busy to deal with diversity issues or to elevate those issues to a higher place on their agendas? Or is it because CEOs and other opinion makers in the Valley exalt themselves as having Teflon shields that will insulate them from any negative consequences or blowback emanating from their decided lack of attention to the diversity issue?

Unfriendly to Women: The Frat House Ambiance in Tech

A principal factor, one somewhat removed from the CEO suite, that is said to dominate Silicon Valley and information technology companies is the prevalence of what author Katherine Losse has termed "an unrepentantly boyish company culture."[23] Ms. Losse joined Facebook in 2005 as customer-relations manager, at a time when Facebook had fifty employees, all but one of whom were male. On her first day, she confronted a bevy of "young, plain looking guys in T shirts, gazing at their screens, startled—if not displeased—to see a strange new woman in the office."[24] The surrounding Facebook workroom resembled the firehouse wall of forty or fifty years ago: "Much of the graffiti in the room featured stylized women with large breasts bursting from small tops that tapered down to tiny waists, mimicking the proportions of female videogame characters."[25]

Wonder Woman's Return

On the cover of its inaugural issue, in 1972, *Ms.* magazine featured Wonder Woman on the cover. Wonder Woman's appearance heralded the dawn of a new day in which, increasingly, women would be able to enter business, the professions, sports, and most or all other pursuits. In those callings, women would be able to scale heights the likes of which they had never been able to scale before. Yet, historically, Wonder Woman had only one weakness. She would lose her strength if a man were to bind her in chains. Women have gone on to climb many of those rock faces standing before them, perhaps not in the numbers they would have wished but with increasing frequency nonetheless.

Information technology stands in marked contrast to all of that. Have the men who hold the reins of power tied aspiring Wonder Women in chains, or is there some other explanation for this paradox in information technology? In 2017 *Wonder Woman* returned to the motion picture theaters, taking a place among the leaders at the box office. Can Wonder Women throw off those chains that have held them down in the IT industry and at the companies that populate its ranks?

3

QUALIFICATIONS AND RESERVATIONS

Chapter 1, "Industries That Do Not Hire or Promote," paints a negative picture of women's participation in tech industry leadership. Chapter 2, "The Paradox," points out the number of women who have become CEOs (in fact, celebrity CEOs) of large information technology companies, a rosier development. This chapter returns to the dark side. There are a number of reasons to believe that in the future the level of women's participation in the industry may be no better—and, indeed, may be less—than at present. Events of the last decade, such as they are, may represent a high-water mark in female participation in tech. Those reasons include the following:

> *The Glass Cliff Theory.* According to this hypothesis, boards of directors tend to select women to fill CEO positions almost as a last resort, when companies are in extremis. The women so chosen must begin their tenures in far less than ideal situations. As a result, these female CEOs have reduced chances of future success because of the circumstances under which they began their tenures. A last implication of the theory is that women will be chosen for the highest positions only on an episodic basis.
> *Poor Performance by the Current Crop.* Once they have assumed the reins, women as IT CEOs have presided over extended periods of lackluster or declining stock prices, declining earnings, "dumb" acquisitions, little or no "top line" (revenue) growth, declines in the rate of innovation, and failed corporate strategies. The current female CEO crop would include Marissa Mayer at Yahoo! (dumb acquisitions, flat revenues, and the on-again, off-again sale of Yahoo!'s stake in Alibaba, and a near—fire sale to Verizon) and Meg Whitman at Hewlett-Packard (layoffs of large percentages of the workforce and, as a last-ditch effort, split of a large, unwieldy entity into two large, unwieldy, and probably underperforming entities). The poor or lackluster CEO performances,

in some measure attributable to glass cliff circumstances, could lead to reduced selection of women for future CEO vacancies.

> *Poor Performance by the Predecessor Crop.* The first generation of female CEOs in the industry did not set healthy precedents for the women who would follow. Carol Bartz at Yahoo! never was able to project a vision for the company, or, alternatively, her attempts at doing so were screened from view by her use of salty language and abrasive ways. Carleton Fiorina ("Armani Carly") at Hewlett-Packard spent most of her time promoting Carleton Fiorina, meanwhile trashing the iconic HP Way and slashing tens of thousands of jobs. The HP stock price went down, went down further, and stayed there for six years, while Ms. Fiorina presided.

> *The Paucity of Women Rising through the Ranks.* In information technology, women occupy approximately 5 percent of senior management positions, as compared to 23 percent for publicly held companies overall. Just 27 women, more or less, hold top management positions in 110 publicly held U.S. information technology companies surveyed (see appendix A).[1] Extrapolating, only about one in three companies in the industry, or even fewer, has a woman in the top executives' ranks.

The lower ranks of managers (middle management and lower levels of senior management) are where candidates for board positions and the senior-most executive positions will begin to emerge five years from now and ten years from now. In information technology, the "pool" of likely female successors, as compared to female employees among the rank and file, is inordinately small. Down below, in the innards of companies, pickings from the pool are slim, will become slimmer as the years go by, and do not bode well for the future. The "pool problem" is common to—indeed, pandemic in—industry in general, but it is particularly acute in information technology.

> *The "Adult in the Room" Scenario.* Engineers, inventors, and scientists often staff fledging businesses. Historically, that has been triply true for information technology companies, often pictured with employees bringing dogs to work, playing Frisbee (the dogs playing as well), and spending half their time (the engineers, not the dogs) playing video games. At some point, as the enterprises grow, it is necessary to superimpose on the chaos some tenets of modern organizational and business methods, such as having meetings, setting agendas for those

meetings, hashing out strategies, keeping books, and preparing projections and financial statements. Implementing those things has traditionally been thought to necessitate the introduction of "an adult into the room."

The "adult supervisor" at Google was Eric Schmidt, who in 2001 joined Google, "then a young company brimming with intellect but lacking traditional approaches to product development and management."[2] Meg Whitman at eBay, Carol Bartz at Autodesk, and John Sculley at Apple were the adults in the room at their companies.

A school of thought postulates that women managers are adept at filling this role. The skill set thought to be particularly endemic among women managers could provide an enduring space for women in the upper ranks of information technology management, as companies develop, grow larger, and move toward being acquired or conducting a public offering of shares.

The Glass Cliff Theory Revisited

A recent take on gender and corporate governance, from British scholars, is the glass cliff theory.[3] Professors Michelle Ryan and Alexander Haslam posit that corporations are likely to turn to a female for an officer or CEO position when events magnify the risk of failure. Professors Ryan and Haslam found that businesses appoint women to corporate leadership positions in problematic circumstances. Their appointments hence are more precarious than males' appointments. If a woman CEO succeeds, directors and senior executives say, "We expected nothing less." If the woman falls from grace, many, including directors, will say, "I told you so," leaving unstated that failure and the ensuing fall must have been due to her gender.[4]

When we use U.S. Fortune 500 female CEOs as the sample, the glass cliff theory seems to bear up under examination. Patricia Woertz became CEO after Archer Daniels Midland had reached a nadir, with the former CEO's son beginning a term in prison for price fixing on ADM's behalf.[5] In 2004 Susan Ivey, now retired, became CEO at Reynolds American, when the $246 billion settlement with forty-six states and other adverse judicial outcomes had laid the tobacco industry low.[6] Brenda Barnes got the reins at Sara Lee after over-diversification and lackluster returns had driven the company down.[7] Mary Sammons became the CEO of Rite Aid in the midst of deeply troubled times, with former CEO Martin Grass and other Rite Aid executives beginning prison terms and with the share price reduced to a few dollars and cents.[8] The Rite Aid share price was flirting with $1.00 per share, which would have necessitating de-listing by the New York Stock Exchange.

In more recent times, Sheri McCoy left Johnson & Johnson to become CEO of Avon Products, at a time when Avon's share price was in free fall, the company was ensnarled in a government investigation into illegal bribes Avon had paid in violation of the Foreign Corrupt Practices Act, and the door-to-door selling method for which the company had been famous had become outmoded and largely ineffective.[9]

In fact, a near-majority (ten of twenty-two) of the women who had become Fortune 500 company CEOs by 2010 had come to power only when corporations faced uncertain circumstances, or worse. Those women CEOs who came to power in precarious corporate settings include Jill Barad at Mattel; Andrea Jung at Avon Products; Anne Mulcahy at Xerox; Patricia Russo at Lucent; Susan Ivey at Reynolds American; Patricia Woertz at ADM; Brenda Barnes at Sara Lee; Mary Sammons at Rite Aid; Christina Gold at Western Union; and Carol Bartz at Yahoo!.[10]

Facing a Glass Cliff at General Motors

A good example of a glass cliff hire occurred early in 2014 when General Motors appointed to the CEO position Mary Barra, a GM "lifer" who had begun her career as a manager at a GM automobile assembly plant. Her days at GM had begun even earlier than her employment. She received her bachelor's degree at General Motors Institute (now Kettering University). Her father, a die maker, had been a lifelong GM employee.[11]

Within days of her appointment, Ms. Barra had to face an expanding imbroglio involving a fatal ignition defect in Chevrolet Cobalts and other GM automobiles. The defect had been the subject of a long-standing cover-up that went on as scores of operators of GM cars were severely injured. Deaths of an estimated 124 persons were attributed to the long-standing, and uncorrected, defect.[12] Ms. Barra claimed, quite genuinely, to be taken completely by surprise, as her first weeks and months as CEO were preempted by the all-consuming need to respond to the growing scandal.[13] One can infer that those in the know at GM knew of the impending storm and that insiders put at least a thumb on the scale in the process leading to Mary Barra's appointment as CEO.[14] The glass cliff phenomenon has explanatory power in the United States as well as in Great Britain, where it originated.

The Glass Cliff in Information Technology: Recent Cases

Does the glass cliff hypothesis have power to shed light upon the appointment of women as CEOs in information technology? A good case can be made that eight of the twelve women who became CEOs of tech companies did so under circumstances described by the glass cliff theory.

Marissa Mayer at Yahoo!: Women's groups and other lauded Ms. Mayer's appointment as CEO at Yahoo!, where she received a five-year "hello package" of $100 million in salary, guaranteed bonuses, and retention awards.[15] Her task, emblematic of the glass cliff theory, was to resurrect "a once great bloated and struggling Internet company."[16] While "2011 revenue per average employee was $1.4 million at Facebook and $1 million at Google, . . . at Yahoo it was $316,000." Only just inside the front door, Ms. Mayer would face the daunting task of reducing in size Yahoo!'s 15,300-person workforce.[17]

Before Yahoo!, Ms. Mayer had a successful career at Google, being employee number 20, and Google's first female product engineer.[18] Much more publicized was that Ms. Mayer was the first pregnant woman a board of directors appointed to a CEO position at a major U.S. public company. She gave birth to a son a few months after her appointment. Later she became the mother of twin daughters.[19]

Very soon Ms. Mayer became the target of criticism from both inside and outside the company. Inside, a well-equipped nursery/day care center soon materialized adjacent to the CEO suite, leading to criticism of Ms. Mayer as among the wealthy and powerful elite whose success was backed up by having "hot and cold running nannies."[20] Other women at Yahoo!, as well as women managers at other companies, did not have the benefit of on-site day care, or at least convenient on-site day care, the way Ms. Mayer had, which her critics were quick to point out.

Outside Yahoo!, matters were less than auspicious for Ms. Mayer from the get-go, as the glass cliff theory would predict. First, she was the sixth CEO in three years, after Jerry Wang (the founder), Tim Koogle, Terry Semel, Carol Bartz, and Scott Thompson (seventh, if interim CEO Ross Levinsohn is counted).[21] Second, the parade of CEOs had proceeded from Yahoo!'s rejection of a $45 billion offer from Microsoft for more than twice Yahoo!'s then market value. The shadow of remorse at the rejection of Microsoft's offer still hung heavily over the company and Ms. Mayer when she came into office. Third, Ms. Mayer caused Yahoo! to embark on a series of acquisitions, fifty of them, for $1.4 billion by one count, capped off by acquisition of the networking company Tumblr for $1.1 billion.[22] Contributions to Yahoo!'s bottom line from those acquisitions amounted to nil.

Fourth, Mayer inherited a jewel within Yahoo!, which eventually morphed into a millstone around her neck. Yahoo! owned a 24 percent stake in Alibaba, the Chinese equivalent of Amazon. This seemingly stellar attribute proved to be one with which Ms. Mayer and Yahoo! were deficient in managing. Fifth, although Yahoo! has value to users as a content provider (Yahoo! Finance, for example) and as an Internet service provider (Yahoo! Mail and yahoo.com), neither Ms. Mayer nor her predecessors were able to capitalize on those strengths by garnering advertising revenue or otherwise.

The denouement came in the summer of 2016 when Verizon agreed to pay $4.8 billion for Yahoo!, a company that at its height had a market capitalization of $125 billion and for which Microsoft had offered $45 billion in 2008.[23] The causes of Yahoo!'s decline were many, including a string of failed leaders, with fluctuating strategies that confused employees and consumers. Former employees saw "the root of Yahoo!'s slow decline as simpler." The company and its CEOs, including Ms. Mayer, missed all three of the watershed changes in information technology, "the phenomena of search, social media, and mobile."[24]

Ms. Mayer, of course, claimed that the sale represented a victory, but experts saw it as a defeat both for the company and especially for Ms. Mayer, who once "had immediate star power, appearing on the cover of *Fortune* and in *Vogue* magazine." "Experts say it is tough to rebound from a rookie reign many observers see as pocked by mistakes complicated by an already-difficult turnaround." For Ms. Mayer, "it will be like the pilot who flew the Hindenburg to then be asked to fly the Goodyear blimp during the Super Bowl." Ms. Mayer has departed from Yahoo! With an estimated $55 million severance.[25]

Meg Whitman at Hewlett-Packard: Ms. Whitman had a prior incarnation as a CEO, a successful one, in ten years at eBay, the "c to c" (consumer to consumer) shopping/auction Internet site. After an unsuccessful 2012 try at election as governor of California, losing to Jerry Brown, Ms. Whitman returned to information technology, as CEO of a company much larger than eBay, Hewlett-Packard.

As at Yahoo!, HP's top echelons (board and senior executives) appeared to be another gang that couldn't shoot straight. HP and its directors had gone through five CEOs (four permanent, one "acting") in seven years. In 2005 the HP board had dismissed Carly Fiorina as CEO. Fiorina had consistently over-promised and under-delivered, failing to make her numbers (quarterly and annual revenue and profit projections) time and time again. She laid off tens of thousand of workers, from whence came the nickname "Chainsaw Carly." Many H-P employees detested Ms. Fiorina, and she drove out from the board of directors or any active role in the company the descendants of the company's legendary founders, Bill Hewlett and David Packard.

The straw that broke the camel's back was Ms. Fiorina's ego-fueled refusal to appoint a COO, or chief operating officer, despite board requests and then board demands that she do so. Every even modestly successful admiral, ship captain, general, president, chancellor, or CEO has had a loyal number two, whether denominated chief of staff, executive officer, vice president, provost, or chief operating officer, but Ms. Fiorina refused to have one, despite what her Stanford degree in medieval history should have told her. So the HP board dismissed her.

New CEO Mark Hurd turned things around at HP, and relatively quickly. He came to HP as a cypher, from the company known as National Cash Register (which now manufactured point-of-sale computer terminals rather than cash registers). At HP, Hurd oversaw increases in revenues and profits. The stock price went all the way back up and then some. In 2008 Hurd engineered HP's acquisition of Electronic Data Systems for $13 billion. The combination of a tech hardware company (HP) and an outsource services entity (EDP) produced "the largest IT company in the world," with its market capitalization over $100 billion eclipsing even that of IBM.[26] That pinnacle later proved to have been the high point.

Reminiscent of Jimmy Carter when he was president in the 1970s, Mr. Hurd committed adultery—in his heart. Mr. Hurd confessed carnal desires toward an attractive public relations consultant HP had hired. The HP board then did the unthinkable: it fired Mark Hurd, a successful CEO who had not actually done anything wrong. Oracle CEO Larry Ellison called the Hurd dismissal unfathomable, hiring the recently dismissed Hurd for his own company.

Soon thereafter the revisionists took over. A sample:

> Mr. Hurd steadily increased H-P's profits—but he did so partly by cutting spending on programs that could have set the company up for future growth [research and development, for instance]. . . . Among the areas where Mr. Hurd cut most aggressively was the services business, eliminating thousands of employees brought over from a $13 billion purchase of outsourcing giant Electronic Data Systems.[27]

Perhaps Mark Hurd's actions as CEO did begin the HP slide, helping form the glass cliff Meg Whitman confronted when she became HP CEO two years later. In those two years (2010–2012) preceding Ms. Whitman's arrival, HP's market capitalization fell from over $100 billion to $30 billion. In November 2012, HP's share price hit a ten-year low, dwindling downward to the low achieved in the bursting of the tech bubble, 1999–2002.

Why the dramatic slide at HP? To replace Mark Hurd, HP bought Leo Apotheker aboard. Mr. Apotheker had been an executive with SAP, Germany's and the EU's leading developer of business software. After coming to HP, Mr. Apotheker began scratching around for an entry "into the high-margin software market, which constituted less than 3 percent of HP's sales at the time."[28] Mr. Apotheker found Autonomy, a UK software developer known for programs to manage large unwieldy databases. Despite being in a business similar to Autonomy's, Oracle earlier had passed on acquisition talks with Autonomy, regarding Autonomy's $6 billion market capitalization as unjustified.

Not so HP and Leo Apotheker: they plunged onward, paying $11 billion for Autonomy, only to find that the acquired company had cooked the books, among other things prematurely recognizing revenues that had not been earned. HP took an immediate $8.8 billion write-off. Lawsuits followed. The HP board dismissed Leo Apotheker from his position as CEO.[29]

Meg Whitman was coming off a general election loss in her quest to become California's governor. The HP board reached out to her and she accepted the CEO position.[30] Let's summarize the glass cliff that Ms. Whitman faced and over which she could drive the company. Between 2007 and 2012, HP had made two gargantuan acquisitions (one for $13 billion and one for $11 billion) that largely had failed; HP's profit had gone from a positive $5.1 billion in 2007 to a $5.8 billion loss in 2012; long-term debt had ballooned from $4.9 billion in 2007 to $24.1 billion in 2012; and the price-earnings ratio had dwindled from the 25X earnings of a growth company to the 5.5X earnings of a tired old industrial.[31]

As CEO, Ms. Whitman rolled up her sleeves. She announced that she would not split up the company, as analysts had wanted. Taking a page from predecessor CEO Carleton Fiorina or *enfant terrible* CEO Chainsaw Al Dunlap ("Rambo in Pinstripes"), Whitman announced that HP would lay off 8 percent of its workforce, or 30,000 of 349,000 employees, which would come on top of the 75,000 workers whom HP, bloated by acquisitions, had laid off since 2005.[32]

We leave Ms. Whitman as another female CEO peering over a glass cliff. In a retrospective entitled "H-P Faces a Long Hard Grind," UBS stock analyst Steven Milunovich "argued that . . . H-P should revisit the spinoff [idea], punting printing along with PCs. This would free Ms. Whitman to focus on H-P's other businesses—data center gear, software and services."[33] But that is another temporal phase, and the subject of another chapter, beyond the glass cliff Whitman faced when she came first to office.

The Glass Cliff in Information Technology: Other Recent Cases

> *Virginia Rometty at IBM*: In January 2012, Virginia Rometty became CEO of IBM, "only the ninth leader of the 112-year-old company."[34] The reason IBM has been able to exist and, indeed, prosper for such a long time is that time and time again it has been able to reinvent itself, while preserving its core values of loyalty and service both to the company

and to its customers.[35] For many years, IBM and its employees pushed "big iron," mainframe computers such as the fabled IBM 360, out the door. The company leased the hardware and then sold applications, other software, and services to its customers.

The PC revolution overtook the days of big iron. Belatedly, IBM entered the world of PCs, in which it had to sell rather than lease the hardware, and networks linking those PCs, servers, and routers. The IBM PC business is gone now, sold to Lenovo, a Chinese company, replaced by a near-complete corporate focus on services and consulting. Former CEO Lou Gerstner's book *Who Says Elephants Can't Dance?* captures well this IBM ingredient, the ability to remake itself.[36] Some companies, such as IBM, have this ability, and some don't (HP perhaps, Yahoo! for certain).

The thesis is that, at the time of Rometty's elevation, IBM's future prospects represented yet another glass cliff, providing a stage for the appointment of a female CEO. A bloated workforce (434,000 employees) had become preoccupied with internal status and company politics, losing concern for and responsiveness to its customers. "Where we haven't transformed rapidly enough, we struggled. We have to step it up with that . . . and that is on all levels," summarized Ms. Rometty.[37] IBM's transformation also involves increased emphasis on what Ms. Rometty terms "strategic imperatives." "Foremost among these are IBM's own cloud-computing applications and Watson, its artificial intelligence platform." So far, however, Rometty may be proving that elephants cannot dance, at least not always. She has presided over five years of quarter-by-quarter revenue declines at Big Blue.[38]

As of late, candidate and then president-elect Donald Trump criticized Ms. Rometty and IBM for closing plants in the United States, shipping the jobs to India. "If a company wants to leave Minnesota, fire their workers and move to another country and ship their products back into the United States . . . we will make them pay a 35% tax."[39] Google, Facebook, and other technology companies also have either moved jobs to or created numbers of support positions in India (see chapter 15).

> *Carol Bartz at Yahoo!:* Press releases at the time described Bartz as "the exact combination of seasoned technology executive and savvy leader that the board was looking for" (comments of Yahoo! board chair and founder Jerry Yang).[40] Bartz had an extremely successful fourteen-year run as CEO of Autodesk, the company that provides CAD (computer-

assisted design) software to designers of everything from boats to kitchen cabinets. The mother of three, and a breast cancer survivor, Bartz was known throughout the industry for "earthy, some say salty, language."[41]

Ms. Bartz also was outspoken. She called the tech industry on the carpet for its lack of introspection about the lack of diversity in the industry's leadership ranks. She believed that men so outnumber women in the industry because a "mine's bigger than yours" mentality prevails, "a game women are loathe to play, or do not play at all."[42] But, apropos of the glass cliff theory, at Yahoo! Bartz inherited a set of glass cliff problems very similar to those Marissa Mayer faced two years later. In the year preceding her appointment, Yahoo! "had navigated a failed acquisition offer from Microsoft and an attempt by investor Carl Icahn to replace its board."[43] "Women are recruited disproportionately into tough jobs, where the title [such as CEO] may be big but the chances for success are quite small."

> *Safra Catz at Oracle:* Larry Ellison, the founder and CEO of Oracle, who in more years than not has topped the CEO compensation chart in the United States, finally stepped down in mid-2014. The Oracle board appointed (or Ellison handpicked) as Ellison's successor Safra Catz, who was to share the position with Mark Hurd, named as a co-CEO. The CEO position at Oracle should be a plum in the tech world. Oracle develops and sells database management software of a type every business of any size needs. But Oracle's preeminence may be fading. "Fifteen years ago, there was no question: If you wanted to store data you go to Oracle." Now, though, a director of engineering at a prominent firm says, "I ask my software architects, 'Build something to handle a billion things.' When you look at that kind of scale, Oracle is no longer the best."[44]

Ten years ago, Oracle acquired PeopleSoft, the leading developer of software for human resources applications. Here, too, Oracle and Ms. Catz faced a sharp drop in their market share. "More companies are opting to pay for such software as a subscription accessed from remote computer[s] rather than buy the software to install on their own computer servers." Oracle has only an infinitesimal share (2.8 percent) of the market for cloud software. So an argument may be made that even the newest of the new among female CEOs, Safra Catz, takes the reins of a company facing daunting prospects, poised at the edge of a glass cliff.

Nonetheless, despite clouds (or the cloud) on the horizon, Ms. Catz may be humming a tune. In 2014 she was the highest-paid CEO in the S&P (Standard & Poor's) 500, earning $43.6 million.[45]

Legacy Female CEOs and the Glass Cliff Theory

> *Anne Mulcahy at Xerox*: Anne Mulcahy got the top job at Xerox only after a sea of red ink flowed and the company's future was uncertain.

> *Carleton Fiorina at Hewlett-Packard*: Several of the reasons for what all analysts and observers agree was a less-than-mediocre performance as CEO undoubtedly originated, partly at least, in the circumstances under which she came into office. As previously stated, she came to a company "that would market sushi as 'cold dead fish.'"[46] She found what had been essentially an engineering company that, despite its iconic reputation ("the HP Way," "Built to Last"), had a plethora of production centers, each with its own products and marketing. "She started the company to reverse what she termed the mentality of 'a thousand tribes,' or 'the silo mentality,' in which each of the 87 centers acted as a separate company, rather than one unified Hewlett-Packard."[47] Whether those circumstances surrounding Fiorina's inauguration at HP fit the glass cliff theory is an open question.

> *Patricia Russo at Lucent*: A female CEO appointment that did fit the glass cliff theory to a *T* was that of Patricia Russo at Lucent. Ms. Russo became CEO of Lucent, the successor entity to Bell Labs, after the government breakup of AT&T. Prior to Ms. Russo's return from a flirtation with Eastman Kodak, Lucent had laid off over 115,000 employees. The share price had gone from $64.69 in 1991 to less than a dollar ($.58) in 2001. Further, the entire telecommunications industry was in transition, indeed in turmoil, going from the days of copper wire, switched networks to an era in which wireless digital would predominate. Yet Lucent was firmly tied to the old and less profitable copper wire era. Ms. Russo had to preside over thirteen consecutive quarters of not only declining sales but losses.

Most commonly, CEOs leave their position due to retirement. Or CEOs depart because a merger has resulted not only in the disappearance of the position but the company as well. Boards of directors remove only a small subset of the CEOs who have left the corner office. This does not hold true, however, for woman CEOs. "Over the last decade, 38 percent of female chief executive officers who left their positions were sent packing."[48] That many of those women faced a glass cliff when they came into office undoubtedly adversely affected their performances later on, leading to an inordinate number of involuntary departures from the CEO position.

In some instances, the past is regarded as prologue. Information technology may not be an exemplar of that dictum. In information technology, the rocky and uneven performances under women CEOs make a good case for the assertion that history will *not* repeat itself. A probability exists that in the future the number of female CEOs may remain lackluster or decline.

4

POOR PERFORMANCES BY FEMALE CEOS

Alongside the glass cliff theory, another predictor of the future fate of women as IT CEOs is the mixed performance of women who have headed up Silicon Valley corporations. That track record includes extremely poor performances, as touched upon in the previous chapter. This chapter amplifies that theme. Along the way, the historical accounts of women CEOs demonstrate how rapidly trends and fads, no matter how ephemeral, influence the industry.

Carleton Fiorina

In her six-year tenure at Hewlett-Packard (1999–2005), Ms. Fiorina saw the HP share price fall to half, and then continue downward. In her 2016 campaign for the Republican presidential nomination, Ms. Fiorina represented that in her era tech company stocks fell 80 percent. That may well have been close to the truth for HP under Ms. Fiorina, but overall, as the "tech bubble" burst, the NASDAQ tech index fell 27 percent, not 80 percent.[1]

To Jeffrey Sonnenfeld, associate dean of the Yale University School of Management, Ms. Fiorina "destroyed a corporate icon." Among CEOs, Mr. Sonnenfeld rated her "the worst because of her ruthless attack on the essence of a great company."[2] The sobriquet "Built to Last" referred both to the company's products and its vaulted "HP Way" of internal governance and product development.[3] Fiorina had respect for neither, lampooning the HP Way. "Carly can market the tar out of herself. That's what she's known for," one Wall Street analyst summary description of Fiorina's reign concluded.[4]

More on Marissa Mayer

Outside Yahoo!, in the press, the latest photographs of the usually attractive Ms. Mayer have taken on that startled, "deer-in-the-headlights" look. Inside Yahoo!, Ms. Mayer misstepped time and time again. For instance, she decreed that employment required employees to be on-site at least four days per week. At Yahoo! as well as at other companies, employees had increasingly chosen the option of telecommuting from home or other remote locales, communicating by email and via the Internet. Indeed, the "work anywhere, any time" culture had become entrenched, a Silicon Valley standard.[5] The prevailing ethic's downsides were that employees no longer knew each other, let alone brainstormed and strategized, at least in the way face-to-face coworkers are supposed to have done. Impersonal, faceless interaction spilled over into the workplace: employees emailed coworkers whose offices were two doors down the hallway.[6]

Mayer instituted other practices unpopular with Yahoo! employees: "She . . . pare[d] down the workforce through a rigorous quarterly review system, modeled after Google [and GE and Jack Welsh's ruthless "rank and yank" system]. [T]op performers receive generous bonuses and the underperformers are dismissed."[7]

Understandably, Ms. Mayer had come from Google, a company that encourages face-to-face employee interaction. Rather than by fiat, Google encourages face-to-face interaction with on-site facilities: restaurants, workout facilities, relaxation areas, rock climbing walls, and more. Google employees dining solo in the company's restaurants are encouraged to take up a flag for their table. Seeing a flag, an engineer might join a product development or sales person's table at lunch. Employees thus have a window on what is going on in other parts of the company. Mayer attempted to emulate that at Yahoo!, with the stick rather than with the carrot, making it immensely unpopular.

The First Year Alone

In her first full calendar year in office, Ms. Mayer committed other missteps, or what many onlookers regarded as missteps:

> Ms. Mayer fired Henrique de Castro, the COO she had bought over from Google a year earlier. "Rather than name a replacement, Ms. Mayer [assumed] leadership of the company's ad operation herself and stepped into the role of Yahoo's top ambassador to Madison Avenue."[8]

> Early on Ms. Mayer expended $1.3 billion in "three dozen small acquisitions," none of which produced significant revenue and which led to accusations that she "has yet to show that she can buy her way to growth."[9]

> After Yahoo! made $5.8 billion in Alibaba's initial public offering, and undaunted by her lack of success, Ms. Mayer announced that she would utilize the funds for further acquisitions rather than distribute them to shareholders.

The latter produced calls for Ms. Mayer's dismissal. Hedge fund Starwood Value "called for Yahoo! To halt its acquisition strategy, which it said has cost the company $1.3 billion and clearly not delivered value to shareholders." An apparently defiant Ms. Mayer pledged to continue on the course she had set.[10]

More Missteps

Ms. Mayer solidified her membership in the gang that couldn't shoot straight with the Alibaba fiasco. The year 2015 began with hope that Yahoo! would earn tens of billions through the sale of Alibaba shares (Yahoo! proposed to sell a 15 percent stake [383 million shares, worth approximately $31 billion]—its total stake amounted to 22.8 percent of Alibaba). The fly in the ointment was the refusal by the Internal Revenue Service to issue an advance opinion that the spinoff would be tax-free at the corporate level. An entire year of highly publicized on-again, off-again proposals ended with Ms. Mayer calling off the proposed sale.[11] Yahoo! shareholders once again were brides left at the altar.

Following her failed acquisitions strategy, Ms. Mayer shifted to her second and third strategies. She axed additional employees, early in 2016 reducing the Yahoo! workforce 15 percent, from 14,000 to 10,700, with further cuts to come.[12] She also announced the third strategy: Yahoo! Would spin off its core business, either into a newly formed company or via a sale to others. Ms. Mayer then began unraveling the ventures at expansion she had caused Yahoo! to enter two and three years previously.[13]

The chorus was all condemnatory. Yahoo! was a "Portal to Nowhere."[14] When one of Ms. Mayer's responses was that the changes she had implemented still "would take a few quarters to translate into higher growth," financial columnists were gobsmacked: "What about the past three years of Ms. Mayer's tenure? [She] has failed to transition Yahoo from a lumbering legacy platform into a streamlined Internet business."[15] Toward the year's end, a news piece observed that "many investors have lost patience, saying the embattled chief executive has no clear sense of direction and has misled investors and advertisers about the company's progress."[16]

Alarmed at the number of executives departing, the Yahoo! directors began a formal process of exploring "strategic alternatives." They took the extraordinary step of excluding the CEO (Ms. Mayer) from the process.[17] In the wings, would-be purchasers (Verizon, AT&T, Comcast, Alibaba, Softbank, Twenty-First Century Fox, Walt Disney, Google, Microsoft, News Corp., IAC/Interactive Corp.) queued up.[18]

Meanwhile, institutional investors (Starboard Value, Spring Owl Asset Management, Canyon Capital Investors) proposed radical reforms at Yahoo!. Starboard said "it would not back down from its fight with Yahoo! Inc. until Chief Executive Marissa Mayer is out."[19] The *Wall Street Journal* featured Ms. Mayer on its short list (an extremely short list, numbering three) of "executives to watch in 2016."[20]

The board of directors engineered the sale of Yahoo! to Verizon for $4.8 billion.[21] *Forbes* labeled the sale "the saddest $5 billion deal in tech history." Yahoo!'s market value had exceeded $125 billion in 2000.[22] Then, following discovery at Yahoo! of a massive security breach of 500,000 subscribers' personal data, Verizon negotiated the price still lower and the Yahoo! board of directors cut Ms. Mayer's pay.[23]

Virginia Rometty

Ms. Rometty has been more a stealth CEO, not much in the news, low in profile compared to Marissa Mayer at Yahoo!. Nonetheless, Ms. Rometty, who took office in January 2012, joins Ms. Mayer and Matthias Muller at Volkswagen as one of the three "executives to watch in 2016": "After 14 straight quarters of declining revenue, International Business Machines Corp. is trying to reinvent itself. . . . CEO Virginia 'Gini' Rometty's challenge is to shift IBM's business from products tailored to large, individual customers to offerings that appeal to entire industries."[24]

Other views are that Ms. Rometty and IBM must square up to another revolution in information technology, the advent of the cloud. "A growing number of analysts fear IBM may be on the wrong side of a major technological shift [to] cloud computing."[25] In the future, software and hardware will be in the cloud, available for prospective users to pull down from above, renting what they need, for the time a user needs the particular application. By contrast, under its business model, IBM "makes much of its money selling software, hardware and computer services installed by its army of technological consultants."[26] In 2013 IBM's net income shrank 21 percent and its earnings declined 15 percent. Institutional investors, including activist hedge funds, blamed Ms. Rometty for the disappointments. The headlines read, "Rometty Feels the Heat."[27]

Fast-forwarding two years, IBM was still trying to turn the corner. The company had shifted significant resources to its Bluemix cloud computing service and to data analytics software. On the other hand, financial results were "not sterling": revenue fell again, to 8.5 percent, "making for 15 straight quarters of declining sales." Through a spokesperson, Ms. Rometty pleaded for additional time: "We're transforming a big company. We've always said that this was going to take time."[28]

Revenues, profits, and stock price again fell in early 2016. Ms. Rometty appealed for still more time: "We are becoming a cognitive solutions and cloud computing company," but as analysts observed, one with "its older businesses shrinking faster than the new business [is] growing."[29]

Carol Bartz

Chapter 14 describes the STEM (science, technology, engineering, and mathematics) education wave that, over less than a decade, has enveloped secondary and post-secondary education, arguing that the STEM movement should be leavened with other ingredients. Carol Bartz's short tenure as CEO of Yahoo! may be evidence for the latter point.

Business leaders and educators see the STEM movement as particularly necessary to move women and girls forward in technology. The history of Carol Bartz as well as that of Marissa Mayer might give STEM advocates pause, for Ms. Bartz and Ms. Mayer represent two of the more spectacular CEO flameouts of our time. The two women have the distinction of having the deepest, highest-quality STEM backgrounds in the female CEO crop, Ms. Bartz from the University of Wisconsin (PhD in computer science) and Ms. Mayer from Stanford University (BS and MS in computer science).

The Yahoo! board dismissed Ms. Bartz in September 2011, two years and four months after her appointment in April 2009. In retrospect, Ms. Bartz's prospects for success were narrow indeed.[30] Earlier, Yahoo! had shifted away from an advertising-dependent, search engine and email format to attempt to become a digital media company that produced original content (Yahoo! Finance, Yahoo! Sports). This opened wide the field for Google, which perfected its DoubleClick Ad Exchange and became overwhelmingly the search engine of choice. Yahoo! could not then go back. Google had preempted the field.

Then social media came to the fore, rendering large chunks of the Yahoo! magazine format quickly obsolete. In many cases, news traveled faster via Twitter or Facebook than it ever could via specialized online magazines. At Yahoo!, Ms. Bartz's biggest failures were that, although she thrived on technology and engineering, she lacked expertise in strategic thinking, marketing, and sales. For example, when asked whether Facebook posed a competitive threat to Yahoo!, Ms. Bartz dismissed the possibility on the grounds that Facebook did not have the revenue to compete globally.[31]

Yahoo! shares declined 15.4 percent in 2010. The disastrous first and second quarters of 2011 sealed Bartz's fate. She had missed the boat on social networking and its effects. She had failed to find a new niche for Yahoo!. Effectively, it remained a company without a mission, as well as one not nimble enough to reinvent itself in a quickly changing environment.

Meg Whitman

The previous chapter left Meg Whitman as the new CEO of Hewlett-Packard, struggling to unwind the Autonomy acquisition and to reduce debt and employee head count (from 375,000) at the bloated company. She resisted calls to split the behemoth in two ("Together we are stronger").[32] In October 2013, as new CEO, she announced that "we are better together."[33] Two years later, one financial columnist wrote that "Ms. Whitman's only tangible achievement has been to reduce net debt about $9 billion [from $27 billion]. [HP] seems as strategically moribund and unmanageable as ever."[34]

Clients, students, and laypersons often ask questions about corporate governance and finance, thinking that there is *an answer*. They are frequently incredulous when they discover that there is no one answer and that, as often as not, fads are extremely influential. Further, Wall Street investment bankers frequently initiate the fads in quests for large fees. The prospect of a fee rather than the merits dictates their answers.

The Split-Up and Spin-Off Trend

In the 1990s the fad was the issuance of "tracking stocks." Instead of spinning off ("hiving off") a subsidiary or a division, a parent company would retain the unit but issue a stock whose revenues and profits tracked the separated but still internal unit. U.S. Steel and General Motors, among others, issued tracking stocks. Fads have included step bonds, TIPs, strip securities, preferred stocks, convertible preferred stocks, convertible debentures, contingent convertible securities (CoCos), and endlessly onward. The fads come and, as often as not, go, receding into the background.

The latest trend, or fad, on Wall Street has been to split a publicly held company into two publicly traded companies, thereby "unlocking shareholder value." Pharmaceutical companies have done it (Abbott Labs with Abbvie and Baxter Labs with Baxalta). Oil companies have bifurcated themselves in to exploration and extraction (the upstream part) and refining and retail (the downstream part). Sunoco and Marathon (now spun off as companies separate from U.S. Steel) are examples. Alcoa and Xerox put plans on their drawing boards for separations, unlocking the higher-tech, value-added part from the older, more staid operations of the companies. Trying to stave off extinction, newspaper companies (Tribune Publishing and Gannett, for example) saw splitting in two as salvation. In the tech field, Ms. Whitman's former company, eBay, split itself into eBay and PayPal. Xerox has also pursued plans to split in two.[35]

The Hewlett-Packard Split-Up

Surprisingly, after three years in office and no progress in turning HP around, Meg Whitman reversed herself, announcing that late in

2015 HP would hive itself in two: "The new HP, Inc. will carry on HP's personal computer and printing operations. . . . The other part, Hewlett Packard Enterprise [HPE] will sell HP's products and services for large companies, including computer servers, data storage, software, and consulting."[36] Ms. Whitman and HPE did themselves one better, later announcing that half of the HPE half would itself be split, the spun-off technology services operation then to merge with Computer Sciences Corp.[37]

The resulting question has been whether Ms. Whitman's reversal of course has been a diversion from HP's dismal performance during her tenure as CEO (H-P shares are down 62 percent since she took over). Or is it a copycat move by Ms. Whitman, imitating what has gone on around her, the current fad or trend, the "restructuring" that investment bankers always seem to be recommending?[38] Opinions are divided. A negative outlook is that "Three years after putting the kibosh on the idea of spinning off its personal computer business, HP is now ready to do just that. . . . The company's turnaround efforts have hit a brick wall."[39] By contrast, Ms. Whitman's spin is wholly positive: "We needed to be smaller, more nimble, more focused."[40] Needless to say, Ms. Whitman will take for herself the CEO position at the more cutting-edge Hewlett-Packard Enterprises.

And, as a final fillip, in the manner increasingly of CEOs everywhere (Chainsaw Carly Fiorina, Rambo in Pinstripes Al Dunlap), Ms. Whitman announced further cuts in the H-P workforce, which had once numbered 375,000 employees. Ms. Whitman and HP announced a further 10 percent reduction from the 300,000-employee level, putting 30,000 additional people out of work.[41] Then Ms. Whitman put herself out of work, in December 2017 announcing that she would step down from all roles at HP and HPE, effective January 2018.[42]

Other Female CEOs in Tech

Taking a page from Ms. Whitman's "sampler," and facing adverse stock market reactions to the financial results during her tenure, CEO Ursula Burns announced that Xerox will split itself in two.[43] The court of opinion also reconvened in order to consider anew whether Anne Mulcahy, Ms. Burns's predecessor as CEO of Xerox, had indeed saved the iconic copier and document-handling entity. Later, Ms. Burns announced that she would relinquish the CEO title and position after Xerox split itself.[44]

All of these tales of mixed—indeed, poor—performance by female CEOs in the information technology field may, in certain sets of hands, argue for fewer rather than more women in senior management of tech companies in years to come.

PART II

A HISTORY OF WOMEN IN INFORMATION TECHNOLOGY

5

ONCE UPON A TIME

In our society and many others, "women hold up half the sky."[1] Here in the United States, for example, women earn 60 percent of the bachelor's degrees and 50 percent of the doctorates. One would think that something similar would be true of the cutting-edge information technology industry. Certainly at one point there were signs of a trend toward a semblance of gender equality.

Precursors

Grace Murray Hopper (1906–1992) was one of the pioneers. In the 1950s she pioneered the use of COBOL (Common Business-Oriented Language), a ubiquitous language for early generations of computer programmers. In doing so, Grace Hopper spearheaded the movement toward computer languages as close to English as possible, rather than machine code or languages close to machine code that others promoted. She was instrumental in the development of the first widely used mainframe computer, the UNIVAC by Remington Rand.[2]

Much if not all of the time she was doing these things, Dr. Hopper was an officer in the U.S. Navy, first as a reserve officer and later as a regular. After Dr. Hopper's retirement, the U.S. Congress took the extraordinary step of awarding her the one-star rank of commodore, just below rear admiral, the Navy's two-star rank (unlike the other services, the Navy ordinarily does not award the one-star rank). Her name "graces" the transom of a U.S. Navy guided missile destroyer, the *Hopper* (DDG 70), known in the fleet as the "Amazing Grace." In 2017 Yale University renamed Calhoun College, originally named after John C. Calhoun, senator from South Carolina and a Yale graduate, Grace Hopper College, after Grace M. Hopper, also a Yale University graduate.

Closer to the subject, each year there is a Grace Hopper Conference, a technical meeting of up to ten thousand women interested in computer science and related subjects. Microsoft Research awards the Grace Murray Hopper prize "to the outstanding young computer professional of the year, selected on the basis of a single recent major technical or service contribution."[3] Aside from significant prestige, the award brings with it a $50,000 stipend. Based upon Ms. Hooper's early-on involvement and genius in the field, one might believe that women would have a significant if not widespread position in the field today. But the idea of numerous Grace Hoppers in more recent years would be inaccurate. It may even be deceptive.

Days Gone By

Women once were as prominent in the field as they have become in law, medical, and MBA programs, in which women have achieved parity. At the peak, in the mid-1980s, women earned 37 percent of U.S. bachelor's degrees in computer subjects.[4] In 1987 women constituted 34 percent of the systems analysts and 42 percent of the computer programmers.[5]

In prior years, the numbers had been even better. In the days of punch card systems, precursors of yesterday's and today's computers, women were a majority of those who operated the sorters, collators, multipliers, and tabulators of the punch card era. When the early computers arrived, and still used what people called the "IBM card," women made the transition from the collator and sorter era to the early computer days. Around 1970, for instance, 89 percent of the keypunch operators still were women.[6]

Once again, however, the trends did not hold. Even then (1970) the 89 percent figure represented a significant presence for women only in the lowest-paying category of jobs. In the early days, the hierarchy was set: first keypunch operators, then, ascending upward, machine operators, programmers, systems analysts, and supervisors and managers, in that order.[7] Women in keypunching jobs "had no prospects for advancement beyond supervision of other clerical jobs," that is, no prospects for advancement to positions higher in the hierarchy.[8]

Since the 1980s, the proportion of women studying computing has "fallen steadily. No other professional field has ever experienced such a decline of women in its ranks."[9] Today, women account for just one in seven undergraduate computer science students (14 percent), down from 37 percent in the 1980s. And the decline continues. In 2010 a mi-nuscule 4 percent of first-year university women students listed com-puter science as a possible major. While women are 36 percent of the university presidents and chancellors, females are only 11 percent of the computer science faculties. Post-1984, computer science is the only one of twenty-one STEM (science, technology, engineering, and mathemat-ics) majors experiencing a steady and prolonged slide in the percentage of women enrolled.

A Wave of Change

In 1951 Prudential Insurance had 13 punch card centers, with 1,000 machines and 660 employees, most of them women.[10]

> The one big [personnel] change with computerization was the addition of a new job: programming. . . . Programming was constructed very dif-ferently . . . as a kind of mathematical labor. It was seen . . . as a hybrid of aspects of the work previously carried out by machine operators. . . . Whereas [previously] instructions created by the analyst were interpreted directly by punch card machine operators, they now had to be translated into the enormously pedantic language of the computer.[11]

In 1955 Metropolitan Life Insurance installed a UNIVAC computer. "While 189 women and 9 men had worked in the punch-card division, the new 20 person computer staff consisted of 12 men and 8 women."[12] As the computer revolution unfolded, gender roles were reversed, and then some. "Punch card work became gender segregated, low skill and low paid."[13] There was "a transformation of feminized clerical work (coding) into the highly masculine, seat-of-the-pants 'black art' of programming."[14]

But then programming, in which women had a reduced presence but a presence nonetheless, in turn began to be relegated to a lower position. The increasing capability and reliability of second- and third-generation software and hardware meant that the baroque work-arounds and be-spoke tailoring so prized by programmers were outmoded, no longer as necessary as they once were. "The development of automatic program-ming systems threatened to make programmers obsolete altogether."[15]

Proliferation of shrink-wrapped and other off-the-shelf software and computer applications ("apps") shoved programmers from their position on center stage.

Bootstrapping by Creation of Professional Associations

Meanwhile, males were busy creating forms of professional certification, imitating the bootstrapping that has occurred in other professions (law, accounting, financial analysis, insurance, speech therapy, audiology, civil and structural engineering, and so on). The computing organizations such as the National Machine Accountants Association (NMAA) (in 1963, changed to Data Processing Management Association) "promised ambitious *men* the chance to elevate their positions within the corporate hierarchy."[16]

In its original incarnation, the NMAA was 2 percent women. Among other things, male NMAA members used membership in the organization to obtain greater pay as they moved away from machine operation and, later, from programming. Now, to advance in what would become information technology, women had to penetrate two or even three barriers: male versus female, nonmember versus member, and woman versus organization man.

In later years, the DPMA's leaders debated whether supervisors of keypunch operators should even be eligible for membership in the DPMA. Keypunch operators (mostly women) already were *personae non gratae*. Then, too, women's jobs as data entry clerks continued to vanish. Women had a presence on the next rung up on the ladder, programming, at approximately 25 percent, but that field had leveled off and had begun to decline.[17]

Tokens and Skewed Groups

Besides tone deafness within the industry and among its leaders, another factor that serves as a barrier to renewed progress, or perhaps any progress at all, for women in information technology was identified by sociologists who studied corporate culture. In 1977, Rosabeth Moss Kanter, a sociologist on the Harvard Business School faculty, published her landmark work, *Men and Women of the Corporation*.[18]

As background, Professor Kanter described the status ("token") and difficulties associated with being the only member of a minority (for example, female, African American, Latino, gay or lesbian, and the like) within a work center, a certain rank in the hierarchy, or a designated place in any other organization. When a token enters a group, "practical jokes become crueler. Coworkers invoke stereotypes with a vengeance."[19]

To protect herself, a token woman may retreat into a stereotype such as mother figure, group pet, class clown, or queen bee. Alternatively, as noted, the dominants in the group may characterize the token by application of a stereotype to that person. While the stereotype may offer protection against downside risks, and therefore enhance job security, application of the stereotype, whether by the dominants or by the minority group member herself, also will serve to mask the token's achievements and performance, or at least cause discounting by the dominants. According to one source, "the problem with stereotypes is not that they [perhaps] are untrue, but that they are incomplete. They make one story become the only story."[20]

So the addition of a second and perhaps a third member of the minority group would improve the situation, so that tokenism would no longer be operative and stereotypes no longer imposed—or so one would think. Exactly the opposite tends to occur. Now sensing a potential threat that they did not feel before, with only a token in their midst, dominants will then attempt to play one minority group member off against another.[21]

When there are three, four, or even five minority group members, the result is what Professor Kanter terms a "skewed group."[22] The dominants in the group now sense an even greater threat to their primacy. "The temperature rises."[23] The men engage in an exercise Professor Kanter describes as "boundary heightening," exhibiting hostility toward skewed group members and increasingly excluding them from the inner circle or excluding them altogether. Based upon her empirical studies, Professor Kanter found that males resorted to macho attitudes and discussion when females were present. They confined discussion to sports, cars, tools, women, hunting, fishing, and other subjects thought to be distinctly masculine. Outside the presence of skewed group members (women, in this case), the males' discussion reverted to more prosaic subjects, such as the schooling of their children, household repairs, and the like.[24]

Token Status and Prevalence of Stereotypes in Tech

These situations are common in the information technology field. Women, for example, are found to "lack the peer support that men get . . . because of [males' much] greater numbers." "Peer support seems particularly important to . . . women . . . or underrepresented minorities."[25] Professor Kanter's research and insights explain why.

The roots of these sociological phenomena are deep:

> Very early in life, computing is claimed as male territory. At each step from early childhood through college, computing is actively claimed as "guy stuff" by boys and men and passively ceded by girls and women. . . . Culture and society [link] interest and success with computers to boys and men. Curriculum, teachers' expectations, and culture reflect boys' pathways into computing, accepting assumptions of male excellence and women's deficiencies in the field.[26]

In the late 1990s the computer science department at Carnegie Mellon University held summer workshops for high school computer science teachers. Nearly a third of the teachers had no girls or only one girl in their classes.[27] The numbers of skewed groups can only be estimated, but it is reasonable to assume that their numbers, and their effect on girls' psyches, are substantial.

Information technology has a "distinctly masculine culture" that is off-putting to potential women participants.[28] That culture does not change, let alone disappear, with the addition of tokens or even of skewed groups.

Absence of a Trickle Down

Another factor that could aid women's entrance into and progress in the industry would be the presence of women in superior ranks in companies and in the industry, discussed in chapter 2. Those women at the upper levels in the hierarchy would take a particular interest in the advancement of other women. This phenomenon is referred to as the "trickle down." The data show that in a corporation with a woman as chief executive officer, the board of directors will tend to include an increased number of women.

Although the sample was small, numbering twenty-two women who had become CEOs of Fortune 500 corporations, one study found good support for the trickle-down hypothesis.[29] At Avon Products, when Andrea Jung was the CEO, four other directors were women. The boards of Sara Lee (Brenda Barnes, CEO) and Alcatel-Lucent (Pat Russo, CEO) each had three women directors. So, too, with PepsiCo (Indra Nooyi, CEO). When Marion Sandler was CEO of Golden West Financial, she presided over a board with four women directors. The theory is that a trickle down would also replicate itself among the ranks of executives.[30]

There is evidence to the contrary. Some women CEOs resort to what advice books term the queen bee syndrome, reveling in being the only woman or one of a very few women in senior positions. Unfortunately, the queen bee syndrome seems to be common in information technology. Carleton Fiorina, for six years the CEO at Hewlett-Packard, appointed no additional women to the HP board or senior positions. She also took pains, at least while in office, to point out that she was gender-blind.[31] She was an example of the queen bee.

"How important are role models? . . . How important are female leaders?"[32] The trickle-down theory would say "very," but little evidence exists that any trickle down has taken place in information technology.

The Nerd Image Turnoff

A thesis with great explanatory power regarding the declining role of women in information technology has been young women's aversion to a nerd stereotype applicable to the younger males who populate the industry. The image begins in high school, continuing into university. Male computer science students are said to have "monitor tans."[33] They have "sunken glowing eyes," and are "withdrawn, relatively incompetent [at anything not related to computers], sexually frustrated, and desperately unhappy when not submerged in their craft."[34] "An exceptionally high level of obsession and expertise has become the expected norm" for males in information technology. It deters women from pursuing either education or employment in the IT field. Many young women find the culture to be "insular, isolating and off balance."[35]

Progressing to employment, the nerd image takes on additional ingredients: pet dogs in the office, Frisbee in the hallways, computer games—very sexist ones at that—in the offices, weekly baths only, no deodorant, poor hygiene all around. Antisocial attitudes, or images thereof, ratcheted up: one "striking characteristic about [male programmers and engineers] . . . was their disinterest in people. . . . They prefer[red] to work with things rather than people." The notion that computer people "lack people skills [and that the deficiency was of no moment] became part of the computer industry. . . . Programmers became excessively independent . . . to the point of mild paranoia, . . . often eccentric and [bordering on] mild schizophrenia. The incidence of beards, sandals, and other symptoms of nonconformity" became prevalent.[36]

On the opposite side of things, that is, from the viewpoint of the industry, "the idea that detached (male) individuals made the best programmers [and engineers] was [incorporated] . . . into the hiring practices of the industry. . . . The idea of the [male professional] as being particularly ill-equipped for and uninterested in social interaction became part of the conventional wisdom of the industry."[37] But those who control the industry regarded males' social backwardness to be not only insignificant but, in many cases, a badge of honor.

Hacker and Nerd Dominance

It was not until 1980, though, that the "computer geek" and "hacker" images became widespread, affecting women's participation in both education and employment.[38] Since that time the images have become even more common, deterring girls and young women even more, the images progressing from nerd to grind, dweeb, geek, tool, "someone with an overwhelming attraction to the innate technical world, . . . an antisocial, malodorous, pasty-faced monomaniac with all the personality of a cheese grater . . . [with a] thin underdeveloped bod[y]."[39]

The actual experiences of Katherine Losse dovetail with the portraits painted above. Ms. Loose was the fifty-first employee and second woman to be hired at Facebook. When she left Facebook in 2010, she was still only one of a handful of women among seven hundred employees. All or nearly all of the women were in fields such as customer support or marketing. They earned only one-third of what Facebook paid to engineers or other computer professionals, all male. The few female employees were regarded as peripheral to the company's mission as, from first to last, Facebook's founder and his lieutenants molded the firm as "an engineers' company."

The latter seems to have resulted in the very conditions the industry critics have described, as recounted above:

> At Facebook, the office was a warren of desks . . . cluttered with open drink bottles, half-wrapped snacks, and video games. [The] desks were occupied by young, plain-looking guys in T-shirts, gazing at their screens. They looked barely awake, having not yet consumed their daily quota of Starbucks coffee drinks and Red Bull and seemed startled to see a strange new woman in the office. The only other woman sat in front of a large piece of graffiti art featuring a cartoonish, heavy breasted woman with green hair.[40]

The Objectification of Women

The Katherine Losse quotation provides a transition to a last reason why many women find information technology distasteful and why their numbers have steadily declined since the late 1970s. At Facebook, Ms. Losse continues, "much of the graffiti in the [technicians' and engineers' work] room featured stylized women with large breasts bursting from small tops that tapered down to tiny waists, mimicking the proportions of female videogame characters."

Women's objections were not to be heard:

> Just because a few women might be let into their [clubhouse] we weren't supposed to complain about things like sexy women on the walls. This was [the male programmers' and engineers'] kingdom and their idea of cool, and we shouldn't mess with it. If you couldn't handle the graffiti, or the unrepentantly boyish culture it represented, the job was not going to work out.[41]

An interesting aspect of this misogynist culture has been the longevity of it. "The routine denigration of women [which took place even as far back as the 1950s] would be shocking to modern sensibilities."

> [In the 1950s] terminal firm Entrex ran a series of advertisements . . . that their data-entry systems were so easy to use it was no longer necessary to hire intelligent women. One advertisement . . . boasted that a data entry clerk could be hired "on her looks alone." Another [ad] consisted of a huge pair of red lips parted for a kiss. The headline read "We taught our data entry system to speak a new language: Dumb Blond. . . . She can be the dumbest blond you ever find."[42]

In April 1967 *Cosmopolitan* ran a feature entitled "The Computer Girls." Those were the young women "who taught the dazzling new 'miracle machines' what to do and how to do it." They had advantages over male programmers because, in the words of *Cosmopolitan*, "programming was just like planning dinner." There were twenty thousand women working as programmers, with an immediate need for twenty thousand more.[43] Around the same time, another *Cosmopolitan* piece extolled "the chances of meeting men in computer work." In fact, the article portrayed the chances as "very good, as the field is overrun with men." A somewhat patronizing male programmer gave the *Cosmo* reporter a catch line: "We like having girls around. . . . They're prettier than the rest of us."[44]

Even IBM, a company one might think would be above the fray, ran condescending, sexist advertisements. A "Meet Susie" advertisement featured a young blond woman in a miniskirt. "Even a pretty girl with no previous experience can program an IBM machine using PL/1 computer language." In part, the sexist attitudes at IBM, Entrex, and other companies were emblematic of the times, but that these attitudes have continued for forty or fifty years seems beyond problematic and worrisome.

Some Takeaways

One estimate is than fewer than 10 percent of computer engineers are women.[45] At Facebook, of the first hundred-plus engineers hired, only one was a woman.[46] If young women do make it to the inner circle, becoming analysts and programmers, they can expect to earn only 72 percent of what comparable males do.[47] At one world-class university, only seven of a matriculating computer science class of ninety-five (7 percent) were women.[48] Those who graduated four years later undoubtedly were fewer yet. Internationally, the rate of participation by women tends to be similar, tending to be low everywhere. For example, information technology and computer science have the lowest percentages enrolled of any course of study at the Norwegian Institute of Technology (8 percent).[49]

The issue is an important one, and not merely from a social justice point of view. "The stakes are high for the national economy [as well]. . . . The information technology profession is . . . [and has been] in the midst of a severe workplace shortage; it is estimated that more than 900,000 jobs [1 million or more by other estimates] are unfilled." The upshot is reflected in one survey of computer software projects: "more than 40 percent had been cancelled and another 35 percent had serious problems, with much of the difficulty attributed to a shortage of skilled workers."[50]

Rather than seriously addressing the problem, the information technology industry's response to the shortage of computer professionals has been a political one. Under the H-1B visa program, discussed below in chapter 15, the industry has been able to sponsor up to 130,000 or so analysts and engineers from countries such as India or Armenia (which the industry understates as only 65,000 or, alternatively, as 85,000). The visas permit the guest workers to remain in the United States for three years. The industry continues to lobby extensively for expansion of the program to 300,000 or more entrants per year. It has been the industry's nearly exclusive response to shortage.

By and large, though, women represent a large untapped pool of brainpower and talent that the information technology industry and its leaders, including female CEOs, largely ignore. These women, or certain of them, can "hold up half the sky," and can do so for significantly longer than three years at a time. What, then, are some of the impediments that the industry and the society as a whole must overcome to make inroads on the gross underrepresentation of women in information technology?

6

BASIC EDUCATION

Impediments to Overcome

As engineering professor Caroline Clarke Hayes notes, "The percentage of women has steadily increased over the last 40 years in almost all science, technology, engineering, and math (STEM) disciplines. However, what is uniquely perplexing . . . is the percentage of women undergraduates [in information technology fields] has been steadily dropping for 20 years."[1] The future prospects do not seem bright either:

> In their enthusiasm for computing, [instructors and other experts at high schools and universities] have created situations in which it is hard for novices to be enthusiastic. Like the overzealous tour guide who forces his charges to climb endless steps for the perfect view [or] to eat sheep's eyeballs for the perfect cross-cultural [gastronomic] experience, . . . a [university IT] organization can produce more dropouts than recruits.[2]

Many of the obstacles that stand in women's way are cultural and deeply ingrained, such as the nerd image of the dominant male or the pandemic objectification of women. But the educational framework, the setting that introduces women to information technology fields, would seem to be more easily changed. And if education can turn itself around, perhaps inroads will be made in ameliorating the other "turnoffs" as well.

An Analogy as Background

Sports coaches and youth activity leaders have narrow vision. And, as the kids in their charge mature, coaches' vision narrows further rather than broadens. At a time when kids have more and more demands on their time (homework, music, ballet, drama, science club, college visits), coaches' vision becomes myopic. They demand monomaniacal devotion to the team and to the sport or activity they supervise. Rather than attempting to accommodate the increased demands on their charges' time, those coaches' and other youth leaders' demands for total dedication is a turnoff for young women whose range of interests broadens as they mature.

Something similar happens in computing and information technology settings. In fact, the dissonance may be greater. "Male students start [computer] programming earlier. They develop a sense of familiarity; they tinker . . . and they develop a sense of mastery over the machine. They are introduced by a parent who is involved with computers . . . [and is] able to seed a budding interest. [Boys] are drawn by [computer] games designed to spark and engage boys' interests."[3]

By contrast, girls and young women have a different early history. "For most, the attraction [to computing] is more moderate and gradual. Most did not have the experience of falling in love at an early age that many boys did."[4] One can see this in a sampling of young women's responses to interview questions:

> "I didn't spend all my waking hours on it [the computer] the way some budding hacker did."
> "I was never the kind of person to sit at the computer and fiddle with things."
> "All of that tinkering never appealed to me."

In one study, three-quarters of the men but almost none of the women stated that they were magnetically attracted to computing when they were quite young.[5] So by the time they (women) arrive there, information technology and computer science already have a "distinctly masculine culture" that is off-putting to young women. Piled upon the masculine culture is the nerd image. "The nerd stereotype is perhaps the most common explanation for low rates of participation by women: . . . the computer nerd [is] eccentric, unkempt, antisocial—and male."[6]

Initial Forays by Young Women

Then, too, when young women begin to explore entry into the field, they have a wider circle of interests and a much broader conception of the place they would like to occupy in society. The contrast with the opposite gender again is stark. Males, most of whom already are there, either as students or teachers, have well-honed tunnel vision.

"For most women students . . . the study of computer science is made meaningful by its connections to other fields. Men are more likely to view their decision to study computer science and the study itself as ends in themselves." Stated another way, "for most men . . . the decision to major in computer science barely reaches the level of conscious consideration: it is a natural extension of their lifelong passion for computing." Women bring "contextual concerns" to their deliberations over whether to study computer science.[7]

Technical computer science curricula lack the larger interdisciplinary framework that women find appealing. Women are excited to learn how the use of computers might relate, for example, to environmental study or to improvements in health care. When men, including especially instructors, do relate computing to a broader context, the context borders on the frivolous, or seems that way, delving into football or professional baseball statistics. "Can a creative person, a 'people person,' care about the world and still be happy in computer science? The stereotype says 'No.'"[8]

The one or two girls who do enroll in a computer class find that they are "perpetually teased about their bodies, their appearance, and their competence."[9] Like injured hermit crabs, the girls retreat into their shells, or they leave the field altogether.

So painted, the picture seems dark and forbidding. The upside, though, actually is brighter than it might seem. The reason for that cheerful outlook is that many or even most of the impediments to entry by females into computer science and information technology are fixable.

The Education Roadmap

The literature on computer education is voluminous. Many of the authors plow the same furrow, albeit in differing, and sometimes enlightening, ways. These are four of the better sources:

> *Women and Information Technology: Research on Underrepresentation*, edited by J. McGrath Cohoon, University of Virginia, and William Aspray, Indiana University (MIT Press, 2008).

> *Gender Codes: Why Women Are Leaving Computing*, edited by Thomas J. Misa, University of Minnesota (Wiley, 2010).
> *Unlocking the Clubhouse: Women in Computing*, by Jane Margolis & Allan Fisher, Carnegie Mellon University (MIT Press, 2003).
> *Tech Savvy: Educating Girls in the Computer Age*, by American Association of University Women, Commission on Technology, Gender and Teacher Education (2003).

Undoubtedly, other excellent sources exist; there will be still more in the future. On the other hand, certain of the source materials relating to diversity, education, and information technology are incredibly dense and technical, accessible only to the most dedicated reader, but the following sections present gleanings from the above sources.

Improved Home Environments

Once students get more deeply involved in academic settings, 40 percent of the males but 65 percent of the females report that one or both parents participate with them in computer-based activities. "Parents impart their computer enthusiasm and skills to their children."[10] Judging from the paucity of girls and young women downstream (they represent only 9 percent of the test takers for the higher-level Advanced Placement examination in computer science) and overall,[11] an insufficient number of girls are receiving this beneficial head start of parental involvement, more important for young women than for young men.

In some cases, parental attitudes may be part of a lopsided home environment. Today's parents want to raise children of both genders with a full range of educational, sports, and career options. "And yet when it comes to toys, activities, room decorations and the like [a subset of parents] seem to forget their overall gender neutral objective. Often this results in unintentionally stereotyped decisions, like placing the computer in the son's room 'because he is using it more.'"[12]

The home environment is also affected by computer-based games and the gaming industry, which are extremely problematic. They are so male-oriented—not only male-oriented but male-dominated—that information technology and its anemic performance overall look good in comparison. Games and educational software are principal gateways to the computer world. Yet "blue software" (for boys) almost completely occupies the field. Almost exclusively, "blue software panders to male fantasies for violence and aggression."[13] Because this is such a turnoff for girls and young women, with the result that they are denied a principal path into information technology, the need for reform of the computer game industry forms the topic of chapter 22 of this book.

Early Nondirectional Exposure

As Margolis and Fisher note in *Unlocking the Clubhouse*, "When girls do receive encouragement or enthusiasm from parents, it usually occurs later—in the form of encouraging daughters to take computer science in high school [or] to major in computer science in college."[14] One could say "Better late than never," but tinkering and feeling comfortable putting your head under the hood often begin in the home environment. "Becoming engaged in game-playing does not constitute technological fluency, but game playing and [introduction to] software culture are important factors in making [girls] comfortable with computing."[15] Professor Sherry Turkle believes that a key ingredient in the computer science world is to be "an intrepid explorer." An intrepid explorer "delights in risk taking and forging ahead into the unknown." She elaborates, "One can't be fearful of 'getting lost' or breaking the computer."[16] A legendary Silicon Valley entrepreneur was said "to have a hacker background" and, as a result, "was not afraid to just go figure things out."[17]

"Parents raise boys to take risks, expecting them to be adventurous and bold, while they encourage girls to be cautious and careful."[18] A positive home environment, one infused with parental involvement and enthusiasm, constitutes an important first step in inculcating in young women the comfort level needed to become a tinkerer or an "intrepid explorer."

Early Academic Surroundings

"In secondary schools . . . a repeated pattern plays out: a further increase in boys' confidence, status and expertise in computing and a [further] decline in the interest and confidence of girls." Teachers and administrators play a role, as "computer science curricula traditionally build upon and reflect the boys' interests and experience levels. The girls, as 'outsiders,' do not see how they . . . fit in."[19]

Physical facilities play a part. In the computer lab, "boys always get there [to the machines] first. Experienced, aware teachers find it necessary to have computer time assigned, specifically dedicating time for the girls to use the machines." The film *A League of Their Own* chronicled the all-female professional baseball league of World War II days.[20] In order to increase girls' and young women's involvement, more than a few computer science teachers advocate "a lab of their own."

Why is this so? One potential explanation is positive—or in its own way more positive—while the other explanation may clause alarm.

The first explanation is that young women's reticence is purposeful. Surveys of young women reveal a strong strain of "We can but we don't want to" among female high school students. "Girls are not computer-phobic: they are computer reticent. . . . They express the 'we can but we don't want to' philosophy." Evidence bears this out: "In focus groups, most girls took offense at any suggestion that there may be differences in how boys and girls interact with computers."[21]

Of course, girls may express an approach-avoidance outlook because they anticipate that teachers and male students will treat them as second-class citizens in the classroom and the computer lab once they get there. Alternatively, the "we don't want to" part of "we can but we don't want to" may be in anticipation of and revulsion at the nerd culture young women feel will surround and possibly swallow them in IT.

A second explanation is more sinister. "Girls' 'computer reticence' stems from a perceived conflict between femininity and an interest in computers. . . . This notion persists."[22]

> Research suggests that boys and girls working together with computers means trouble for girls. . . . Females in mixed-sex groups were likely to have their competence questioned; their work critiqued, laughed at, or publicly criticized; and their concentration interrupted by males [as compared to young women] working alone or in all female groups.[23]

Girls and women report that, in predominantly male computer-related settings, they are exposed to off-color language, references, and jokes; crude comments about their bodies and their dress; crude behavior by males; pornographic pictures and photos on the workplace wall; outright sexual harassment as well as the experience of a hostile environment, and more.[24]

What drives women away from academic IT settings? "Perceptions [originating in] expectations of highly technical work, carried out in isolation . . . and with little social relevance. . . . Female students believe in the stereotype of the solitary nerd pounding away at the keyboard all day."[25] Professors Kathryn Bartol and William Aspray continue, "The nerd hacker image of singular focus, work addiction, and total absorption makes computer science a difficult subject to study for women."

Same-Sex Education, in Whole or in Part?

As computer labs and classrooms "become 'bright white boys' lunch clubs," and as the exclusionary atmosphere continues after the school day ends, two persistent suggestions are to sponsor all-female computer clubs and reserve access to machines and computer labs for young women's exclusive use. A further such suggestion is actually to reconfigure lab and classroom space.[26]

Only three all-male colleges remain in existence today (Hampton Sydney, Morehouse, and Wabash). In contrast, there are fifty-five or so all-female college and universities, including some leading schools (Wellesley, Smith, Mills, Barnard, St. Mary's). Certain of them thrive. One piece of evidence in support of same-sex education's continuing relevance is that Harvard University's School of Business announced that, in recruiting for its MBA program, the school will pay particular attention to women's colleges.[27] Many educational experts advocate the single-sex alternative as a distinct possibility, more so for young women than men. Certain of the experts point to computer literacy in particular.

It is too late in the day to recommend single-sex education in computer subjects, at least across the board, but neither should the notion be gainsaid. An added fillip may come from one coed high school's website "that shows only boys in the computer lab and presents girls only in cheerleading outfits."[28]

Prerequisites

More so at the university level than at the secondary level, requirements for prerequisite courses intervene. Because males are decidedly more likely to have a computer-based educational experience, prerequisite requirements for computer science courses discriminate more against young women. A number of factors exacerbate the likelihood that young women will lack the ability to meet the prerequisite requirements. For example, one factor is that women choose majors generally and commit to nascent interests, particularly in computer science–type subjects, much later than young men do. A second factor may be that insertion of prerequisite requirements constitutes a greater turnoff for women, given the lack of confidence they harbor as they approach the idea of following up on a budding interest or on a parent's suggestion or urging. "Who feels welcome in the computing classroom . . . when undergraduate computer science programs begin requiring prior programming experience for introductory courses?" Requirements for prerequisites "send a negative message to women."[29]

All of the "blueprints—the doors, walls, and windows" for computer education seem to be for "a boys' clubhouse of computing education."[30] Most decidedly, a curriculum with prerequisites is an element of such thoughtless design.

Along similar lines, admissions policies that give substantial weight to prior experience may affect women more than men, particularly at selective colleges and universities. In this area, "an admissions policy should not give preference to more highly experienced students."[31]

Another third negative curricular element is the insertion into the curriculum of a "weed-out" course. In an engineering curriculum, the make-or-break course may be thermodynamics. University chemistry majors come to a major hurdle when they encounter the required organic chemistry course. Business and accounting majors tremble as they face the cost accounting required offering. By contrast, liberal arts curricula (history, English, political science, fine arts, anthropology, sociology, and so on) traditionally do not require a make-or-break course—a weed-out offering—along the way. Moreover, it is extremely uncommon for arts and letters majors to have any type of weed-out course at all.

Studies have found that "weed-out" courses often constitute a major deterrent to students selecting a major.[32] Computer science faculties often design curricula with a weed-out course in mind. Faculty expect the student to "toughen up," or in oxymoronic terms, "to man up," after an introductory course or two.[33] Frequently, word spreads across the campus that the course in advance programming or the required courses in artificial intelligence and data analytics are centerpieces in the obstacle course designated for a major and leading to a degree in computer science.

Overall, "there is an absence of institutional intervention to actively support women students" in computer courses and majors.[34] Requirements for prerequisite courses, admissions policies that give weight to prior experience in the field, and insertion of weed-out courses all work against more extensive female involvement in computer science.

Better Pedagogy and Role Models

In a survey of 892 high school math, science, and computer teachers, one in three (36 percent) found computers "an unpleasant but necessary part of teaching nowadays," while a similar number (35 percent) found introduction of computers into their classes "a time consuming obstacle."[35] Studies of teachers "find high levels of anxiety about technology and little knowledge or experience in how to use it, other than for word processing or administrative tasks."[36]

A driver of teachers' insecurity is the inadequacy of training for them. When teachers do receive training, the training is done with the "drive-by approach," consisting of an hour here or an hour there, or an in-service day at most. Only 11 percent of the 892 teachers surveyed responded that they had received training on how to integrate computers into their teaching and into their courses. Most often the in-service training consisted of basic "how-to" instruction on use of a computer.[37] All teachers the survey canvassed agree that what is needed is "sustained and ongoing" teacher training on integration of computers into courses.[38]

Another defect in the pedagogy is the unavailability of role models for young women in computer science. Women constitute 42 percent, more or less, of full-time university faculty and 36 percent of the university chancellors and presidents.[39] By contrast, women number only 11 percent of computer science faculty.[40] At one prestigious university, women constitute only 10 percent of the computer science department faculty. Moreover, the proportion "has held steady for years."[41]

Another in-depth study includes as the fourth and last of its recommendations: "Pay more attention to teaching. Put experienced, senior, better, and more emphatic teachers into the earliest [computer science] courses. Incorporate diversity training into teacher assistant training."[42] Teacher training is one area in which the IT industry easily can mount a coordinated effort, with particular attention paid to introduction and training of young women in the field.

Contexts

Two points here. First is a subject already discussed, namely, that teachers weight teaching materials heavily toward contexts, such as baseball or football statistics, that have little interest for most young women and that usually have a decidedly masculine tone. The second point is that, anticipating the settings students may encounter in the future, teachers and curricula direct young women more toward instrumentalist contexts and skills such as word processing and data entry. Meanwhile, teachers point young men toward longer-lived subjects such as theory and skills such as programming and systems analysis.

Being directed toward entry-level, mechanical skills (such as word processing) becomes a turnoff for girls. They realize that teachers are downgrading them, mindlessly in their opinion. "That self-assessment causes many young women to turn their backs" on IT.[43] To many teachers, administrators, and quite a few young women, "gender equity" means "girls' mastery of tools such as PowerPoint, email, Internet research, information retrieval, word processing and data base management." In turn, later on, those attitudes "cause women to be dramatically underrepresented in [true] IT jobs: systems analysis, software design, programming, and entrepreneurial roles."[44]

For young women, the goal for teachers and academic experiences "must be 'the fluency model' of computer and information technology, not glorified clerical computer-based skills."[45] Administrators and planners "need to broaden the concept of computer literacy to include numeracy, cognitive science, problem solving and logic as well as systems planning, programming, software design, hardware usage, and so on."[46]

To reiterate, female students want to use computer-based skills to study disease, urban planning, environmental concerns, and so on.[47] An experienced teacher notes that "most software . . . is targeted for boys: action packed, scoring points, winning situations." "Only [6] percent of computer science students could think of any software with female characters."[48] Another teacher relates, "If it calls for knocking things down, the girls perceive it as just for boys."[49]

One Caveat: There Are Limits

The organization One Laptop Per Child raises funds and receives equipment from a myriad of sources, with the goal of providing every child in K1–12 with his or her own computer. Too much of a good thing may be one result of attempting to reach computer science utopia. Researchers found, for example, that "impoverished students who received free laptops spent more time on games and chat rooms and less time on their homework than before."[50]

Other findings in the Duke University study by economics professors Jacob Vigdor and Helen Ladd may just as alarming and may be more widespread among all students, not just those from impoverished backgrounds. "Students who gain access to a home computer between the 5th and the 8th grades tend to witness a persistent decline in reading and math scores. . . . The license to surf the Internet was also linked to lower grades [with] younger children."[51] Balance in all things includes the reminder that overemphasis on computer subjects can result in the neglect of history, English, geography, art, music, and other subjects. The Vigdor-Ladd study found that "with no adults to supervise, many kids used their networked devices not for schoolwork, but to play games, troll social media and download entertainment (And why not? Given their druthers, most adults would do the same)."[52]

Real-World Connections

Women, much more than men, want an ultimate link, or connection, between what they do in academic settings and the real world:

> Women seem to differ from their male colleagues . . . in the high
> value they placed upon their work contributing to solving real world
> problems—which might range from turning abstract theories into usable
> software, to providing tools for firefighters and air traffic controllers . . .
> to helping business users satisfy their customers. . . . Interviewees [female
> computer programmers] wanted to see a connection between their tech-
> nical work and the needs of real users.[53]

Computing is linked to investigations in medicine, public health, environmental science, epidemiology, famine control, art, and music. Yet
textbooks and teachers focus on dry, abstract subjects or on professional
sports. "The common practice of grouping computer science with math
and science, both informally and organizationally, exacerbates the gender gap in computing."[54]

When surveyed about what they value most in life, women IT majors
gave the highest ratings to family, friends, a rich cultural life, and joy in
living. By contrast, male IT majors rated occupation as having the highest importance. "Women placed a higher value on having a multifaceted
life rather than being focused on only one dimension."[55]

Computer science departments, programs, and classes must add
meaningful context to technical subjects, demonstrating links from
computer-based subjects to problem solving and betterment of the
human condition. An influential study of university departments included as second of its four principal recommendations: "Add context.
Relate [computer-based subjects] to solution of real world social and
similar problems. Introduce curricula that exploit the connection between IT and other disciplines."[56] Additions could be recommendations
to implement the intrepid explorer and fluency models for educating
young women.

7

THE DISTANT PAST AND NEAR FUTURE

This chapter provides bookends for the previous chapter, that is, looking at the more distant past and then looking at recommendations for the future. First, however, the chapter must delve into one more subject involving information technology, young women, and education beyond K1–12: the tendency to switch majors and transfer out of IT subjects at the university level. The problems associated with a lack of women in academic IT studies do not end once the women arrive on campuses and choose IT subjects and majors; they spill over into the first years of college study, as young women enter and then leave the field.

The Transfer Phenomenon

As a university major, English, for example, has one of the lower transfer rates at 15 percent. By contrast, the switching rates in engineering range from 38 percent to 40.5 percent. And the highest rates of all are for mathematics and computer science, up to 63 percent.[1] The problem's magnitude, too, is larger than that. Losses "come from a pool of disproportionately able undergraduates (45.3% with A or A- high school grade averages as compared to 26.3% in other [college] majors)."[2]

Then there is a second confounding factor relevant here. "Switching was the highest among women who have chosen [STEM] majors (52.4 % overall). . . . The majors in which women switchers exceeded women entrants by more then 55% included mathematics/statistics (72.3%) . . . [and] computer science (62.9%)."[3]

Several causes of the switching-out phenomenon are easily identified. First, "weed out classes have the unintended effect of driving away some highly talented students." The previous chapter has already discussed that subject. Second, "slaughtering people in the first exam or two" has a similar negative effect.[4] Third, academic experts have spoken of the "counterproductive effects of grade curving."[5] All three negative practices—weed-out

classes, slaughter-type assessment practices, and grading on the curve—
are found frequently in computer science. Moreover, these deleterious
practices affect young women more than young men.

Why These High Transfer Rates?

In addition to the three practices just mentioned, "losses from [STEM]
majors were thought to reflect a poor balance between faculty research
and teaching, large classes, [and] inadequate academic and emotional
support for students." Women in particular feel the latter. "Studies of
female [STEM] students reported psychological alienation and lowered
self-esteem as factors in their decisions to leave."[6]

A key finding is that, in academic STEM settings, the most marked difference between men and women "lay in their levels of self-confidence."[7]
The biggest factors women cite in recounting their decisions to leave are
"loneliness, intimidation, and discouragement":

> "It is intimidating to be in a class of 97 men and just 3 women."
> "Women just can't break into these solid ranks of men. . . . It's always
> been male and they're gonna keep it that way."
> "I think perhaps the worst thing is, it's lonely. . . . You don't have the
> support you get from talking with other women."
> "I was very intimidated."[8]

No one seems to suggest that a cause of women's reactions is faculty
sexism. "Dissatisfaction with faculty was high" but was not markedly
dissimilar from that of males' (80.3 percent for women, 66.2 percent for
men).[9]

No one suggests either that coddling or hand-holding of women is
the answer to curbing high transfer rates. Instead, efforts at elimination
of the three pedagogical practices outlined above would be a start, one
that undoubtedly some university teachers have undertaken. In addition, the curriculum should allow for, and indeed encourage, more ex-
perimentation in the first place. "In the humanities, faculty commonly
encourage students to experience different disciplines before making a
final choice. By contrast, [STEM] faculty demand an early [often total]
commitment from students."[10]

The First Bookend: A Long-Term View of Women in Business

On at least three occasions, women's employment numbers seemed to suggest a profound cultural change in the offing and a significant increase in women's role in business. The second and third decades of the twentieth century saw a geometric increase in administrative and other front office functions in American business. Labor shortages in World War II resulted in an increase in women's employment (the Rosie the Riveter phenomenon). And the 1950s and 1960s, the early years of the computer revolution, saw the rise to prominence of women in data entry and machine operation, as discussed in chapter 4.

On each occasion, however, the reality failed to live up to expectations, and women's efforts at parity in the workplace evoked images of Albert Camus's myth of Sisyphus. Sisyphus's punishment in hell, you will recall, was to push a large boulder up a hill. As he neared the top, the boulder escaped his grasp, rolling back to the base. He was destined to push the large rock up the hill, only to have it roll back down the slope, for eternity.[11]

In the years preceding World War I, as American manufacturing and retail operations expanded greatly, companies were "faced with a shortage of clerks, willing to be paid low wages . . . [and] turned to women to be operatives in the office workplace." "The office . . . was increasingly full of females, . . . ideal candidates for clerical jobs."[12] Women then began to agitate for and receive new, expanded roles in business at the same time that suffrage activists were achieving some successes in obtaining for women the right to vote. Wyoming became the first U.S. state to grant that right, which it did in 1890, while still a territory.[13]

For example, in the midst of all this, as Jeanette Eaton and Bertha Stevens described it, "Women [in 1915] are thinking of themselves as professional workers, and men are thinking of them with a new seriousness. . . . This new professional awareness of women comes fortunately at a time when . . . the [business] professions themselves are acquiring an unprecedented public importance and new flexibility of mind."[14]

A Pushback by Men in Business Pursuits

Males—or certain of them—worked to cap the level to which women could rise. At that time, "a growing [counter-]trend was toward requiring . . . standards for professional status, including college degrees, certifying examinations, licensure . . . and, frequently, postgraduate training as well. While some of these changes were aimed at improving training, they were also designed to limit access" for women.[15] These, too, were the times of advocacy for "scientific management." In 1911 Frederick Taylor published his manifesto, *The Principles of Scientific Management*, which quickly became the bible for Taylor's admirers and followers ("Taylorites").[16]

The purported ability of the male business professional to employ the "scientific method" was a critical aspect of males' power. "The Taylorites acquired the mantle of science . . . partly by the simple fact of changing the term *systematic management* to *scientific management*."[17] At times, the backlash from males and schools of scientific management became ridiculous: "employing subjective ideas about women's biology, commentators tried to argue that women were simply unsuited to the rigors of scientific thought."[18] Some male business professionals made these ideas explicit, excluding women. "At the General Electric Company . . . male managers and executives were sent to summer camp, beginning in 1922, to encourage company loyalty and solidarity. They performed forest rituals and dressed up like lumberjacks or Roman soldiers. No women were ever invited."[19] The dominant males circled the wagons tighter. One advocate of scientific management, an engineer, illustrated what he termed "principles of efficiency": "Women make tepees, but men build skyscrapers."[20] A prominent mining engineer publicly announced that "women would be as welcome in engineering as would be snakes in Ireland." A Pittsburgh engineer named John Needles Chester did "not approve of women entering any field [that would] subtract from their womanliness." He went on to apply his principle to his profession: "Next to military leadership, the profession of engineering is the most masculine. . . . Engineering incorporates . . . the roughest and most hazardous. . . . It will be years before women could place themselves . . . in this field."[21]

Economic events intervened. The Great Depression pushed unemployment rates to 25 percent. Widespread unemployment crowded many women out of the workplace, arresting and then reversing the movement of women into middle management and then even into clerical roles. The boulder Sisyphus had pushed rolled back to the base of the hill.

The War and Rosie the Riveter

A second foray of women into occupations previously monopolized by males occurred in World War II. Replacing males who had gone off to fight, Rosie built airplanes and ships. WASP and WAVE members flew airplanes to places where they were needed. Of necessity, women occupied a myriad of positions and professions, as the Army and the Navy sent males overseas to prosecute war on not one but two disparate fronts.

Almost as quickly, as men returned from the war, they resumed their prewar callings, professions, and occupations. From the mid-1940s to 1950, women's presence in the workplace and the front office dwindled once more. Women continued to have an increasing presence in a few fields, such as bookkeeping, a calling in which women occupied more than 63 percent of an estimated 721,000 to 738,000 positions.[22] There was even a backlash against female bookkeepers. Some industries and firms, such as insurance companies and investment firms, kept women confined to "women's departments." "Banks in particular remained bastions of male privilege."[23] Overall, though, the trend was downward once more.

The Punch Card and Computer Eras

A third expansion of women's foray into businesses and offices occurred in the 1950s, 1960s, and 1970s in the fields of data entry, machine operation, and some lower levels of programming, in part an outgrowth of the earlier female presence in bookkeeping and similar fields. Males, though, intervened once again, to dominate the upper ranks of IT—namely, programming, systems analysis, and hardware and software development. From the 1980s onward, women's presence even in IT's lower ranks has dwindled at an increasing rate.

In many ways, these three epochs of women's entry into business and information technology resemble one another, bringing to mind not only the myth of Sisyphus but the shopworn statement "The more things change, the more they stay the same."

The Other Bookend: Peering into the Future

Some policy prescriptions for the future may help things change:

> Mentoring and sponsorship at the educational level in addition to the occupational monitoring that may enter the picture at a later stage;
> Rethinking the near-total reliance on the H-1B visa alternative and the industry's reliance on programmers and engineers from other nations;
> Partial revival in some form of a relic from the 1920s called "vestibule training";
> Encouragement of same-sex activities and outlets such as lab time, computer club activities, and computer science majors;
> Elimination of the snobbishness and elitism that permeate information technology's thinking and hiring.

Mentoring

The "how-to" literature for women is full of assertions about the absolute need for mentoring.[24] Recommendations are that mentors are like stocks: women should have not merely one or two but a diversified portfolio of them. An aspiring woman should have not only one or two mentors in her own company, but also mentors in other companies in the same or similar industries, a couple in her field (finance, marketing, manufacturing, information technology, and so on), and perhaps a few mentors in her city or region.[25]

The voluminous discussion in the literature, discussed at length in chapter 12, seems to be devoid of any thought about mentoring in educational and pre-employment contexts. Historically, much of science and mathematics are approached and taught as if they existed in a vacuum. There are lab sessions and clubs, but they only go part of the way in answering students', particularly women students', question, "What's the point?"

Computer classes and clubs, as well as math, chemistry, and physics offerings, would benefit greatly if representatives of companies and industries demonstrated to high school and university groups not only the relationship of academic studies to the real world but the actuality of it. "I work for so and so, it is a large company, this is what I currently work on, this is how I use what I learned in the classroom, these are some of the things I have worked on in the past, these are some of the matters we possibly will encounter in the future." A mentor from government or industry could appear, in the flesh, not on one but several occasions. An intrepid mentor could pass out her business card, saying, "Call me if you have comments or questions."

Replacement of Portions of H-1B Visa Sources with Recruitment and Training of Women

This subject has been touched on previously and will be explored in depth in chapter 15. The IT industry seems disingenuous in its relentless push for H-1B visa program expansion compared with its neglect of half our society's brainpower, that is, females. Leavening the mix so that it does not consist solely of programmers and engineers (mostly male) from India and other foreign nations such as Armenia seems to be a no-brainer but has made little headway in information technology.

Vestibule Training

With the expansion of office functions and the resulting need for clerical workers, companies established "vestibule or corporation schools to train workers" for newly created and vacant positions.[26] On corporate premises themselves, company representatives taught young women about filing systems, composition of business letters, billing and collection procedures, and other subjects. Complete training for programming or software development roles would not be possible, for the simple reason that such on-site training could not go nearly as deep as the positions required. Some form of vestibule training could, however, compensate for the overwhelming head start males have had in information technology roles.

Same-Sex Extracurricular and Similar Activities

I attended a boys' high school and a men's college, followed by several years as an officer in the Navy and then law school, predominantly but not exclusively male back then. My ex-wife blamed many of my myriad deficiencies on my same-sex educational and military backgrounds. Nonetheless, I am a great believer in same-sex education, particularly for young women. I have two daughters, now in their thirties, who share my beliefs, or say they do. The importance of same-sex education, or at least same-sex extracurricular activities, in information technology seems amply supported by surveys of young women about their opinions and experiences. Chapter 6 discussed the subject in greater depth.

Eliminate Snobbishness and Elitism

In her book about women's employment at Facebook, Katherine Losse relates how the company's hires were almost exclusively those with Stanford or Harvard degrees.[27] Having graduated from Wesleyan, she considered herself lucky to be hired, albeit at a much lower salary than that of the males. She was, after all, coming from a university few on the West Coast may have heard of, even though Wesleyan is a "little Ivy." Ms. Losse had a master's degree from Johns Hopkins, presumably a university that would be known in Silicon Valley, though her graduate degree was in English literature.

Google and Microsoft, other giants in information technology, exhibit the same or an even greater level of credential consciousness. They screen job applicants' credentials with extreme vigilance. Prevalent throughout the IT industry is this overreliance or overemphasis on credential screening and collecting. Today especially, excellent quality people come from everywhere. Even conservative college counselors consider there to be 150 or more elite colleges and universities. Many university-level students cannot afford the travel, room, and board that would be required to attend a more distant university. They may be "place-bound," by marriage, by children, by a job needed to defray the costs of education, or a need to care for a dependent parent or sibling.

In addition to place-bound students, other college-bound students and their families cannot afford the $35,000 or $40,000 in yearly tuition that private colleges and universities charge. Even tuition and fees at state-supported institutions of higher learning have ratcheted upward dramatically in the last fifteen years. Some or all of these considerations bear down harder on young women than young men. Some parents with anachronistic attitudes may be more willing to pay money for sons' as opposed to daughters' educations.

In recruiting and hiring, the information technology industry has to cast a much wider net. The industry's elitist attitudes are unwarranted and, in particular, discriminate against women.

Increased Industry Involvement and Coordination

In addition to the above measure, the information technology industry has to face the issue of women's roles in their industry, get more deeply involved in attempting to solve the problems thought to exist, and to the degree possible mount coordinated, comprehensive plans to ameliorate them.

In San Francisco, the AltSchool bases itself on the premise that while "a three year old today isn't different, . . . largely because of technology a thirteen-year old [girl] is *really* different [from a boy]."[28] The school has 150 professionals, evenly split among educators and technologists, bent on ameliorating such differences. Venture capitalists have invested $110 million in equity and a further $20 million in loans in the school.

The Founders' Fund, which includes as members Silicon Valley legends Marc Andreessen (*The New, New Thing*), John Doerr (partner at Kleiner Perkins, the leading venture capitalist firm), and Mark Zuckerberg (Facebook founder) have been extremely generous in financing the venture. The philanthropic Silicon Valley Foundation invested $15 million in the AltSchool.

> None of these backers want to own part of a chain of boutique microschools. Rather, they hope that AltSchool will help "reinvent" American education: first, by innovating in its micro-schools; next, by providing software to educators who want to start up their own schools; and, finally, by offering its software for use in public schools across the nation, a goal that the company hopes to achieve in three to five years.[29]

Although not always directly responsive to the lack of female involvement and leadership in technology, the AltSchool goes a long way toward addressing certain of the problems.

There are other, similar efforts. The Bill and Melinda Gates Foundation and the Emerson Collective (funded by Laurene Powell Jobs, Steve Jobs's widow) have invested tens of millions, and more, in similar educational efforts. Mark Zuckerberg made a highly publicized $100 million investment in the Newark, New Jersey, public schools. These and other attempts at educational advancement aim at overcoming deficits in much of traditional education. To a great degree, the perception has been that educators have forgotten the need to think about how children learn and what they need to be successful in life, in a world that has undergone vast change in the last decades.

What is needed is similar industry commitment to the subset of problems unique to women's involvement in information technology. Those problems have led to the most dismal record in hiring and promoting women, with IT topping the list of offenders.

PART III

SOLUTIONS ADVANCED

8

WOMEN TO TRY HARDER

"Lean In" and Similar Recommendations

For several years now, occupying center stage have been Sheryl Sandberg and her 2013 book on gender and business leadership, *Lean In: Women, Work, and the Will to Lead*.[1] Because Ms. Sandberg is the chief operating officer (COO) of Facebook, a successful information technology company, and previously had been an executive at Google, an even more successful IT company, the book and its recommendations have particular relevance to women in information technology.

Lean In's central thesis is that women must "lean in," that is, work actively to overcome the barriers that have prevented the ascension of women in the same numbers and with the same speed as their male counterparts. Women in business should sit at the conference room table rather than on the periphery of the meeting room; women in business must take steps to prevent males from plagiarizing their concepts and ideas; women should put in extra effort (more not less) during pregnancies and prefatory to leaves of absence; and women in business should insist that spouses share equally in household and child-rearing tasks. Sandberg coins the useful term "nudge techniques," "small interventions that encourage people to behave in slightly different ways at critical moments," that women should implement in the workplace.[2]

"Sandberg . . . drills down on one [obstacle for women] in particular, the one she says receives the least attention: the invisible barrier in women's minds."[3] "Compared to our male colleagues, fewer of us aspire to senior positions. It's not exactly that they're to blame. Females are raised from birth to have different expectations. There's an ambitions gap, and it's wreaking havoc on women's ability to advance."[4]

Ms. Sandberg introduced that theme early in her book: "Women are hindered by barriers that exist within ourselves. We hold ourselves back . . . by lacking self-confidence, by not raising our hands, and by pulling back when we should be leaning in. We lower our expectations of what we can achieve."[5]

Near-Unanimous Praise for Ms. Sandberg and Her Book

The Sandberg book met with instant adulation. The *New Yorker*'s Anna Holmes wrote that *"Lean In* is inauguration, more than the last word, and an occasion for celebration."[6] Sheryl Sandberg's photograph featured prominently in national publications such as *Time* (on the cover) and the *Wall Street Journal*. The author appeared, and still appears, on television talk and news programs, proselytizing on her book and her new organization, Lean In.

Ms. Sandberg, her book, and her new organization were not without critics. The *New York Times* columnist Maureen Dowd focused on the book's recommendations: "[Sandberg] seems to think that she can remedy social paradigms with a new kind of club—a combo gabfest, Oprah session and corporate pep talk."[7]

Criticism and Drawbacks

Lean In is another book that puts the onus on women, albeit one with more than a few new wrinkles and tweaks, and is of significantly higher caliber than the books that preceded it. Almost all of those books are how-to and advice books for aspiring women. Ms. Sandberg denies that her book is the same, early on stating that "this book is not a memoir. . . . It is not a self-help book. It is not a book on career management."[8] In fact, the book is all of those things. *Lean In* suffers further from the author's repeated denials that the book is personal coupled with a refusal to admit that she comes from an elite—indeed, rarefied and elite—background that other women do not share.[9]

Work/life issues aside, none of the available literature focuses on what corporations and industries can and should do to address this important social issue. *Lean In* continues in that shopworn vein. Of course, Ms. Sandberg's high office at a tech company handcuffed her. She was the COO of Facebook, a corporation that at the time had one of the worst records in hiring and promoting women (it has since righted itself). Ms. Sandberg could not very well criticize her own company or the industry in which it functions, namely, information technology. She undoubtedly felt she had to pull her punch, at least if she had a punch to pull.

Deficient Paradigm?

As aforesaid, another central criticism of Ms. Sandberg's recipe for success is its inherent thesis that what worked for her will work for all, or many, other women. This has been recognized as a doubtful proposition at best. In her book review, tongue in cheek, journalist Ann Belser concludes that "[*Lean In*] is more than just a plea for women to stay engaged. It is also a memoir: the story of how a young woman rose from her upper-middle-class upbringing as a doctor's daughter with a stay-at-home mom to attend Harvard and subsequently rise to the upper 0.1 percent."[10]

I ran that comment by an accomplished woman colleague, ending with my conclusion that perhaps Ms. Sandberg lacked standing, or perspective, from which she could advocate for more typical women executives. She lacked standing, I said, because "Sandberg was born with a silver spoon in her mouth." My colleague replied, "What silver spoon? Born with a diamond-encrusted gold—nay, platinum—spoon in her mouth."

Ms. Sandberg's career trajectory has been extraordinary:

> As a sixth grader she placed second in a statewide oratory contest that included high school students.
> She was at the top of her class in a large Miami high school, was voted "most likely to succeed" by her senior class, and was a National Merit Scholar.
> She was at the top of her class as an undergraduate at Harvard College, graduated with honors, and was elected to Phi Beta Kappa.
> She worked for two years as special assistant to Larry Summers when he was president of the World Bank.
> She was first in her MBA class at the Harvard University School of Business and was awarded the Ford prize as the best student in the class.
> She served as chief of staff to Larry Summers when he was secretary of the treasury (youngest chief of staff in Treasury history).
> She was employee number 200 at Google, 2001–2007.

> When she was hired by Mark Zuckerberg, CEO, to be COO of Facebook, she was the only woman among the top fifty executives at the company.

Fostering Harmful Stereotypes

The "lean in" school of thought and Ms. Sandberg's pronouncements have good points as well as bad. A deficiency is *Lean In*'s constant refrain that women are markedly different from men. Ms. Sandberg ascribes this purported difference to "society" for sending "cultural messages" loaded with "gender stereotypes" that discourage women from taking leadership roles in business or even from aspiring to them. "Society discourages women from taking risks and from promoting their own achievements."[11] Ms. Sandberg fosters "a single gender stereotype" of women and it tends not to be a positive one.[12]

Women may be different from their male counterparts, but it is a slippery slope to advocate that people should think that way. Historically, just such a view has been the pretext by which males in positions of power have retarded women's advancement. They did and still do so by saying that "she's a woman and therefore too emotional," "she's a woman and therefore not analytical," or, as the Supreme Judicial Court of Massachusetts once remarked, "after all, she was only a housewife."[13]

The opposite view is that those in power, including corporate directors and corporate CEOs, repeatedly announce and promulgate decrees "tell[ing] everyone that the organization will bend over backwards to treat everyone equally and fairly" and to think of them in that way.[14] All employees should receive equal pay for equal work, equal benefits, and equal opportunities for increased responsibilities and promotions. A CEO should send the message that disparate impacts and hostile environments will not be tolerated: as an organization, the corporation constantly will revisit the issues to ensure fair and equal respect and treatment for all.[15]

Ms. Sandberg's philosophical viewpoint, from the perspective of women rather than corporations or an industry, feeds directly into an outmoded and dangerous way of thinking. The "old guys" or "nerds and geeks" who dominate selection processes may venture little beyond lip service, putting women on a different track, for different positions (so-called pink-collar jobs) on the grounds that candidates are women and, therefore, different. Search committees may eliminate female finalists on the grounds that they are women, that women lack the requisite "charisma," and that the position to be filled somehow requires that ineluctable quality.[16]

Fostering Positive and Constructive Stereotypes

Sheryl Sandberg did introduce some helpful elements to the discussion. For example, she encourages an aspiring woman to think of her career path "as a jungle gym rather than a ladder."[17]

> Ladders are limiting—people can move up or down, on or off. Jungle gyms offer more creative exploration. There's only one way to get to the top of a ladder, but there are many ways to get to the top of a jungle gym. . . . The ability to forge a unique path with occasional dips, detours, and even dead ends presents a better chance for fulfillment.[18]

Women beholden to the ladder approach, as Ms. Sandberg describes it, become frustrated by phenomena such as "glass walls" and "glass elevators." Corporate organizations tend to slot women into positions that, longer term, offer less opportunity for advancement. Often the positions are infelicitously termed "pink-collar" jobs: positions in human resources or with the corporation's captive charitable foundation. Glass walls around certain corporate work groups such as the pink-collar ones allow women to see but not to venture into other work centers, positions, and career tracks in which upward advancement is a better possibility. The glass elevator is a related concept. Women in an organization can see male counterparts ascending vertical tracks. Yet an impermeable see-through barrier permits the female executives to see but not join the upward movement the males enjoy. The jungle gym perspective is a useful antidote.

The refrain "Don't leave before you leave" is a useful heuristic as well.[19] Ms. Sandberg's advice is that when the decision to leave is on the horizon, to have a child or care for an aged parent, for example, that is a time when younger women should lean in rather than lean out. Put in extra effort, "show your stuff," bend over backward to demonstrate your dedication and your proficiency. "The time to scale back . . . is when the child arrives—not before, and certainly not years in advance."[20]

Mimicking Her Predecessors

Sheryl Sandberg spends a chapter echoing advice that has been central in many of the other "how-to" and advice books for women in business.[21] The CEO of Catalyst, Sheila Wellington, authored an acclaimed book, *Be Your Own Mentor*.[22] Ms. Sandberg describes the difficulties women encounter in obtaining mentors, followed by entreaties to gather mentor relationships nevertheless, despite the difficulty.

As previously noted, mentors are like stocks. An aspiring executive should have a diversified portfolio of them: one or two senior executives at her own company; one or two executives at other companies; a go-to person on, say, accounting issues; the same as to marketing; ditto for intellectual property issues; one or more women business leaders who can advise on obstacles to expect; and so on.[23]

A downside of the quest for mentors is that men do not resort to senior women as mentors (Ms. Sandberg noted that she could not "recall a single man asking me to be a mentor").[24] A related issue is that certain senior women relish the notoriety or ego boost that comes from being the only woman in a work group or at a certain management level. They do not willingly serve as mentors for other women or, if they do, they steer them in circles or wrong directions. Organizational psychologists and sociologists have written extensively about the phenomenon, the queen bee syndrome, at times citing it as evidence of women's cruelty to other women.[25]

Other Sides of the Issue

There are two sides to every story, or at least to most of them, and Ms. Sandberg frequently ignores the downsides to the courses of conduct she recommends. Obtaining and maintaining mentor relationships is one such subject. As I will develop further in chapter 12, there are three major downsides to a mentor-mentee relationship:

> At some organizations these relationships morph into a "star system" in which the upside may be greater for a chosen few but downfalls are more numerous, quicker, and more pronounced for the many.
> Unwittingly, mentors may shield women mentees especially from problems, or attempt to shunt them into safer positions (pink-collar jobs again), rather than advising a female mentee on how to work through a problem or providing background on the political landscape. Scholars term these phenomena the "office uncle" and the "glass bubble" hazards that women in particular may encounter in a mentoring relationship.
> Based upon lengthy experience, many observe that more often than not mentor-mentee relationships do not lead anywhere, or fall short of expectations. They have not been a propellant for many women executives who aspire to higher positions in business, as traditionally advice givers have billed them to be.

Indeed, some would say that Sheryl Sandberg was a beneficiary of a star system not once but twice, first at the World Bank, and then at the Department of the Treasury, as she rode the coattails of her powerful mentor, Harvard economics professor Larry Summers. Undoubtedly, Ms. Sandberg's accomplishments and abilities played a central role too, but the question is a legitimate one: mentor-mentee relationship or a star system? A woman in business should be alert to the difference, keeping a weather eye in that direction.

Outright Bum Steers

At a few points, Ms. Sandberg's advice book goes completely off the tracks. Without citation to authority, she throws out the statistic that the average American has eleven jobs—eleven positions prior to age forty-six, let alone prefatory to her final or "nth" position.[26] Women, she says, should not be afraid to take risks. She quotes Eric Schmidt, then Google's CEO, when offering Sandberg a position at Google: "If you're offered a place on a rocket ship, don't ask what seat. You just get on." Women in more established industries "can look for rocket ships within their companies—divisions or subsidiaries that are expanding."[27]

Women should be less averse to taking risks, Sandberg advises. "Women only apply for jobs if they think they meet 100 percent of the criteria listed. Men apply if they think they meet 60 percent of the criteria." Men look for stretch assignments while women hang back.[28]

This may be good advice, but it is buttressed by dangerously inaccurate statistics. In 2010 I published *The Last Male Bastion: Gender and the CEO Suite in America's Public Companies*.[29] The book tracks the education and career patterns of the twenty-two women who at that point had become CEOs of Fortune 500 corporations. In 2010 there were fifteen women in office (there are something like twenty-three or twenty-four today) coupled with seven who had retired or been removed from office. I wanted to find out what successful women actually did, as opposed to the myriad advice books for women in business. All of the latter base their recommendations on anecdotal evidence and armchair empiricism: "I did this," or "my friend says she did it that way." What actually had successful women done?

In that exercise, I found that women CEOs had an average, or mean, of 3.3 jobs, not the 11 toward which Ms. Sandberg points, up to and including their position at the top. The mode (most frequently encountered) was 3. Several CEOs, such as Anne Mulcahy at Xerox or Ellen Kullman at DuPont, were lifers, having spent their entire careers at one company. The outlier was Meg Whitman, now CEO of Hewlett-Packard, whose "Whitman's Sampler" included eight jobs. Excluding the outlier (Whitman), the mean number of jobs in a trek for women to the CEO position was three.

The danger of a woman heeding Ms. Sandberg's advice, jumping from job to job, or within a company from position to position, is development of an appearance that the woman is a "job jockey." Admittedly, a woman may justify jumping around for good reason. Meg Whitman, for example, is married to an academic neurosurgeon whose career has taken him to disparate geographical areas. Ms. Whitman and her two sons have followed Dr. Harsh's career moves. Besides, Ms. Whitman has a bachelor's degree from Princeton and an MBA from Harvard. A person with those credentials undoubtedly has an easier time moving from job to job and position to position, as would Sheryl Sandberg with a bachelor's degree from Harvard College and an MBA from Harvard University. As in other areas, Ms. Sandberg's advice may not be for everybody, or even for a significant number of women in business.

Two Bottom Lines

The first bottom line is that although Ms. Sandberg wrote a good book, filled with useful anecdotes and recommendations, it is just another "how-to" advice book for women. Moreover, it is a typical "how-to" advice book, filled with personal anecdotes and memoirs from her own privileged business career.

Lean In says nothing about the other side: what corporations—for example, those in information technology—might do. A comprehensive treatment would suggest methods a corporation could adopt to increase the numbers of women as directors or in senior management positions. What aspiring women should do or the paths they might follow is a closely related topic—relevant but only half of the story.

The second point to make about *Lean In* is that the market is awash in how-to "I did this" or "I did that" books such as Sheryl Sandberg's, although none from the vantage point of her *uber*-privileged background. The following is a sample of such books, including the good with the not-so-good:

> Susan Adams, *The New Rules of Success for Women* (Celebrity Press, 2013).
> Esther Wachs Book, *Why the Best Man for the Job Is a Woman* (Harper Business, 2000).
> Ann Crittenden, *The Price of Motherhood* (Metropolitan Books, 2001).
> Nina DiSesa, *Seducing the Boys' Club* (Ballantine, 2007).
> Gail Evans, *Play Like a Man, Win Like a Woman* (Broadway, 2000).
> Carol Gallagher, *Going to the Top* (Penguin, 2000).
> Jill Griffin, *Earn Your Seat on a Corporate Board* (Jill Griffin Books, 2016).
> Pat Heim & Susan Golant, *Hardball for Women* (Plume, rev. ed. 2005).
> Pat Heim & Susan Golant, *Smashing the Glass Ceiling* (Simon & Schuster, 1995).
> Sylvia Ann Hewlett, *Forget a Mentor, Find a Sponsor: The New Way to Fast-Track Your Career* (Harvard Business Review Press, 2013).
> Sylvia Ann Hewlett, *Off-Ramps and On-Ramps: Keeping Talented Women on the Road to Success* (Harvard Business Review Press, 2007).
> Linda Hirshman, *Get to Work* (Penguin, 2006).

> Jean Hollands, *Same Game, Different Rules: How to Get Ahead without Being a Bully Broad, Ice Queen, or "Ms. Understood"* (McGraw-Hill, 2000).
> Kelly L. Johnson, *Skirt Rules! For the Workplace* (Skirt Publishers, 2008).
> Debora J. McLaughlin, *Running in High Heels: How to Lead with Influence, Impact and Ingenuity* (Balboa Press, 2014).
> Deborah Rhode, *What Women Want: An Agenda for the Women's Movement* (Oxford University Press, 2014).
> Deborah Rhode & Barbara Kellerman, *Women and Leadership: The State of Play and Strategies for Leadership* (Jossey-Bass, 2007).
> Karen Salmansohn, *How to Succeed in Business without a Penis: Secrets and Strategies for the Working Woman* (Three Rivers Press, 1996).
> Sheila Wellington, *Be Your Own Mentor* (Random House, 2001).
> Christy Whitman & Rebecca Grado, *Taming Your Alpha Bitch: How to Be Fierce and Feminine (and Get Everything You Want)* (BenBella Books, 2012).
> Joan C. Williams, *Unbending Gender: Why Family and Work Conflict and What to Do about It* (Oxford University Press, 1999).
> Joan C. Williams & Rachel Dempsey, *What Works for Women at Work: Four Patterns Working Women Need to Know* (New York University Press, 2014).

Many, perhaps all, of those books advise aspiring women to be more assertive, to demonstrate their assertiveness, to be a "quarterback," noted from above for their can-do spirit and their potential leadership abilities. The books tend to utilize sports metaphors ("Throw knockout punches," or "Shoot the three," or "Score a goal").[30] Some of the books make astrology look learned and respectable.

Of course, the path to senior positions is far more nuanced than the advice books depict it. In fact, aggressiveness and assertiveness may gain a woman her first or even second promotion but afterward will backfire. Her aggressiveness may result in her removal from the upward-bound group, or pool, on the grounds that she lacks the ability to think strategically or to inspire and lead others.

Ms. Sandberg has contributed, in a positive way, to all the reservations about the existing literature. In doing an annual survey about women in business, Ms. Sandberg's Lean In organization teamed with McKinsey

& Company, the consulting firm.[31] Reviewing the 2016 study's results, which noted that women do not negotiate on their own behalf, Ms. Sandberg noted that women who do negotiate "face social pushback— and are viewed as 'bossy' or 'aggressive' simply for asking."[32]

> Women who negotiate are 67% more likely than women who don't to receive feedback that their personal style is "intimidating," "too aggressive," or "bossy." . . . We *expect* men to be assertive, look out for themselves. . . . But women must be communal and collaborative, nurturing and giving, focused on team and not themselves. . . . So when a woman advocates for herself, people often see her unfavorably.[33]

So, for overly aggressive women in business, in tech as well as elsewhere, pushback and unfavorable responses may result even before that first or second promotion.

The "How-To" Literature versus *Lean In*

Literally scores of advice books comparable to *Lean In*, as well as articles in magazines and learned journals, have surfaced in recent years.[34] *Lean In* makes a worthy contribution to that body of literature, but it does not supplant it, and that is a principal criticism of Ms. Sandberg's book.

Perhaps a more important criticism is that "more great women don't lean in because they don't like the world they are being asked to lean into."[35] Jody Miller, CEO of Business Talent, concluded her review of Ms. Sandberg's book as follows:

> "Leaning in" may help the relative handful of talented [and privileged] women [such as Ms. Sandberg] who can live with the way top jobs are structured today—and if that's their choice, more power to them. But only a small percentage of women will choose this route. Until the rest of us get serious about altering the way work gets done in American corporations, we're destined to howl at the moon over the injustice of it all while changing almost nothing. In the main, her book is beside the point.

Add to that how corporations hire and promote women, accommodate childbearing and child-rearing, and deal with work/life balances, and you have some of the most important questions facing information technology and other industries today. While informative, Ms. Sandberg's book largely ignores those issues.

A Postscript

In May 2015, while vacationing in Mexico, David Goldberg, Sheryl Sandberg's husband, went to the hotel's fitness room. While exercising on the treadmill, Mr. Goldberg experienced a severe cardiovascular trauma. Hitting his head, he collapsed and lay there for a long period of time, eventually succumbing to cardiac arrhythmia.[36]

In the ensuing months, Ms. Sandberg rethought several of the treatments in her book, including "the difficulties women face when they have an unsupportive partner, or no partner at all." She has spoken out in Facebook posts and at university commencement exercises about her grief.[37] Most recently, in 2017 Sandberg coauthored a book (*Option B: Facing Adversity, Building Resilience, and Finding Joy*) about her bereavement, the obstacles that may result, and overcoming those seeming roadblocks.

9

MANDATORY QUOTA LAWS

In 2003 Norway's Parliament adopted a statute mandating that in Norwegian publicly held companies at least 40 percent of directors be of the gender opposite the other percentage of directors. The drafters phrased the law in observance of Norway's long allegiance to gender blindness in all pursuits.

By 2008, Norwegian companies had achieved that goal, raising their percentage of women directors from 6 percent to 40 percent or more in six years.[1] Meanwhile, Belgium, Spain, and the Netherlands adopted quota laws of one sort or another. Subsequently, France (40 percent) and Germany (30 percent) adopted quota laws calling for female directors on public corporations' boards of directors.[2] In 2012–2013, European Union (EU) Commission vice-president Viviane Reding pushed hard for the Commission to promulgate a quota law applicable to the then twenty-eight EU nations.[3] She failed in that endeavor, but "vowed that she will not give up on the idea."[4]

Quota laws and debate about them have been much-discussed topics for a decade or more, since Norway's adoption, eliciting support in some quarters and adamant opposition in others, for example, the United Kingdom, the United States, and New Zealand.[5] In the latest iteration of its corporate governance code (2015), the influential Organization for Economic Cooperation and Development (OECD) backed away from any firm endorsement of quota laws, despite urging to the contrary, providing only that "countries may wish to consider measures such as voluntary targets, disclosure requirements, boardroom quotas, and private initiatives that enhance gender diversity on boards and in senior management."[6]

Nonetheless, advocates press onward. In 2015 Cambridge University Press published *Challenging Boardroom Homogeneity*, a 315-page paean to adoption of a quota law in Canada, authored by a law professor at Osgoode Hall School of Law (York University, Toronto, Ontario).[7]

Joining that chorus, and possibly hoping against hope, scholars in the United States have advocated quota laws in America.[8] Other advocates have demonstrated that, empirically, quota legislation "generates the most substantial change to the representation of women on boards—far greater that any individual firm, industry or country-level factor previously identified."[9]

Opponents have likened the enactment of quota laws in the United States to using an elephant gun to kill a mouse, or a mallet to kill a moth. On a more elevated plane, "many [U.S.] corporate leaders worry that preferential treatment [of women] will encourage tokenism, result in unqualified appointments, stigmatize beneficiaries, and diminish [women's] credibility. [A] majority of American female directors oppose quotas," citing similar purported reasons.[10]

Applicability to Management Positions

Quota laws, of course, relate to female representation on corporations' boards of directors rather than to representation in senior management. Nevertheless, the former would spill over into the latter. To ensure a robust supply of women directors, companies must place additional emphasis on the pool from which corporations and their boards are likely to select candidates for board positions (see chapter 17). A large segment of that pool is, of course, made up of women who inhabit the upper management ranks in publicly held U.S. enterprises. More slots for women as corporate directors would result in not insignificant pressure to increase women in senior management, that is, pressure to enlarge the pool.

How about the other side of the coin? Will the actuality of additional female directors aid in the elevation of additional women to the upper ranks of middle management and on into the ranks of senior management? "A study by economists in the United States and in Norway found that legislative mandates did not do much in the short run to increase women's representation in the executive ranks."[11] In other words, although there is evidence that female CEOs bolster other women's rise as executives (see the discussion of "trickle down" in chapter 2), the evidence suggests that females as directors have little or no such influence.

Of course, the first generation of activist efforts has concentrated on board seats for women candidates. Most individuals in business consider a seat on the board of directors of a major corporation to be the pinnacle of a career. Also, scholars and advocacy organizations can easily track diversity statistics on board composition for large companies. Annual proxy statements ("Definitive 14A's") that corporations file with the SEC contain extensive data on boards' makeup. By contrast, gathering statistics on the composition of management is more difficult. In the required compensation table, SEC-filed proxy statements do contain disclosure about who are in most instances the five senior-most managers (see the statistics presented in chapter 1). Rounding up statistics about female or other diversity representation in the remainder of senior management, including the lower ranks of senior management, is difficult.

That said, no great leap is required for advocates of quotas to postulate an analogy, arguing that a quota system be extended to management levels as well. So any discussion of female leadership in information technology, whether at the director level or lower down in the management ranks, should delve into the subjects of quota laws, regulations, and programs.

A Principal Argument in Favor of Quota Laws

Advocates of quota laws assert that no progress has been made in promoting the ascension of women to board seats and senior management positions. Appearing on the front page of *USA Today* under the banner headline "Women Have Made No Progress at the Top," a smiling Sheryl Sandberg, labeled "Tech icon feminist," asserts that there has been a "10 year stall."[12] Professor Aaron Dhir makes similar claims in his manifesto in support of a quota law for Canada. Both are incorrect.[13]

Even without any one specific measure or reform, let alone a legislative enactment, national jurisdictions have made gains. U.S. Fortune 500 boards of directors went from 9.6 percent women in 1995 to 20.2 percent today, not breathtaking progress but progress nonetheless, at least if one takes a view of more than ten years.[14] There are twenty-three or twenty-four women CEOs in U.S. Fortune 500 corporations (the exact number varies); prior to 1997, there were none.[15] Similarly, without law, Canada has progressed to a census figure of over 20 percent for women on boards of directors.[16] Elsewhere, formalized but still voluntary programs have worked well. For example, the mentoring/sponsorship initiative in Australia has played a role in rapidly moving the needle from 8 to 20.1 percent among ASX 100 corporations.[17]

Ms. Sandberg and others use a fictionalized lack of progress as a principal plank in their arguments. Although the progress that has occurred falls short of the rate we might like to see, the progress that has occurred does significantly undercut a principal argument for adoption of quota laws or other mandatory measures.

A History of Quota Laws

As aforesaid, in 2003 Norway enacted a quota law that as many as 40 percent of public corporations' directors had to be of the opposite sex of the other directors. The deadline for achievement of that goal, which public companies in Norway reached, was 2008.[18]

Several European Union (EU) member nations (Belgium, France, Italy, the Netherlands, Germany, and Spain) have followed Norway, a non-EU member, in adopting quota laws, as have Iceland, Israel, Switzerland, and Malaysia, among nonmember states.[19] Impatience with the continued male dominance of seats on corporate boards has been growing throughout Europe and among developed countries.

As stated, parliaments in Italy, the Netherlands, and Belgium have followed Norway, enacting gender-based director laws.[20] Yet the quota statutes vary considerably, most particularly in the teeth they have and in how sharp the bite will be in cases of noncompliance. For example, Spain, the second nation to act, ordered achievement of the 40 percent level by 2016, a significant jump from the 5 percent level that prevailed in Spain at the time of the law's adoption.[21] The Spanish statute, though, is aspirational, while the Norwegian law has severe penalties. Norwegian companies that fail to comply are not subject to modest penalties, such as delisting on the stock exchange or monetary penalties, but rather to the extreme penalty of outright dissolution.[22]

France, the third nation to act, adopted a 40 percent quota law early in 2011.[23] Looking northward to Norway, a deputy of the Assemblée Nationale had introduced a 20 percent quota bill in 2006. Thereafter the notion of gender parity, at least in French corporate governance, had to negotiate a twisting route. In 2009, besides looking northward toward Norway, and adding to the momentum for adoption of a quota statute, the French quota measure's supporters found that only 8 percent of directors in France's largest hundred corporations were women. Further, they bemoaned that in that year French public companies added only six new women directors to corporate boards.[24]

The recently enacted French quota mandate was staged. Public companies' boards had to have 20 percent women directors within three years of the enactment and 40 percent within six years (2017).[25] Large French corporations were out in front of the 2014 objective, early in 2012 having passed the 24 percent mark of women directors on boards.[26]

Opposition to Mandatory Quotas

Sweden, Finland, Germany, and the United Kingdom have all come out in opposition to quota laws, at least initially, for various reasons. Sweden (28.2 percent) and Finland (26 percent) already have meaningful representation of women on their corporate boards.[27] Majorities in those countries view adoption of a quota law as unnecessary.

On the other hand, Germany and the United Kingdom have middling to poor and so-so records, respectively, on the issue. The United Kingdom remains openly opposed (see chapter 10), but in 2015 Germany adopted a quota law, albeit a modest one (30 percent representation), for supervisory boards (versus managing boards, for which no requirement exists) of large German publicly held companies.[28] Both countries, Germany and the United Kingdom, have long traditions of bucking trends, becoming even more recalcitrant when told what to do.[29] Besides Norway, EU nonmembers Israel, Iceland, and Switzerland have adopted quota laws. On the other side of the world, the Malaysian government has imposed a quota that publicly held companies there have 30 percent women directors by 2016, especially noteworthy as Malaysia is a Muslim country.[30]

The Dark Side of Quota Enactments

Quota laws have unintended consequences. In the rush to name females to directorships, for instance, Norwegian companies named one—no doubt very capable—woman to eleven corporate boards.[31] No one, not even Superwoman, can serve adequately on more than three or perhaps four boards, especially in the current era with its emphasis on proactive, hands-on directors. Quota laws produce a surfeit of women trophy directors—figurehead (token) directors who are possibly unqualified. Another unintended consequence of a quota law is that a public company may go private and thus go dark rather than attempt compliance with the law.[32]

Quota laws also may result in a surfeit of celebrity directors, who also may be regarded as tokens. Allegedly, that has happened in France, where board seats have gone to former first lady Bernadette Chirac (luxury goods retailer LVMH); Nicole Dassault, wife of the controlling shareholder (Dassault Aviation); Florence Woerth, spouse of the former minister for labor (Hermes); Brigitte Longuet, wife of the former minister of defense (broadcaster Canal Plus); and Amélie Oudéa-Castéra, former tennis professional and wife of Société Générale CEO (media group Lagardère).[33] After adoption of a quota law, "in France, in private, chief executives say they will look for female board members . . . who will look decorative and not rock the boat."[34]

Of course, free of a quota law, the United States has witnessed the celebrity director phenomenon as well, with an opera diva, a faux television "judge," and spouses of U.S. senators as directors, the television judge to three and senators' wives to five and six Fortune 500 boards of directors.[35] The incidence of U.S. celebrity appointments, though, falls far short of what has occurred in France, which might be laid at the feet of France's adoption of a quota law, concomitant with a vast increase in pressure to appoint women directors and to do so relatively quickly.

Another consequence of quota laws could be that companies downsize their boards of directors so as to reduce the number of women candidates necessary and thus lower search costs. Again, an extreme consequence may be that some companies may go private in order to evade a quota law's requirements altogether.[36]

The Other Side of the Coin: Opposition to Quotas

Opposition to enactment of quota laws or regulations is strong in nations such as New Zealand, a country in which women make up 59 percent of the workforce and which recently was and now again is governed by a female prime minister (Jacinda Ardern took office on October 26, 2017), yet in which many corporate executives oppose mandatory or other guidelines.[37] The New Zealand Stock Exchange has publicly stated that it will not even follow its Australian counterpart, the Australian Stock Exchange (ASX), which has a requirement for companies to set and meet "voluntary" quotas for increasing the number of women at the top.[38]

In the United Kingdom, a recent government report urged a voluntary quota of 25 percent by 2015 but pointedly stopped short of any recommendation that the nation adopt a compulsory quota, as France, Spain, Belgium, the Netherlands, Norway, and other states have done.[39] Scholars and women's rights advocates view New Zealand and the United States as representing the forefront of the opposition, nations in which "the political climate remains firmly opposed to the notion of quotas."[40]

Lopsided Nature of the Norwegian Example

Norway may be the most unrepresentative example to which advocates of a quota law could point. First, Norway is among the wealthiest nations on the globe, ranking fourth on one list.[41] Second, Norway has a homogeneous, cohesive, and small population, numbering a shade over five million persons.[42] Third, Norwegian society is among the world leaders in honesty, forthrightness, lack of corruption, and transparency.[43] Fourth, last, and as previously noted, Norwegians have a bred-in-the-bone sense of gender neutrality. From play school onward, children—and later adults—are more gender-blind than the citizens of any other nation on earth, with any variance between sexes not tolerated.

The foregoing considerations make Norway the ideal candidate for imposition of a director quota law, with near-universal acceptance by the business community and the citizenry both before and after the policy's adoption. A few other nation-states, such as Canada, may exhibit similar characteristics but are more pluralistic, since many of its citizens are imbued with libertarian attitudes. Those attributes would render adoption of quota laws improbable, or opposition fierce. Norway, or Norway alone, is a poor example from which to draw conclusions and proselytize about quota laws.

Political Feasibility of a Quota Law in the United States

Whether progressive, liberal, or conservative, Americans have a libertarian streak. An ample majority of U.S. citizens, from all levels of society, would find a European-style quota law or regulation an extensive and unwarranted incursion into the affairs of private businesses.[44] The same would be doubly true were government or a government agency to attempt to reach downward into private corporations, imposing gender quotas at various levels of senior management and on downward into middle management ranks.

Widespread American opposition may arise from several sources. Americans, or a significant percentage of them, balk at being told what to do. A major impetus to the opposition to the Affordable Care Act (the ACA, or "Obamacare") was the "mandate."[45] Under the ACA, U.S. citizens must have health insurance, provided by their employers or, if they are unable to obtain insurance through an employer or on their own, obtained through an insurance exchange. If as citizens they had not obtained health insurance coverage, Americans had to pay not insignificant fines. A great deal of opposition to the ACA, from conservatives, libertarians, and many moderates, centered on the mandate. Americans don't like being told what to do, nor do they want their government telling others, including corporations, what to do.

More Nuanced Explanations

The number of director seats on larger U.S. public corporations actually is declining. Between 2000 and 2007, for example, the number of Fortune 500 corporate board seats declined, from 5,821 to 5,161.[46] U.S. corporations are tending toward British, Australian, and similar governance models in which boards are significantly smaller: five, six, seven, or eight directors rather than ten, eleven, twelve, or thirteen, as in the United States.

By contrast, the number of senior management positions may be expanding. Although no statistics are available, one factor in support of the proposition is the creation or elevation of the position of chief risk officer in the last decade or so, often as an addition to the C-suite. In addition to the CEO, and the chief risk officer, the C-suite may contain the COO, CIO, CLO, CCO, CMO, and CFO.[47] Regardless of the ebb and flow of available positions, many directors and aspiring senior managers regard availability of top positions as a zero-sum game. One person's elevation to a seat or position crowds out another equally credentialed and experienced candidate. The elevation of a female to a senior position translates to fewer available openings for the majority group, in this case white middle-aged and older males.

Does such a view feed into the notion that the majority group (older corporate males) is made up largely of chauvinistic misogynists? Perhaps so (although the rhetoric seems out of the 1960s). But the explanation for opposition to quota laws and similar mandates may be more subtle.

Vilfredo Pareto (1843–1923), an Italian professor of economics at the University of Milan, accomplished many things in his life but is perhaps best known for the concept of Pareto optimality, also termed Pareto efficiency. The term describes the point at which, in the distribution of resources (in this case, executive positions), it is impossible to make any one individual better off without making another individual or group worse off.[48] Promotion of women to senior executive and board positions violates inbred notions of the proper distribution of wealth and emoluments. In other words, such promotions violate the principle of Pareto optimality, or Pareto efficiency. Elevation of women and other minorities makes others—namely, the opponents to quotas and guidelines—worse off.

One of the most important twentieth-century political philosophers was John Rawls, James Bryant Conant Professor of Law at Harvard University. Professor Rawls espoused a theory somewhat parallel to Pareto's. In *A Theory of Justice*, Professor Rawls attempted to build upon Rousseau's social contract.[49] What are the ingredients of an ideal social contract? A principal one is distributive justice, what Professor Rawls first termed "social justice" and later described as equivalent to basic notions of fairness.[50] Social justice exists, or persists, when an unequal distribution of goods and wealth (again, here, positions in corporate hierarchies) is permitted if and only if those inequalities also benefit the worst-off members of the social unit.

If we define the social unit as those wanting to occupy and those actually occupying executive-type positions, admittedly a privileged group, the elevation of women and minorities crowds out the worst-off in Raw-ls's terms: those others who are not members of the privileged subgroup (women and/or minorities). Aspiring males perceive themselves as potentially in the group made worst-off. As such, they do not receive any benefit, and possibly perceive themselves as becoming worse off, from the elevation of women, which they perceive as an unequal distribution of positions.

Application of Pareto and Rawls to explanations of the American deep-felt opposition to quota laws may be half-baked, or inarticulately presented. Be that as it may, there exist other possibilities for increasing the representation of women not as strong or hard and fast as governmentally imposed mandatory quotas.

Variants

Corporations, of course, are subject to many imperatives and quasi-imperatives that are not imposed through laws, executive orders, or agency regulations. Every day companies act pursuant to stock exchange regulations, accounting standards and bulletins, industry and trade group pacts, and so on. These quasi-governmental and nongovernmental pronouncements fit under the heading of soft law, as opposed to law, or hard law (government mandates). Soft law further breaks down into "hard" soft law or "soft" soft law. A regulation in the New York Stock Exchange or NASDAQ listing manuals constitutes hard soft law. By contrast, an "acceptable practices" guideline from a corporate governance blueprint, or an association of widget manufacturers' guidelines, would fit more easily farther down the spectrum, perhaps under the heading of "soft" soft law.

Apropos here, the Rooney Rule, a self-imposed regulation, has been taken up and enforced by a governing body, the National Football League, and therefore fits into the category of hard soft law. The rule applies not to the ultimate hiring decision, as a quota law would, but to the penultimate decisions informing composition of the candidate short list, for head coaching and general manager positions. Football clubs that do not comply face stiff fines and other sanctions. Chapter 20 discusses the Rooney Rule and its application to information technology.

By analogy, industry groups and self-regulatory organizations could deliberate about and possibly adopt soft law variants to the hard law requirements European nations have imposed upon corporations. Voluntary acceptance of quota-type guidelines begins to resemble the pledge programs adopted in the Netherlands and in the United Kingdom and, at one time, urged in France as an alternative to a quota regulation. Advocacy groups such as the Thirty Percent Coalition, which has as its objective 30 percent women on corporate boards, or the Moving the Needle pledge/quota program of the American Council on Education, furnish further soft law analogies. Through bylaw amendments or board resolutions, many corporations have adopted self-regulatory provisions.[51] While not promoting women, these bylaws and resolutions have imposed quotas on how many board seats directors may hold, reversing the growth of "trophy directors." They thus reduce the chance that a trophy director's appointment may crowd out qualified and younger female candidates for open positions.[52]

One takeaway from this chapter is that while mandatory quota laws are unpalatable, in reality many other alternatives (pledge programs, Rooney Rule variants, industry group guidelines) are soft law variants of a hard law quota system, or can be viewed in that way. Another takeaway is that while physically we leave behind quota laws and regulations, we should take with us a summary of the drawbacks to such laws and the reasons we, possibly, oppose their imposition.

10

CERTIFICATE AND PLEDGE PROGRAMS

In the main, the pledges exacted from corporations in various countries relate to increasing the number of women directors, often with a goal stated, such as 25 or 30 percent representation. Nonetheless, similar pledge programs could specify objectives regarding proportions of senior management positions women hold. The information technology industry, of course, could use both types of pledges to increase the number of female directors *and* the number of women in senior management.

In particular, countries and business groups operating in the shadow of but opposed to quota laws, such as in the United Kingdom, have resorted to pledge programs as an alternative. Overall, pledge programs have a mixed record: some have failed to gain traction, while others claim to have reached the goals they set for themselves.

An Early Precedent: The Netherlands

The Dutch 2008 Talent to the Top pledge required public corporations to add women to their boards if the corporations subscribed to the pledge, which was termed "voluntary."[1] All 110 large corporations domiciled in the Netherlands signed the pledge.[2] This included some very large entities such as Royal Dutch Shell, Phillips, Heineken, Reed Elsevier, and Unilever.[3] The Dutch pledge program, and the corporate actions that ensued as a consequence, played a part in raising women's representation in Dutch corporate boards of directors from approximately 7 percent in 2006 to approximately 16 percent in 2010.[4] Since that time, however, the whirlwind of activities promoting adoption of quota laws across Europe, including in the Netherlands, and the actual adoption of laws by countries such as Germany, Belgium, France, and others have obscured attribution of further advances to the Talent to the Top program.

Pledge Programs Proposed as Alternatives to Quotas

France adopted a quota law to take effect early in 2011, calling for publicly held companies to have 40 percent female directors by 2017. In the run-up to adoption of the law, French business leaders advocated a pledge program instead. For example, Claire de Montaigu, CEO of Leaders Trust, attempted to gain support for a pledge system requiring French companies to set objectives for addition of women directors and to stipulate that the companies would undertake to achieve those objectives. A newly chartered nongovernmental organization (NGO) would solicit the pledges. Afterward, the NGO would monitor companies' progress toward the goals.[5]

Needless to say, the French adoption of a mandatory quota law superseded any push for a voluntary program involving pledges and monitoring, a quasi-hard soft law variant on a softer notion (wholly voluntary pledges). According to one poll taken at the time, 71 percent of French citizens favored the quota law alternative.[6] Laurence Parisot, head of the powerful employers' union MEDEF, spoke in favor of a quota law: "Improvement without a law is so slow that we cannot stay doing nothing."[7] Catherine Chouard, president of the French Equal Opportunities and Anti-Discrimination Commission, seconded Parisot's comment: "[A quota law] is an excellent way to change mentalities. The law will be a first step to a 'new way of life' in companies."[8]

The Failure of a European-Wide Pledge Program

In 2011 the European Union (EU) attempted to follow the Netherlands' example when it requested large publicly held companies throughout Europe to voluntarily pledge to achieve the 30 percent level of female directors. Companies would stipulate to reach that objective by the end of 2015.

The proposed EU program failed miserably. After a year, only twenty-four corporations in the European Union had agreed to the pledge.[9] Calling for quota laws, instead of corporate pledges, EU justice commissioner Viviane Reding explained why her allegiance had shifted: "One year ago, I asked companies to voluntarily increase women's presence on corporate boards. . . . I regret to see that despite our calls, self-regulation so far has not brought about satisfactory results."[10]

The Rooney Rule: A Pledge Program That Seems to Work

There are advocates for a pledge program in the United States. Inspiration for such a program in the corporate sphere comes from an unlikely source: the National Football League (NFL). The late Dan Rooney, an owner of the Pittsburgh Steelers professional football club (and later U.S. ambassador to the Republic of Ireland) chaired the NFL's Committee on Diversity. The committee's charge was to inquire as to why few, if any, of the head coaches or general managers in the NFL were African American when 70 percent of the football players were black.[11] The committee drafted and the NFL owners adopted the so-called Rooney Rule, which requires each team in the league to pledge to include a minority candidate among the finalists for each head coaching and each general manager vacancy that arises. The signatories agree to conduct at least one on-site interview with one or more minority group finalists.

The Rooney Rule has met with success in solving the problem it addressed. Since 2003, when the NFL adopted the rule, the number of black coaches in the NFL has increased from 6 percent to 22 percent, and seventeen teams have hired African American or Latino head coaches.[12] A good deal of that success, though, may be attributed to the Rooney Rule's nature: although styled as a pledge program, compliance is not voluntary. Member teams must agree to the rule's provisions. Failure to abide by what the teams pledged to do has consequences. The league office fined the Buffalo, New York, team $225,000 for an instance of noncompliance; the Detroit team was fined a similar amount.

In the United States, calls for a pledge program modeled after the Rooney Rule and aimed at increasing the number of women corporate directors have multiplied.[13] Chapter 20 delves more deeply into the Rooney Rule and adoption of a version for publicly held companies in the United States. Whether the looming threat of a quota law (a remote possibility in the United States) and continued advocacy for one motivate recommendations for adoption of a Rooney Rule–type pledge program is a further question.

Adoption of a Pledge Program in the Shadow of Quota Law Adoptions

The many calls for an EU-wide quota regulation and various European states' adoption of national quota laws made many business executives and government officials in the United Kingdom feel that they had a gun to their heads. A large subgroup of them opposed any quota law or regulation that would have applicability in the United Kingdom.

Nonetheless, in 2008 the United Kingdom's Equality and Human Rights Commission had reported that "at the current rate of change it would take more than 70 years to achieve gender-balanced boardrooms in the UK's largest 100 companies."[14] Despite ardent advocacy, the number of women on Financial Times Index (FTSE) 100 companies' boards had increased only from 6.2 percent in 1999 to 9.4 percent in 2004 to 12.5 percent in 2010.[15] Taking note of the lack of progress, in 2010 the British government pledged to "look to promote gender equality on the boards of listed companies."

The British business minister and minister for women invited Mervyn Davies (Lord Davies of Abersoch, CBE), formerly chairman of Standard Chartered Bank, to review the situation and make recommendations. Thus was born the "Davies Report," named after Mervyn Davies as chairperson of the committee that authored the report, which appeared in February 2011.

In the letter accompanying the report, Lord Davies sided with opponents of any quota law, albeit in euphemistic terms:

> Some people told us that the only way we could make real change in increasing the number of women on boards was by introducing quotas. . . . Many other people told us that quotas would not be the preferred option as they did not wish to see tokenism [that quota laws would produce] prevail. On balance, the decision has been made not to recommend quota laws.[16]

Instead, Lord Davies's committee's report set out for implementation in the United Kingdom a ten-point recommendation list that may be characterized as a robust pledge program.[17] Among the salient points are the following mandates (couched as recommendations):

> FTSE 350 companies should set out the percentage of women "they aim to have on their boards in 2013 and 2015." FTSE 100 companies "should aim" for 25 percent female representation.
> Company chairmen specifically should be charged with implementation of the report's mandates. (In the United Kingdom, company chairperson is a powerful position compared to the United States, where typically, but not always, the chair is little more than a figurehead, as discussed below).
> The Financial Reporting Council should amend the UK Corporate Governance Code (called the Cadbury Code after the late Sir Adrian Cadbury, or the "Little Yellow Book," after the volume that contains the code as well as synopses of the Cadbury, Hempel, Greenway, and other milestone governance code contributions) "to require listed companies to establish a policy regarding boardroom diversity, including measurable objectives."
> Companies "should" report on these matters annually, beginning with the 2012 Corporate Governance Statement required in annual reports.
> "Company Chairmen will be encouraged to sign a charter supporting the recommendations."
> In the section of the annual report mandating a description of the work of boards' nomination committees, companies "should disclose information about the company's [board] appointment process and how it addresses diversity."
> "Executive search firms should draw up a Voluntary Code of Conduct addressing board diversity."

Robust Success for a Strong-Form Pledge Program

The British program is a pledge program, termed "wholly voluntary." Companies "should set out" diversity goals, "should aim" at 25 percent female composition of their boards, and "should report" on programs and results achieved with those programs. Given the self-description of the program and the various conditional phrasings used, the Davies gender equality corporate governance program might be concluded to be a voluntary one—but it is one with teeth. The Financial Reporting Council has amended the disclosure requirements applicable to public companies. The London Stock Exchange governance recommendations (the "Little Yellow Book") have diversity "comply or explain" reporting requirements effectively tantamount to "comply" disclosure requirements. Those requirements subsume and render mandatory adoption of a program and pledging objectives the signatory company intends to meet.

On the fourth anniversary of their report and its recommendations, Lord Davies and his committee reported across-the-board compliance by large and not-so-large British public companies: 26.1 percent female directors at FTSE 100 companies and 19.6 percent at FTSE 250 firms.[18] Lord Davies hailed "the near-revolution which has taken place in the boardroom" in the United Kingdom. Looking toward Continental Europe, Davies pronounced "the introduction of legally enforced quotas . . . unwarranted." "The voluntary approach is working." The president of the British Chambers of Commerce backed Davies: "There is no need for 'overbearing governmental regulation.'"[19]

There were naysayers. One critic pointed out that companies were appointing women to non-executive board positions, leaving men dominating companies' executive boards and suites. Another pointed out a fact obscured by celebrations over the 26.1 percent figure. In fact, the proportion of executive positions held by women stood at only 9.6 percent, even though women in the United Kingdom constitute 47 percent of the workforce and 53 percent of the university graduates.[20] Naysayers to one side, Lord Davies and his committee announced a new objective for British publicly held firms: 33 percent by 2020.[21]

Could There Be a Lord Davies Pledge Program in the United States?

There are several reasons that a pledge program similar to the British one would probably not succeed in the United States. First is the strong libertarian streak running through not only the business community but all of American society. Second is the lack of any threat from without (imposition of quota laws) that undoubtedly galvanized the British efforts (the Davies Report and ensuing events). Third is the lack of any corporate officer to act as a point person for implementation, as board chairmen have in the United Kingdom. And fourth, related to the first, is the proclivity of British people to forestall even a hint of negative publicity, as compared to the ruggedly individualistic American *zeitgeist* that bends only to real, imminent threats (court orders, legislation, possible confiscation).

The Board Chair Position in the United States versus the United Kingdom

In England, as well in most other countries, different persons hold the position of board chair and the CEO position (in the United Kingdom known as the managing director, before the switchover to the more modern CEO parlance). Moreover, in Britain the board chair usually is intimately involved in convening board meetings, presiding at meetings, conducting board and individual director evaluations, reviewing committee personnel, initiating amendment of committee charters, and so on.[22]

The United States is one of the few nations, if not the only nation, in which the dominant public company arrangement is the reverse of that pattern. The U.S. practice is to combine the position of chair with the CEO position rather than to separate the posts. Eighty percent or more of the public companies in the United States followed this pattern until recently, when activist investors and good governance advocates have made separation of the offices central to their reform agenda. Nonetheless, combining the offices remains the most common practice in the United States. In fact, in an exercise of megalomania, many U.S. CEOs insist on three titles: board chair, CEO, and president.[23]

The highest calling for a board of directors is to monitor and evaluate the performance of the chief executive and, if necessary, remove a CEO deemed misguided or underperforming. Critics ask how a U.S. board would be able to do that when the person charged with convening the board and presiding at the meeting would be the very person, that is, the CEO, whose removal is sought.[24]

But that riddle aside, another factor that might result in the British pledge program being "lost in translation" is the difference between the two views of the board chair position. As has been seen, the board chair has a number of duties and plays a hands-on role in the United Kingdom, regardless of who holds the office. By contrast, in the United States, under states' laws, the position of chair has no legal status other than what the company's bylaws state (usually little if anything). The position of chair thus is an empty vessel into which various companies pour various things, but generally not very much.[25] Quite often, if the current CEO does not hold the board chair position, the corporation's board "kicks" the former CEO "upstairs," where he or she acts as a figurehead or, at most, as a father confessor figure to the current CEO.

The point of all this discussion is that under the typical U.S. arrangement, no one except the CEO is occupying the bully pulpit. Under the U.S. schematic, CEOs have a myriad of tasks assigned to them. Most (many) CEOs would have too full of a dance card to be able to assign a high priority to recruitment of female directors and advancement of women managers. It is highly unlikely, then, that many U.S. corporations would have a focal point for administration of a pledge program high enough in the hierarchy of managers in the way U.K. and other nations' corporations would.

Soft Law and Best Practices Compared: The United States and the United Kingdom

The English Bill of Rights is said to "live in the hearts and minds of English men." Hence there is no need for enactment of a written statement of liberties. When asked what prevents, for instance, the majority in the society from rounding up all the red-haired, freckled persons and placing them in internment camps in Cornwall, all knowledgeable English have an answer. "It is just not on," they unvaryingly reply. A similar retort would be given to more realistic hypotheticals as well, involving, say, free exercise of religion, freedom of speech, freedom from racial and gender discrimination, and so on.

By contrast, U.S. institutions and individuals display a more pronounced individualist trait, some would say a rebellious one, even a swashbuckling one at times. They often do not feel bound by any principle that is not written down or enacted into positive law. Individual corporate boards and CEOs would not sign a voluntary pledge, or, if they did so, would not feel bound by it, especially if the phrasing were similar to that used in the Davies Report: that companies' boards "should aim," board chairs "are encouraged," companies "should draft" programs and reports, and so on.

Negative or Adverse Publicity as a Deterrent

Another salient difference between the United States and the United Kingdom is the effect of adverse publicity to which a company would be subjected if it refused to sign a widely accepted oath or pledge. The effect in Britain usually is severe, leading companies and individuals to be far less prone to get out of line in the first place. One can theorize multiple reasons for this phenomenon. The corporate and publishing worlds in the United Kingdom are very centralized, focused on the City (the original London of one square mile, which now contains the financial district) and Fleet Street, which adjoins the City, epicenters for the entire country of 64 million plus. Members of the City's financial community and the press can and will quickly subject a nonconformist to embarrassment and censure by its peers. Business and corporate reporting is more detailed than in the United States. Business editors and reporters do not hold back on criticism of noncompliance or of self-regulatory efforts.

In the United Kingdom, then, "public censure or adverse publicity is quickly generated and quickly heeded."[26] By contrast, the United States is not so centralized, sprawling from Portland, Maine, to San Diego, California, and from Anchorage, Alaska, and Seattle, Washington, to Miami, Florida. U.S. companies are much more likely to risk adverse publicity, weathering the storm and waves of public censure such as those that would result from non-adherence to pledges.

Can the Robust Successes of the U.K. Voluntary Pledge Program Override Differences in Corporate Governance and in National Psyches?

On October 29, 2015, the Davies Committee released its five-year review a year early, pronouncing the British pledge program a runaway success.[27] Among its highlights:

> "The FTSE 350 has more women than ever before serving on boards, with 550 new women appointments in just over four years."[28]
> Having reached its original goal, and then some, with 26.1 percent, the "voluntary business lead approach is to continue for a further five years," with a new goal of 33 percent women on corporate boards.[29]
> The new push forward is to have a *second prong, that is, pledges by corporations to increase dramatically the number of women holding "senior-most leadership positions"* in addition to the original prong, pledging to increase the number of female directors.

> In 2011, 152 of the FTSE 350 boards were "all-male," but by 2015 that number had decreased to 15; in 2011, 21 of the FTSE 100 boards were all-male, but "there are now zero."[30]

The Davies Report presented comparative statistics as "evidence to show that the voluntary regime is working," and by inference that mandatory quota rules are unnecessary. With 26.1 percent reported, "the UK is sixth in Europe behind Norway [35.1 percent], Sweden [32.6 percent], France [32.5 percent], Finland [29.4 percent] and Belgium [28.5 percent]."[31] Six European countries have quota laws: Norway (40 percent), Spain (40 percent), France (40 percent), Belgium (33 percent), Italy (33 percent), and Germany (30 percent).[32] The United Kingdom is not far behind, and with the Davies 33 percent pledge it will surpass some nations with quota laws. "Let's prove to them that this [a voluntary pledge program] is a better way to do it," said one FTE 100 company chairman.[33]

At the risk of being criticized the way Mozart was ("too many notes"), I will risk a few more comparative numbers from the Davies Report ("too many numbers," as an editor of a business magazine told me):

> Rounding out the top ten are the Netherlands (23.7 percent), Denmark (21.7 percent), Germany (21.3 percent), and Spain (19.5 percent).
> Across the Atlantic, the United States is eleventh (16.9 percent, according to Lord Davies, or 20.2 percent according to Catalyst); moving further across the Pacific, Australia is thirteenth (16.2 percent), although the Australian press computes higher numbers, as discussed in chapter 12.
> Some surprises: on the high side, India ranks seventeenth (12.1 percent) and China ranks eighteenth (11.1 percent).
> On the low side, public companies in Ireland have only 12.7 percent of directors who are female.

A Concluding Judgment

While a quota law or regulation seems unworkable, by contrast, a pledge program may work in the United States, both at the director level and at the senior management level. Any program advanced would have to contain modifications, taking into account the issues raised above, such as who would serve as a focal point for monitoring and compliance in individual corporations. More importantly, to lend moral force to the pledge program and to the need for compliance following the pledge, the industry's leaders would have to join in spearheading the effort. A substantial number of companies within a given industry would have to back business leaders in implementing the pledge program. The latter could prove difficult, given the variety of companies, the diversity in what those companies do, and the numbers of mavericks who populate information technology, especially as one descends downward through the industry's ranks.

11

COMPLY OR EXPLAIN REGIMES

Increasingly, in the United States, laws and mandatory regulations impose corporate governance requirements. The 2002 federal Sarbanes-Oxley Act (SOX), which grew out of the Enron and WorldCom scandals, marks the first federal foray into the subject, which previously had been the exclusive province of state laws.[1]

The 2010 Dodd-Frank Act[2] then layered upon SOX's requirements a host of additional mandatory governance requirements.[3] Thus, U.S. public companies must have a review by independent accountants of internal accounting controls; CEOs and CFOs must certify quarterly and annual financial reports; companies must have an audit committee staffed by independent directors; audit committee rosters must include at least one director who is a "financial expert"; if accounting results have to be restated due to misconduct, corporate officers must repay incentive-based compensation; loans of corporate funds to directors or officers are now forbidden, and much more. These are mandatory requirements.

Much of the rest of the world goes about corporate governance in a different, softer way. Rather than laws passed by the parliament or legislature, codes of best practices govern the area. Rather than legislatures and regulatory agencies such as the SEC, foreign stock exchanges, either directly or through corporate governance councils, promulgate codes of best practices that are aspirational rather than mandatory. The Organization for Economic Cooperation and Development (OECD) in Paris also maintains a corporate governance code that has become the starting point for the evolution of many country-specific codes.[4]

The approach is further softened by the adoption in many of these codes of a "comply or explain" regime rather than absolute, mandatory rules and requirements. For example, the Swedish Corporate Governance Board explains this feature of its code of rules and recommendations: "Companies that are obligated to apply the Code do not always have to comply with every rule in the Code."[5] The board continues, explaining the rationale behind the approach: "If a company finds that a certain rule is inappropriate . . . it can choose another solution than that found in the Code. The company must, however, clearly state that it has not complied . . . along with an explanation for the company's preferred solution."

The Australians refer to such a regime as the "if not, why not" approach.[6] From time to time, the approach pops up in U.S. regulation. For instance, rather than requiring that corporate boards have a compensation committee, Dodd-Frank requires only that companies disclose when they do not have one and state the reasons they do not have such a committee.[7] Sarbanes-Oxley requires similar public corporation disclosure in the case of boards' audit committees or the adoption of a code of ethics for financial executives. U.S. laws and regulations, however, do not incorporate a broad, across-the-board comply or explain regime.

Actually, Dodd-Frank is more indirect than that. The statute requires the SEC to direct the various stock exchanges to adopt comply or explain rules in their listing requirements.[8] "Requiring individuals to give reasons for particular actions [or inactions] improves decision-making quality, reduces reliance on stereotypes, and helps level the playing field for underrepresented groups [e.g., the gender diversity comply or explain requirements of the London and Australian stock exchanges]."[9] But the United States has chosen not to go down the comply or explain road.

Comply or explain exists in the United Kingdom, Germany, the Netherlands, much of the rest of the European Union, Hong Kong, Singapore, Australia, and New Zealand, to name a few.[10] In particular, many of those countries, or at least those without quota laws, single out diversity, most particularly gender diversity on corporate boards and among senior management, for comply or explain treatment.

Comparison with Other Types of Regulatory Approaches

One can theorize at least four types of regulatory schemes that would compete with the notion of "comply or explain."

First, in contrast to mandatory requirements, discussed below, a regulatory regime may consist wholly of disclosure requirements. Beginning with the Securities Act of 1933, the U.S. securities law regime governing the issuance and trading of investment securities follows the disclosure approach. If a company seeks to raise capital to put a person on a celestial body, say, Pluto or Mars, the company may do so, provided it makes full disclosure about the difficulties and risks in the mission it has set out for itself.

Second, a comply or explain scheme is very much about disclosure as well, but inherent in it also is an imperative. Circumstances being normal, the governance code expects, but does not require, that companies will comply. If not, the company not only can but must explain the "why not." If the "why not" explanation is flimsy or off-the-wall, adverse publicity and peer pressure will result. Scholars have written about the effects of shaming that results from adverse publicity and its effects on corporate behavior.[11]

Third, a comply or explain regime could have definite consequences that flow from noncompliance or compliance with the letter but not the spirit of the recommendation. Stock exchanges, for instance, could levy a fine or suspend a listing for disingenuous or egregious noncompliance with the explain dictate.

Fourth, as noted above, corporate governance directives can take the form of mandatory commands. The "Thou shall do X" or "Thou shall not do Y" phrases found in statutes and regulations are substantive requirements, in contrast to disclosure regulations.[12] A further dichotomy is the division of statutory and legal commands into hard law and of stock exchanges' and codes of best practices' provisions into soft law, as discussed in the previous chapter.[13] This chapter deals with comply or explain regimes and, tangentially at least, with the option of comply or explain with consequences.

A Brief in Support of Comply or Explain

I once heard a law student speaker compare the use of Socratic questioning in legal education with caning in the Singapore judicial system: "It's hard, it hurts while they're doing it, and the British invented it."[14] So, too, with the idea of a pervasive, wall-to-wall "comply or explain" corporate governance approach. The British invented it.

The Institute of Chartered Accountants in England and Wales (ICAEW) describes its breadth:

Comply or explain is an approach that covers much of the content of the UK (Corporate Governance) Code. Today, the Code contains over 50 provisions which set out over 110 instances of what companies, boards, directors and others "should do." And yet there is no requirement to comply with these provisions and companies can decide not to do so provided that they give an explanation for any non-compliance.[15]

In a paean to the wisdom of the British approach, a commentator outlines a few of its perceived advantages ("where comply or explain can serve businesses and investors and have advantages over other alternatives"):

> Innovation: when introducing aspirational new ideas and changes to company governance.
> Proportionality: a measured application of more demanding requirements, especially for smaller businesses.
> Avoiding box-ticking: encourages companies to think through overarching principles before automatically complying. . . .
> Long-term learning: assisting cultural change in companies that think deeply and regularly about how to meet the purpose and principles of corporate governance.[16]

Gender Diversity in the United Kingdom

The United Kingdom Corporate Governance Code emphasizes that "the comply or explain approach is the trademark of corporate governance in the UK. It has been in operation since the Code's beginnings [in 1993]. It is strongly supported by companies and shareholders and has been widely admired and imitated internationally."[17] In 2010 the council folded a gender diversity statement into the comply or explain regime. The Corporate Governance Code now provides that "the search for board candidates should be conducted, and appointments made, on merit, against objective criteria and with due regard to the benefits of diversity in the board, *including gender*."[18]

Thus, in the United Kingdom, two solutions to the paucity of women in corporate leadership work side-by-side: the Davies pledge program, discussed in the previous chapter, and the London Stock Exchange/Financial Reporting Council Corporate Governance Code provision, as supplemented by the comply or explain principle that modifies the gender diversity recommendation.

Gender Diversity in Australia

I taught the intensive course in corporate governance at the University of Melbourne School of Law each May from 1994 to 2009 and have lectured in Australia and New Zealand since that time, mostly on the subject of gender diversity in corporate governance.[19] From a late start, female leadership both in director positions and as senior managers has become a hot-button issue in Australia (by contrast, it remains on low heat in New Zealand).

In 2010 the Australian Stock Exchange (ASX) stepped up its efforts to add women to corporate boards. Effective January 1, 2012, the ASX required that listed companies comply or explain with regard to diversity. The ASX provided that "companies should establish a policy concerning diversity and disclose the policy or a summary of that policy."[20] Further, "the policy should include requirements for the board to establish measurable objectives for achieving gender diversity for the board to access annually both the objectives and the progress in achieving them."

The Australian guidelines, unlike the British ones, reach beyond the boardroom to recommend disclosures on the proportion of women in the company's workforce overall and in the ranks of senior management.[21] Most corporations, or at least the larger ones, have complied, disclosing what steps they have taken and their progress toward the goals they have set, adding to the pressure to enlarge the pool from which women candidates for board positions and senior management positions may be chosen.

Monitoring Compliance

Along those lines, in 2012 the ASX appointed KPMG, the international accounting firm, to canvas the field to test compliance. ASX Listing Rule 4.10.3 supplies the comply or explain component: listed entities are required to benchmark their corporate governance devices and practices or to disclose why the company has not complied. The good part:

KPMG found that of 211 listed corporations, *all* had either reported that they had established a gender diversity policy or explained why they had not done so. The not-so-good part: only 76 of the 211 companies reported that they had established measureable objectives for achieving gender diversity.[22]

Since the time of its original pronouncements, the ASX has firmed up its gender diversity approach, incorporating gender diversity in the listing standards themselves (but still heading them as a "Recommendation"):

> A listed entity should:
> (a) have a diversity policy which includes requirements for the board or a relevant committee . . . to set measurable objectives for achieving gender diversity and to assess annually both the objectives and the entity's progress in achieving them [and] . . .
> (b) disclose at the end of each reporting period . . . the respective proportions of men and women on the board, in senior executive positions, and across the whole organization (including how the entity has defined "senior executive").[23]

In 2014 the ASX commissioned another audit of compliance with its comply or explain requirements. In April 2014 KPMG reported its findings. Among the largest companies (198 of the ASX 200 surveyed), compliance was excellent. All corporations in the ASX list had either adopted a diversity policy or explained why they had not done so. Nearly all of that group (98 percent of 198) actually had adopted a policy. Eighty-six percent (170 companies) had set measurable objectives as a component of their policy. Those objectives pertained the most to the company as a whole (92 percent) and in relation to senior executive positions (91 percent). Paradoxically, companies were not as diligent when setting measurable objectives for board membership (86 percent).[24]

Compliance, however, was demonstrably lower among midsize and smaller companies. KPMG reported that only 56 percent of ASX 201–500 companies (200 surveyed) had set measurable objectives, although 85 percent had adopted a diversity policy. Among smaller companies (ASX 501+, 200 surveyed) compliance trailed off still more: 66 percent had adopted a policy but only 20 percent had set objectives.

This latter KPMG finding is crucial. Smaller companies play a key role in supplying women who enter the pool from which midsize and larger companies choose directors and senior managers. With this in mind, larger companies and organizations such as the ASX, the AICD, and women's groups should place more emphasis on encouraging smaller companies' compliance with the initiative.

Australia, too, has a two-pronged approach to the issue of women in corporate leadership: a comply or explain requirement spearheaded by the Australian Stock Exchange and a mentorship/sponsorship programs headed up by the Australian Institute of Company Directors (AICD) (discussed in chapter 12). The United Kingdom has a two-pronged approach as well, albeit a differing one: the London Stock Exchange comply or explain regimen and the Davies Committee pledge scheme.

By contrast, the New York Stock Exchange (NYSE) has done nothing to improve gender diversity in corporate leadership. The closest the NYSE has come (which was not close at all) was to adopt Listing Rule 303A in 2005.[25] The rule requires that a majority of the directors be "independent" (neither insiders nor "gray insiders," such as the company's outside lawyer or investment banker). In theory, the rule would create more space for appointment of women and other diversity candidates to the board of directors.

Comply or Explain in the United States

Would such a regime work here, in the promotion of gender diversity among directors and senior management positions?

Where it has been adopted, specifically in the United Kingdom, "it is not without difficulties. Investors often say that the explanations provided [for noncompliance or a differing approach] are perfunctory and do not do a good job of explaining how a company's alternative arrangements support the corporate governance principle."[26]

Then too the United States has a much more freewheeling or even swashbuckling business community, or at least in certain quarters such as information technology or among elements within those quarters. Against such a background, the explain prong could become what the English term a "coach and horses exception" and what we might describe as a "loophole big enough to drive a truck through." Companies and their lawyers would obfuscate, offering gibberish by way of explaining difficulties in compliance.

With regard to senior management positions, U.S. boards might consider a comply or explain requirement to be an overreach. The chief executive of a company has as one of her most central prerogatives the power to hire and fire the executives and managers on her team. The central role of a CEO consists of getting "the right people on the bus, the wrong people off the bus, and the right people in the right seats."[27] Any attempt, even an indirect one such as a comply or explain requirement, would be regarded by CEOs and boards as an intrusion on the CEO's central role.

Last of all, comply or explain is a cultural artifact that infuses most facets of corporate governance in the United Kingdom, Australia, New Zealand, Hong Kong, Singapore, and elsewhere. We in the United States have no experience in or facility with it. In fact, we have gone down quite a different path, namely, that of a few mandatory requirements and commands at the core, layered with increasing latitude for private ordering ("unless otherwise provided" statutory provisions), and disclosure requirements that are devoid altogether of mandatory or substantive content. Companies and their representatives would in all probability view comply or explain gender diversity guidelines as in effect mandatory requirements. The pushback against the imposition of any such comply or explain regime would be long lasting and significant. A prevalent view would be that it constitutes a *de facto* quota system.

Overall, and in the last analysis, one senses that a comply or explain regime would not be a good fit here in the United States or for the information technology industry.

12

MENTORING AND SPONSORSHIP

Calls for mentors to take on mentees and entreaties for women to seek out mentors are constant. They appear in business magazine articles, serious books, not-so-serious "how-to" books, and newspaper articles.[1] One rather melodramatic female interviewee emoted to an author, "He [the mentor] believed in me, more than I believed in myself, and it changed my life."[2]

Strictly speaking, these incessant offers of wisdom ("Get a mentor," in fact, "get several of them") are beyond the scope of this book.[3] This is because this book attempts to approach issues of women's advancement into leadership positions from the perspective of corporate employers and the industry, not that of aspiring women; nor am I interested in putting the entire onus on women (lower your voice, avoid having children, dress for success). What individual women should do (avoid stereotypes, build a network, obtain mentors, lean in) is not a subject for this book, at least not directly.[4]

Following the lead other advice book readers have mapped, "most researchers on gender and IT have noted the importance of mentoring for all students, but particularly women." Universally, those researchers fail to mention reservations about and the downsides to mentoring. Since its founding in 1997, MentorNet has attempted to match IT students with mentors, but its success in matching them has been reported as insignificant (ten thousand overall since its founding).[5]

From an institutional standpoint, the real question to ask is, Why, despite thirty years or more of calls for mentoring, women have made little progress? To be sure, individual testimonials abound. "My favorite mentors guided me to act, respond and manage to my long term potential and aspirations. They helped me understand how IQ got me in the door and in my seat, but EQ [Emotional Quotient] would take me the distance."[6] But if mentoring worked so well, wouldn't we have gotten much further along? If mentoring were that great, we would expect to find many more success stories. If mentoring lived up to the claims its adherents make for it, even some empirical study demonstrating its efficacy might exist. Is there something missing? Something perhaps from the industry side? If the answers to some or all of those questions might be "yes," is institutional involvement of some sort an answer to curing the deficiencies?

Some Reservations about Mentoring

The entreaties for and praise of mentoring are extremely one-sided. They express no reservations, tending even to be over-the-top. "Mentors are more important to career success than hard work, more important than talent, more important than intelligence. . . . You need to learn how to operate in the work world . . . and mentors can teach you how."[7] More than a few caveats about mentoring are in order, and may be part of the reason mentoring has not produced the results foreseen for it. Mentors disappear. They transfer to another location within the company. They move on to a competitor entity. They themselves may become victims of downsizing or reorganization. They retire.[8] Mentoring often is a herky-jerky proposition.

According to many women, even when mentors stay in place, they may become overprotective, losing sight of how they can help women work around or over obstacles, replacing it with efforts to shield their mentees from obstacles or roadblocks altogether. Professor Rosabeth Moss Kanter describes the phenomenon:

> Many women object to the protectiveness that they perceived in their sponsors that "encased" them "in a plastic bubble," . . . rendering them ineffectual. . . . Women complained about the "people who want to move walls for me instead of saying, 'Here's a wall. Let's strategize working through it.'"[9]

Certain sponsors thus may engage in "negative mentoring," advising women to move sideways into human resources, staff positions, or "pink-collar," female-dominated jobs not likely to lead toward advancement. Earnest mentors may offer such advice out of a well-intentioned conclusion that the female mentee needs sheltering from the sudden storms that may arise in line and operations positions.

Overprotective mentors may morph into avuncular or patriarchal figures. Male mentors come to regard female protégés as ersatz daughters or nieces. The British critics of certain forms of mentoring may refer to a mentor of that sort as an "office uncle."[10] With many mentoring relationships, it has been said, an element of the parent-child dynamic creeps in, rendering the relationship very different from what mentoring advocates and mentees had envisioned.

Mentoring may encourage a mentee to engage in conduct that may backfire, many times severely so. Thus, a mentor's presence may provide an impetus for "the lower level organization members to *bypass the hierarchy*: to get inside information, short-circuit cumbersome procedures, or to cut red tape. . . . [They] also provide an important signal to other people, a form of '*reflected power*.'" Proper use of a mentor may be an elusive thing, capable of abuse by the mentees, who must "be careful about the way they use the reflected power of the sponsors." For instance, "you can't use" reflected power "with your own manager or you will get into trouble."[11] A "fast tracker" or a "rising star" should never use sponsorship to avoid or run roughshod over the chain of command.

Those, then, are a few of the seldom-heard criticisms of mentoring, mostly from the female manager's side rather than from the perspective of what corporations might do.

Formalized Mentoring Systems

Institutional involvement in mentoring does emerge from time to time on the corporate side. Companies formally install a matrix form of organization under which a manager, including a female manager, has not only a black line responsibility to the person or persons above her in the organizational chart or chain of command, but also a "dotted line" responsibility or responsibilities to others in the organization who may have a comparable position at another or a larger subsidiary. Or the "other" may exercise supervision over that subject area from a perch at corporate headquarters.

To set out an example, consider a European subsidiary and the second-in-command of marketing whose charge is clothing and accessories. Her direct reporting is to the subsidiary's chief marketing officer (CMO) and perhaps then upward to the subsidiary's CEO. She may also, however, have a dotted line responsibility to a counterpart at a larger subsidiary in East Asia, or to a smaller one in Australia. She may have a further dotted line responsibility to the head of design or to a marketing person at corporate headquarters.

What do dotted line responsibilities entail? Everything under the sun, everything from A to Z—with a wide range of variations. Some managers communicate along dotted lines once a year, or not at all. Others compare notes twice a week. In certain companies, the dotted line responsibility involves affirmative reporting requirements and veto authority from above. In still other cases, the relationship is a much softer one, resembling a penitent–father confessor or nephew/niece–uncle/aunt tie. The matrix form of organization then is an empty vessel into which various companies and organizations pour various things. Most often, though, corporations utilize the matrix form of organization to introduce to their company the framework for mentoring, although companies seldom articulate it as such.[12]

When the company installs a mentoring-like system from above, the company also may ameliorate certain of the pressures older males especially feel in wholly voluntary mentoring setups. Fully two-thirds of men fear that attention toward younger women would be wrongly perceived by coworkers and superiors.[13] "Men who would like to fill gaps in mentoring [for women] frequently are worried about the appearance of forming a close relationship with women."[14]

Degeneration of Mentorship into Star Systems

Another reason mentoring relationships as they presently exist in many companies may not produce the results their supporters envision is that mentoring quickly evolves into something else. What one person regards as mentoring may in reality be, or evolve into, a "star system," incorporating a patronage rather than a merit pathway to promotion. In many corporations' management echelons, probably far too many, a star system holds sway. Stars of the first magnitude, those managers within one or two reporting levels of the CEO, may assemble around or beneath them one or several stars of lesser magnitude. Merit becomes less and less relevant. Personal loyalty and obeisance replace it. The lesser stars rise because they are the favorites of stars of the first magnitude.

As Professor Kanter explains,

> Sponsorship is sometimes generated by good performance, but it also can
> come . . . "because you have the right social background or know some
> of the officers from outside the corporation [for example, the golf course
> or the tennis courts] or look good in a suit." . . . Boy wonders rise un-
> der certain power structures. They are recognized by a powerful person
> because they are much like him. When women acquired sponsors, the
> reasons were often different from the male sponsor protégé situation. . . .
> Officers were looking for a high performing woman they could make into
> a showpiece to demonstrate the organization's openness toward women.[15]

In many or even most cases, at some point the leading star will fall
out of favor. Eventually he may fall, either temporarily or permanently,
from the firmament, in which case the lesser star will fall farther yet. The
whims of the CEO and the trickle down from that may determine who
is in favor that day, week, or month. The system resembles a medieval
court.

At a major Fortune 500 forest products company, the CEO "managed
through chaos," acting on whims and changing favorites every month or
two. An MBA from a quality business school, with over twelve years at
the company, suddenly found himself out of a job when his mentor, or
star, fell out of favor with the CEO. He ended up working for a firm that
imported tires from Korea.

Both from the corporate governance standpoint and from the standpoint of individual employees, a star system within a corporation's
management structure is a snake pit. Backstabbing, rumormongering, ex-
tortion, and conduct resembling blackmail become everyday occurrences.
Any rising woman manager should ask herself whether what she sees
within a corporation is a good-faith monitoring system, a corrupt "star"
system, or something in between. She should be aware of the possible detriments, as well as the benefits, and the ins and outs of mentoring, a subject markedly absent from the reams of advice authors write for women
in business. Aspiring women should be aware that a thin line separates
sponsorship (a good thing) from a whimsical star system (a not-so-good
thing). They should periodically make the attempt to discern between the
two. On the other side of the equation, periodically corporations should

ask themselves whether their mentoring arrangement, sponsorship, or a matrix form of organization is degenerating into a star system.

Where Precisely Does Mentoring Most Often Lead?

The most oft-stated criticism is that mentoring leads nowhere. Women who have assiduously courted mentoring relationships far too frequently feel that their efforts produced few, if any, results. After four, five, six, or seven years in one or more mentoring relationships, women remain at a rank equivalent to the rank they had at the beginning. Whether because of the office uncle, the glass bubble, the pink collar, the star system, or some other phenomenon, mentoring relationships do not yield anything resembling the efforts women have put into them.

It has been found that "no significant relationship exists between having a mentor and receiving a promotion." One female executive explained, "I'm going to get mentored to death before I get promoted."[16] Another executive opines, "If you look around . . . we're putting women in mentoring programs, we're giving them special leadership programs, [and we're] telling them how to ask for a promotion, but we are *not* promoting them."[17]

Women in Australia voiced these complaints about mentoring and its role in increasing gender diversity on Australian companies' boards of directors. The Australian Institute of Company Directors (AICD) listened, and acted. The AICD theorized that what the situation demanded was not mentorship but mentorship combined with sponsorship. To meet that demand, the AICD launched its mentorship/sponsorship program in March 2010.[18] Mentee applicants for board memberships must attend either the AICD's "Directors' Course in Mastering the Boardroom" or its "International Company Directors' Course."[19] Once they have become "ASX 200 board ready," through attendance at one of the courses, and through their experience as lawyers, accountants, financial officers, corporate managers generally, or in not-for-profit entities, women candidates join with a mentor who is board chair of an Australian public company.

Initially, sixty-three women qualified. On the other side of the equation, fifty-six ASX 200 chairpersons had signed on in the first wave. Those board chairs pledged not only to mentor the candidate with whom the AICD had conjoined them but, after one year, to place that woman mentee on the board of a publicly held corporation.[20]

Between April 2010 and November 2010, the percentage of women directors on Australian corporate boards increased 2 percent, from 8.5 percent to 10.4 percent, and continued to increase thereafter.[21] As the program gathered speed, the percentage reached 13.8 percent by March 2011. In 2011 alone, ASX corporations "made more than 20% of their board appointments to women." In subsequent years, the AICD program has continued steadily to move the needle, moving the proportion of directors who are women from 8 percent to 20.1 percent in publicly held Australian corporations.[22]

Caveat: at first blush, numbers such as sixty-three or fifty-six may seem small, but boards in Australia tend to have five to seven directors, whereas the average U.S. board has about 10.6 members, according to one study. In addition, the Australian base is much smaller: compare the Australian Stock Exchange (ASX) 200 to the Fortune 500 (and probably more comparable, the Fortune 1000).

What's the Difference? Mentoring versus Sponsorship

The realization has come to some women that an aspiring woman needs both a mentor and a sponsor, not one or the other. "You can survive a very long time in your career without a mentor but you will not survive without a sponsor," states Carla Harris, a vice chair of global wealth management at Morgan Stanley.[23] The mentor is an experienced person to whom a female executive on the rise can tell the good, the bad, and the ugly. She should feel comfortable sharing with that person the bad and the not-so-good as well as positive achievements and recognition. She can hypothesize goals and objectives and how to get there, as well as mistakes and how to learn from them. "A mentor talks *to* you, offering advice and sharing experiences. A sponsor talks *about* you, advocating on your behalf, lending . . . his or her reputation and credibility."[24]

By contrast, then, a "sponsor is not the person you tell the good, the bad and the ugly. They're the person you tell the good, the good and the good."[25] Ms. Harris expands on that sponsorship role and why the difference exists:

[A] sponsor is the person who carries your resume into the room when it comes time for a possible promotion. He or she is the person who will go out on a limb and vouch for you passionately, behind closed doors. They are expending valuable political and social capital on you, and you have to articulate to them [the potential sponsor] why you are worthy of that capital.[26]

Does the recommendation to have a mentor and a sponsor both seem duplicitous? Not particularly, because the aspiring executive is not telling one thing to one person and the other the opposite. Can the need for and actions of the sponsor morph into a far less desirable "star" system? Yes, in certain instances. The mentee has to evaluate and, if necessary, change course as she goes along.

Mentoring/Sponsorship Programs in the United States

A few of the better American diversity gurus have finally cut through the volumes of hoopla about mentoring, noting that "what aspiring leaders need most is not simply mentors but sponsors. . . . Women in management are over-mentored and under-sponsored relative to their male counterparts."[27] A respected authority on diversity concludes that women "should not be shy in asking for mentoring and especially for sponsorship." That expert, Sylvia Ann Hewlett, published *Forget a Mentor, Find a Sponsor: The New Way to Fast-Track Your Career.*[28]

Some mentoring programs do exist in the United States, but by and large confine they themselves to preparing women aspirants for director positions. Only 16 percent of these mentoring programs have been judged to be "well-implemented."[29] In varying degrees, these programs offer a hint toward sponsorship but nothing resembling a firm commitment as in Australia. Catalyst, with offices in New York, Toronto, and Sunnyvale, California, conducts programs for women aspirants from time to time.[30] Catalyst also maintains a database of boardroom-ready women (Catalyst Board Resource).[31] Boardroom Bound, which operates from Washington, D.C., and Chicago, does something of the same.[32] In 2008 the American Bar Association launched its DirectWomen program, which offers a yearly weeklong program of instruction for thirty aspiring women attorneys, in its beginning years held at the Waldorf

Astoria hotel in Manhattan.[33] WomenCorporateDirectors (WCD), also a New York City–based organization, runs a short course entitled "On Board Bootcamp" for female director aspirants.[34] Deloitte & Touche, the international accounting firm, conducts evening sessions, in select cities, on "financial oversight, business strategy, risk, and securities regulation" in its Board Ready Women Initiative.[35] The Women's Forum of New York, an affiliate of the International Women's Forum, maintains another roster of women deemed to be boardroom ready.[36] Again, though, these programs dispense advice on potential pathways toward board seats but stop considerably short of active sponsorship.

Would an AICD-Type Program Easily Transplant to the United States?

It is possible that an AICD-type program could be transferred to the United States, at least for corporate directors. The applicability of a mentoring/sponsorship program to senior managers would be more problematic, for the simple reason that while appointment to a board position is binary (one is either on the board or not), appointment or elevation to a senior management position is subjective, more complex. How does one judge whether a transfer or promotion actually is a step up, or is sufficiently a step up to satisfy a program's goals? It is not a simple binary proposition.

A second difficulty is similar to the difficulty with pledge programs discussed in chapter 10. The Davies Report in the United Kingdom assigns to the company chair the role of focal point in signing the pledge, in implementing it, and in monitoring progress. In this respect, the AICD mentoring/sponsorship is much the same. Company chairs, who occupy important positions in Australia similar to company chairs in the United Kingdom, play a key role (*the* key role) in guiding, nurturing, and sponsoring female candidates.

In Australia, for example, and in most other industrialized nations, non-executive chairs predominate.[37] But in the United States a different pattern plays out. In approximately 70 percent of U.S. publicly held companies, the same individual holds the offices of both CEO and chairperson of the board.[38] U.S. companies tend to have two-fisted, all-powerful CEO-chairpersons and, in many cases, experienced and influential directors who act as "lead directors" in companies that combine the CEO and board chair positions. CEOs tend to be extremely busy individuals. Whether they would agree or have the time to act as mentors and sponsors to women candidates for directors is problematic. Reluctance of CEOs to participate may be a large—but not insurmountable—obstacle to adoption of an AICD-like mentoring program for women in the United States.

Undaunted, in May 2016 Catalyst announced a program combining mentoring with sponsorship that will attempt to enlist CEOs of public companies to act as mentors/sponsors to women who aspire to board seats.[39] In fact, indifferent to any obstacles that might exist, Irene Lang, former president and CEO of Catalyst, put the onus squarely on CEOs: "Your CEO should commit to sponsor high-performing female leaders as 'boardroom ready.' . . . These are women with whom your CEO has worked or whom he or she assesses as qualified for corporate service."[40]

Later in 2016, Ellen Kullman, former CEO of DuPont, spoke on behalf of a newly formed organization that she chairs. Titled Paradigm for Parity, the organization also has adopted the mentoring plus sponsorship model. In its initial foray, the organization signed forty highly placed, "influential" business executives who have indicated a willingness to act as a mentor/sponsor for women managers aspiring to higher ranks.[41] Further, Paradigm for Parity also "demands that businesses set measurable targets for women at every level," a subject developed in chapter 19. Thus, a bit late to the table, and with modest initial forays, some U.S. organizations have perceived the weaknesses in mentoring alone and have followed the Australian path.

An additional problem would arise in attempts to evaluate such programs to increase female advancement not only at the director but also at the senior management level. Who or what positions within corporate hierarchies could or would act as focal points for such a program? How, again, would success be determined, as it no longer is a question of a binary proposition?

So sponsorship combined with mentoring, perhaps in conjunction with a matrix form of organization, should remain on the list of possibilities for adoption by individual companies, groups of companies, or the entire information technology industry.

13

MANDATORY DISCLOSURE

The U.S. Experience

The mandate for the U.S. Securities and Exchange Commission (SEC) has always been to require disclosure in registration statements, annual reports, proxy statements, and other documents that companies file with the commission, as chapter 11 discusses. When the SEC has attempted to meddle in corporate governance, at least when it has no specific legislative mandate, the courts have slapped the commission's wrist. Ordinarily, without a specific legislative grant of authority, the SEC may not exceed its disclosure mandate.

Among the general public, of course, the belief is widespread that the SEC's mandate is to act as a near-despot over public corporations. That belief is, of course, erroneous, as by and large the SEC's mandate is to require disclosure and disclosure only.

In *Business Roundtable v. SEC*, the SEC attempted to meddle in corporate governance.[1] As a result, the powerful Court of Appeals for the District of Columbia, known as the little supreme court because of its jurisdiction over cases by persons aggrieved by administrative agency rule making, took the SEC to the woodshed. In the mid-1980s, beset by corporations who wanted to issue super voting stock, say with ten votes per share, mainly as a defense against hostile takeover bids, the New York Stock Exchange (NYSE) quickly folded, deleting the supposedly sacrosanct "one share, one vote rule" from its regulations. Using its power to review exchange rule changes, the SEC rejected the revision, reinstating the one share, one vote rule upon which the NYSE had always prided itself. The Business Roundtable, a conservative organization composed of the CEOs of the largest American corporations, challenged the SEC and won, hands-down.

So, given the SEC's traditional fiefdom, and its resounding loss in the *Business Roundtable* case, undoubtedly the SEC felt that it had at its disposal only one tool to deal with boards' composition, a corporate governance rather than a securities law subject. The tool, of course, would be a requirement for disclosures in documents companies file with the commission.

The SEC Gets Its Feet Wet

The SEC's first and only foray into diversity concerned diversity on boards of directors. Without fanfare, in December 2009, the SEC issued a release entitled "Proxy Rule Disclosure and Enhancements."[2] The release amended SEC Regulation S-K, the umbrella disclosure regulation that dictates what material public companies must disclose and sometimes in what format they must disclose it.[3] For example, in tabular form, and as Regulation S-K outlines, companies must disclose the five most highly compensated executives and both the cash and the non-cash remuneration they received in the most recent year. Regulation S-K applies across the breadth of documents companies file with the commission, including registration statements, tender offer documents, proxy statements, and periodic disclosure reports (8-Ks, 10-Qs, and 10-Ks).

Effective February 28, 2010, publicly held companies had to disclose concerning several diversity-related issues:

1. whether diversity is a factor in considering candidates for the company's board of directors;
2. how diversity is considered in the process of selecting board candidates; and
3. how the company assesses the effectiveness of whatever policy and processes it has chosen to adopt.[4]

Based upon SEC filings, in recent proxy seasons, a graduate student (Bryce Holzer) at the University of Washington (Seattle) sorted a sample of twenty-four large cap companies into four groups.[5]

Early Gleanings: Spotty Compliance

The first Holzer group consisted of a large number of companies (twelve of twenty-four) who gave lip service only to the new SEC requirements.

The companies merely disclosed that diversity was a factor in selecting director candidates. They disclosed nothing further, such as how the corporation considered diversity in the selection process or how effective the company's efforts (if any) had been.

A second group of companies (three of twenty-four) more closely adhered to but still did not meet the SEC guidelines. Disclosing that, indeed, diversity was a factor, these companies disclosed only tidbits about how their processes encapsulate their diversity commitments. One large company, for instance, disclosed that it instructs the executive search firm it hires to give diversity weight in culling candidate names to present to the board. Another proxy statement provided that "the Governance Committee assesses the composition of the board [including its diversity] at least once per year."

Third, a fair number of companies (seven of twenty-four, including Boeing, Microsoft, Home Depot, Altria, Century Aluminum, and Amazon), but still constituting a minority of the sample, met the SEC requirements. These companies described the racial and gender composition of their boards of directors. They stated that diversity is considered and stated how they factored it into the selection process.

Fourth, a group of two all-stars (Proctor & Gamble and Citigroup) exceeded the SEC's bare-bones disclosure requirements. Mr. Holzer found these two companies to be "head and shoulders above the rest." They fully articulated their policy and their process (instructions to search firms, annual assessment by the governance committee or by the full board, or both). They calculated the results: "two nominees are women and five nominees—including the chairman and the chief executive officer—are Asian, African American or Hispanic."[6] Finally, these two companies attempted to elucidate how diversity affects the operation of their businesses and what they are attempting to achieve.

An Assessment

Early on, then, Mr. Holzer found that only nine of twenty-four corporations met the newly enunciated standards. Later, based upon its examination of the disclosures it had received, the SEC reported that only 8 percent of the companies indicated that they had any sort of formal diversity policy.[7] In 2016 Professor Deborah Rhode of Stanford

University reported that only an approximate 6 percent of public companies substantially complied with SEC requirements.[8]

Viewed charitably, many corporate draftspersons may not have developed a feel for the newly amended Regulation S-K and the disclosure the SEC sought to require. If that assessment were accurate, however, as the years progressed, the quality of efforts and the disclosure both would improve. As a result of being required to disclose, companies, boards, and board committees would enhance the diversity-oriented processes. By and large, they have not.

In contrast, viewed less charitably, the SEC regulations contain an obvious "coach and horses" exception. Under the rules, companies may opt out of the diversity disclosure policy altogether by stating that they have no fixed policy within the company regarding diversity of candidates for board positions.[9] Brazen corporations can thus short-circuit the SEC's requirements, negating the regulation's intended effect. The "no policy" alternative seems to be the SEC board diversity disclosure standard's Achilles' heel.[10]

A second Achilles' heel is that the SEC fails to define diversity. A frequently quoted line is that "a responsibility to all [or to many] may be a responsibility to none." Companies may define, and many do define, diversity in their own way. In their SEC filings, many corporations define diversity broadly, as including race/ethnicity (African American, Asian American, Latino), gender, business experience, governance experience, international background, and the like. Not only is the SEC requirement not pinpointed toward gender diversity, but the regulation permits companies to adopt a scattershot approach.

Meaningful Research?

For two obvious reasons, carrying out up-to-date research on compliance with the SEC's diversity regulation is an academic exercise. One reason is that there appear to have been no enforcement efforts by the SEC of its diversity policy disclosure regulation. A second reason may be that, whatever the level of increased compliance or enforcement, disclosure has not proven effective, at least in information technology. Information technology companies have as poor a record in selecting women as directors or in hiring or promoting women to executive positions as they did before the SEC promulgated the regulation. That record has been as poor after the regulation as it was before adoption. As chapter 1 illustrates, in information technology, disclosure requirements and compliance with them have not moved the needle at all.

In fact, one can pinpoint several other deficiencies in the commission's regulation:

> At most, a requirement for disclosure such as the SEC enacted is a nudge. It contains no substantive content such as one for goal setting or record keeping.
> Companies are able to equivocate, complying with the regulation nonetheless. As discussed, by defining diversity broadly, or proceeding under the umbrella of a vague or overly broad definition, companies can observe the letter but not the spirit of the rule.
> The rule contains a loophole allowing behavior tantamount to complete evasion. Companies simply state that they have no formal policy concerning selection of board candidates or senior managers, as previously discussed.
> Most importantly, also as previously stated, the rule has not moved the needle.

As concerns diversity, requirements for disclosure are weak tools at best. Regulation through disclosure is too little, like trying to irrigate a desert with a garden hose.

Disclosure's Biggest Drawback

But that is not the biggest objection to a disclosure regime. The biggest objection is that requiring disclosure of some sort is the only tool at the SEC's disposal. Partly because of circumstances, compounded by judicial decisions such as *Business Roundtable v. SEC*, the SEC painted itself into a corner. It can do little else than devise some broad-based disclosure requirements concerning gender diversity, or diversity generally, for publicly held companies.

In this country, and unlike, say, European nations that have adopted quota laws, the only avenue open is self-regulation. State legislatures are not going to provide authority for more stringent measures. Neither will Congress. The industry, therefore, and self-regulatory measures by it, are the most means by which the industry will become more inclusive. It will take leadership, a summit, and continuous monitoring for information technology to increase the number of women serving as corporate directors or senior executives. A pure disclosure mandate, with nothing more, is not a promising recipe for success on these issues.

14

PROPOSALS FOR STEM EDUCATION

Each morning as I dipped into Panther Hollow on my way to the University of Pittsburgh (Pitt's mascot is the panther), I passed a marginal, not quite ramshackle row house with a porch spanning the length of the building's facade. Behind the row house sat stately, towered Central Catholic High School, a Christian Brothers institution that has produced a number of Pittsburgh's movers and shakers. Then one day the row house disappeared, the lot vacant, covered with straw. A sign went up: site of the new Central Catholic STEM (Science, Technology, Engineering, and Math) building. Announcements of fund raising appeared in the newspaper.[1] Then, with amazing rapidity, up went a four-story, 60,000-square-foot brick and stone edifice dedicated to STEM education.

As I go down the escalator at the Pittsburgh air terminal, in order to catch a train to the landside terminal, a huge banner hangs overhead, measuring at least ten feet tall and sixty to seventy feet long. In large letters, the banner proclaims, "STUDENTS WHO GET SCIENCE GET JOBS," signed by a major oil company.

From time to time a newspaper story relates that Chevron, a large oil and natural resources company, has given another grant to a western Pennsylvania high school to fund STEM education programs. Although not large, averaging approximately $4,000–$5,000 each, the grants are frequent and spread across the entire western portion of the state.[2] Joined by the Benedum Foundation and the Rand Corporation, Chevron and partners will fund the Appalachia Partnership to the tune of $20 million, spreading STEM grants over twenty-seven counties in Pennsylvania, Ohio, and West Virginia.[3]

STEM education overtures are the major thrust the U.S. education and corporate establishments have made toward addressing the growing paucity of young people, especially women, who pursue technological positions and technical careers, including in information technology.

STEM education emphasis has surrounded us for a decade or more now. It seems to be everywhere. There is "so much hype around STEM education" that in many quarters it has become "an overused buzzword."[4] Much of the effort seems aimed at young women, although not exclusively so. Central Catholic, for instance, is a single-sex boys' school. The STEM effort is not without critics, although their voices are seldom heard. One has lamented that "resources and emphasis have shifted to 'STEM' (science, technology, engineering and math) programs and away from civics, history, the arts and simply knowing how to form a proper sentence."[5]

STEM at the University and College Level

The emphasis on STEM education continues, though—indeed, intensifies—after high school. Similar to the Chevron program for high schools, the National Science Foundation has an umbrella program (ADVANCE) aimed particularly at encouraging young women to pursue STEM majors and, after graduation, STEM jobs.[6] In catalogues and on websites, numbers of colleges and universities feature STEM and STEM courses prominently. *Forbes* magazine rated these programs, noting that "women are underrepresented in STEM fields. It's a well-documented fact that fewer collegians seek and earn degrees in science, technology, engineering and mathematics-related programs." For example, the article notes, "women make up 14% of the engineers."[7] Nonetheless, "there are several indicators that the number of women in STEM is on the rise." One of those indicators is the number of "schools helping launch women into the STEM professions." *Forbes* then published its list:

1. *University of California at Davis.* In 2016 Cal Davis had 56 percent female enrollment in its STEM majors and 29 percent of the overall female enrollment pursuing STEM.
2. *Cornell University, Ithaca, NY.* The comparable 2016 numbers for Cornell were 51 percent (female enrollment in STEM majors) and 30 percent (of women enrollees overall). Cornell also hosts an annual Empowering Women in Science and Engineering symposium.
3. *Johns Hopkins University, Baltimore* (51 percent and 65 percent). Johns Hopkins has a dedicated program, Women in Science and

Engineering, which includes a semester-long introductory course offered each fall and spring.

4. *Washington University, St. Louis* (51 percent and 73 percent). Washington University has an outreach program, Catalysts for Change, reaching into the high schools, staffed by university students in the four-year Women in Science program. The university has a chaired professorship (Professor of STEM Education), to be assisted by the director of the Women, Gender and Sexuality Center.

5. *Duke University, Durham, NC*. The numbers at Duke: 50 percent of the students in STEM majors are women, and women STEM majors constitute 31 percent of female enrollment overall.

6. *Princeton University, Princeton, NJ* (49 percent and 14 percent).

7. *Rice University, Houston* (49 percent and 20 percent). The university has the Rice Office of STEM Management.

8. *Stanford University, Palo Alto, CA* (49 percent and 12 percent). There is a Women in STEM program.

9. *University of Michigan, Ann Arbor* (49 percent and 57 percent).

10. *University of Chicago, Chicago* (47 percent and 56 percent).

11. *Clemson University, Clemson, SC* (46 percent and 24 percent).

12. *Case Western Reserve University, Cleveland* (45 percent and 88 percent).[8]

Several items stand out on the list. First, the numbers reported—forty-something and fifty-something percentages—seem high. The numbers are so high that they indicate an underrepresentation of males rather than females, which is definitely not the case.

Second, and more importantly, ten of the twelve schools listed are private universities at which a single year of tuition, fees, room, and board can easily top $60,000, or even $65,000.[9] Only Cal Davis and Michigan are state-sponsored universities at which the costs, although much higher than a few years ago, are less, at least for in-state students.[10]

Third, *all* of the universities, including Cal Davis and the University of Michigan, the two state schools on the *Forbes* list, are extremely selective. Only students with near-perfect high school grade point averages, high SAT or ACT test scores, and good recommendations stand a chance of admission.

Fourth, many of these universities are private, highly selective, and appear as well on lists of the most well-respected and selective universities in the United States. Certainly, Cornell, Johns Hopkins, Washington University, Duke, Princeton, Rice, Stanford, Michigan, and Chicago, as well as others, would appear on any list of elite, highly selective colleges and universities. The snobbishness of the *Forbes* STEM university list feeds into and reinforces the predilection of the information technology companies to be overly credential-conscious in hiring and promotion decisions. Recall Facebook, at least in its early years, hiring Harvard and Stanford graduates almost exclusively. These industry tendencies, as reinforced by the list, lead toward discrimination against many women, particularly those who are place-bound, unable to go far afield to attend university. The industry, and the *Forbes* writer as well, need to remember that in this day and age there are good people everywhere.

Another List: Up and Comers in STEM Education

Fortune magazine, one of the other nationwide business magazines, compiled a list that includes some sleepers, trotted out as though they were winners of the Kentucky Derby, as well as prestigious and well-known institutions:

1. Westminster College, New Wilmington, PA.
2. Carnegie Mellon University, Pittsburgh.
3. Harvey Mudd College, Claremont, CA.
4. Colby College, Waterville, ME.
5. Tuskegee University, Tuskegee, AL.
6. State University of New York College of Environmental Science and Forestry, Syracuse.
7. Polytechnic Institute of New York University, New York.
8. U.S. Coast Guard Academy, New London, CT.
9. Worcester Polytechnic Institute, Worcester, MA.
10. California Institute of Technology, Pasadena.[11]

The *Fortune* list suffers from many of the same problems as the *Forbes* list. Eight of the ten colleges and universities listed are private institutions at which expenses are high. Moreover, many of the institutions listed—Carnegie Mellon, Harvey Mudd (one of the Claremont Colleges), Colby, NYU, and Cal Tech—are highly selective. Not only are they not for everyone; few applicants gain admission.

Overall, combining the two lists (*Forbes* and *Fortune*), a fair characterization is that eighteen of the twenty-two institutions are in the elite category, selective in admissions and, for the most part, expensive. Phrased differently, 82 percent of the STEM colleges and universities to which our leading business magazines point are beyond the reach of most (nearly all) aspirants to STEM's siren call.

Of course, many of these elite institutions offer financial aid packages to those unable to afford the costs. Most of that financial aid, though, goes to applicants drawn from the lowest socioeconomic groups. One of the most oft-heard complaints is that almost none of that financial aid goes to the largest group that cannot attend without financial support, namely, the children of middle-class families.

Other Players

One important source below the radar for national business magazines such as *Fortune* and *Forbes* is the for-profit educational sector. At least in information technology, in 2008 for-profits were "the largest producers of women and minorities in IT fields."[12] Schools such as ITT Technical (in bankruptcy), Strayer University, the University of Phoenix, and DeVry University populate this group. Most recently, though, the for-profits have come under enhanced scrutiny revolving around their extensive reliance and misuse of Department of Education Title IV loan funds. Title IV funds account for 65–70 percent of for-profit schools' revenue. Poor job placement records and lack of disclosure about those deficient records have added to the pressure. One large player, Corinthian College, went out of business, while several others are in bankruptcy court. Enrollments at the other for-profits have declined as much as 50 percent. The Trump administration has promised to relieve the for-profit educational sector of government-generated pressures surrounding disclosure of placement statistics and denial of loan funding. At this date, it is too early to assess whether the Trump administration will follow up its rhetoric with actual efforts that generate results.

Professor Karen Chapple at the University of California Berkeley observed that "from 1990 to 2000, women filled almost 440,000 new IT jobs, while computer science departments produced only 100,000 female graduates [over the decade]. Where did the others come from?" She explored the role of "short-term training programs," but concluded that "the number of women who enter IT companies after graduating from short-term training programs is not large: estimates range up to [only] a few thousand a year."[13]

Requiring less in tuition and less in time commitment are the coding schools that have "popped up in recent years, teaching students programming languages such as Python and Ruby on Rails."[14] These programs hold out the prospect that they are able to turn out competent programmers based upon a ten- or twelve-week intensive course. Advertisement leads include "Novice to Hireable in 12 Weeks" (Omaha Code School) and "From Amateur to Professional in 13 Weeks" (New York's Fullstack Academy). Student fees range from $8,000 for an eight-week course (Code Fellows Academy) to $17,780 for a twelve-week course (Hack Reactor).[15]

A last observation is that the focus may be too narrow, at the programming schools and especially at the four-year universities. Computer educators have identified at least twenty IT-related academic disciplines. It is not all about computer science per se. Related fields include information science (computer-related librarianship), graphics, web design, performance analysis, network administration, multimedia design, system security, and a host of other subjects and majors.[16] So, a third source of women entering IT positions has been majors and programs related to but not specifically identified as "computer science" or "computer" this or that. Related fields and majors constitutes a third source that has been under the radar.

Further Observations about STEM

One key finding from a close examination is that STEM education is more amorphous than one would expect. At times, researching providers, programs, and majors was like wrestling with a ghost. Many universities (Rice or Stanford, for example) have an ancillary STEM office, but STEM as a major or a department is somewhat rare. Students interested in a STEM education pursue science (chemistry or physics, for instance), or computer science, or engineering (electrical perhaps), or mathematics (whose department sometimes houses computer science). STEM often tends to be an area of emphasis rather than a school or department.

To illustrate the latter point, one field research task was to inquire of forty-four of the remaining women's colleges in the United States about their STEM programs.[17] None responded that they had a STEM major or STEM department per se, although it must be noted that the overall response rate was very low. The responses that were received pursuant to inquiry about STEM majors and courses were open-ended, some vague in the extreme:

> *Bryn Mawr College, Philadelphia, PA*: "I would recommend that you contact Mary Osirim, the Provost here at Bryn Mawr [to obtain information about STEM majors]."
> *Scripps College, Claremont, CA*: "I am including here the link to our science department page that should give you the information you are seeking."
> *Smith College, Northampton, MA*: "You can find the information you are looking for at www.smith.edu."
> *Mount Holyoke College, South Hadley, MA*: "Mt. Holyoke's listing of majors, minors and certificates is found here, which includes many areas in the sciences, technology, engineering and math. . . . There is no dedicated Stem director [giving a link to mtholyoke.edu]."
> *Wellesley College, Wellesley, MA*: "While Wellesley is a liberal arts college, we offer a great variety of STEM-based programs. . . . There is a great deal of interdisciplinary learning that takes place among different programs under the STEM umbrella."[18]

By contrast, a national leader in STEM education for women, St. Catherine's in Minneapolis, does have STEM majors as well as STEM graduate programs.[19] St. Kate's, as the school is known locally, offers weeklong summer camps for young girls, in coding, robotics, and other STEM subjects. The university has founded and funded a National Center for STEM Education.

Surprise

The biggest surprise, I suppose, is that in some instances, and contrary to St. Catherine's program, the emperor often has no clothes. A relatively exhaustive review of STEM at the university level reveals a scattershot approach in some cases, lip service in others. Fundamentally, students do the same as they always have done: select from various majors and departments in the sciences, engineering, or mathematics. Although many assume that, under the STEM aegis, things have changed, perhaps radically, the reality is that they are not markedly different than they always have been.

Perhaps a consequence of lack of depth in the emphasis on STEM is the mixed nature of the results. Between 2002 and 2012, the number of students selecting a computer and information science major has *declined* 17.5 percent. That period tracks with the major push for STEM emphasis. But the results are mixed. Enrollees in health profession majors increased 129.4 percent in the period, and in biological and biomedical studies 50.7 percent. Perhaps proving nothing more than that students watch television programs, students entering homeland security and law enforcement majors increased 105.2 percent. Those selecting majors in "Parks, recreation, leisure and fitness studies" increased 81.9 percent.[20]

Another surprising feature of the STEM emphasis at most colleges and universities is the apparent absence of any effort to steer students in their choice of courses outside the STEM majors. Instead, the non-major choices for students are open-ended. There is no advice about groupings of courses or mini-tracks that might complement a STEM concentration. A student can fill the holes on her semester or quarter registration form just as easily with French literature or art history offerings.

That may be a good thing for certain students, who need a breather or respite from weighty and difficult curricula. It may not be such a good thing for others who, among other things, wish to marry what they are learning in STEM majors to the real world that will surround the computer science or the electrical engineering courses they are pursuing.

Where Will It All Lead?

No one knows for certain where it will lead, but quite a few believe that the STEM pendulum has swung too far in the opposite direction. One such person is Professor Peter Cappelli, a teacher of management at the Wharton School of the University of Pennsylvania. In his book *Will College Pay Off?*, Professor Cappelli concludes that "many graduates in science, technology, engineering and math—the so-called STEM subjects, which receive so much official encouragement, are having a tough time getting jobs they like."[21] His empirical finding: only about one-fifth of recent graduates with STEM degrees got jobs that made use of their training. "The evidence for recent STEM grads suggests that there is no overall shortage of STEM graduates," Professor Cappelli concludes.[22]

As chapter 15 elaborates, another possibility is that foreign-born and foreign-schooled computer scientists and engineers, great numbers of whom IT companies and IT personnel brokers bring into the United States through the H-1B visa program, will work for lower wages and salaries. The H-1B visa holders crowd out U.S.-based STEM graduates, including young women, depriving them of the employment and the career they thought would be theirs.

An even less rosy prognostication comes from Daniel Gelernter, CEO of Dittach, an information technology company. "Today we insist on higher education for everything" is his conclusion.[23] Mr. Gelernter looks in the opposite direction. "The thing I look for in a [software] developer is a longtime love of coding—people who taught themselves how to code in high school and still can't get enough of it." He is very critical of STEM majors and formal education: "The thing I don't look for in a developer is a degree in computer science. University computer science departments are in miserable shape: 10 years behind in a field that changes every ten minutes." Moreover, Mr. Gelernter says that university faculty have blinders on: "They may teach students how to design an operating system, but not how to work with a real, live development team."

Completing a triad of reservations about the last decade's emphasis on STEM education is the observation author Michael Lewis makes in his recent bestseller, *Flash Boys*.[24] Mr. Lewis notes the superlatives lavished on Russian émigrés for their abilities in programming and software development. He then wonders why so many of them are so superb. Is it because, due to a lack of or restricted access to computers, they learn to write code with paper and pencil, a scenario opposite to that which a STEM-type program offers?

STEM education and the emphasis on it are good things but, again, has the pendulum swung too far?

15

THE INDUSTRY'S ANSWER

An Expanded H-1B Visa Program

Seattle, Washington, is like Rome, they say—that is, built on seven hills. In Seattle, though, only six hills remain. The seventh, extending north from the downtown area to the shores of Lake Union, no longer exists. Early developers excavated the hill, mixed the earth with water, and piped the slurry into Elliott Bay. By the 1960s, the square-mile area, known as the "Denny Regrade," had become a haven for used car lots, small manufacturing plants, and warehouses.

Billionaire Paul Allen, with Bill Gates a co-founder of Microsoft, bought up much of the Denny Regrade real estate in order to build a mall stretching from downtown Seattle to Lake Union. Mr. Allen wanted to make Seattle the bio-tech capital of the United States, with bio-tech companies taking over the Denny Regrade, lining the mall. Alas, always tight with their purse strings, the Seattle voters turned down Mr. Allen's grand plan.

Nonetheless, the Denny Regrade has seen a rebirth, as a center of info-tech in Seattle. The used car lots are gone. Now the area is chock-a-block with new seven-, eight-, nine-, and ten-story buildings housing tech offices and tech workers who labor for Amazon and other information technology giants (not Microsoft, most of whose 126,000 employees work across Lake Washington, in the Bellevue and Redmond suburbs).

Visiting the Denny Regrade at lunchtime, I did not see a single female face. The "tech-bros," as they are known locally, seem entirely male. Moreover, many (most? perhaps 80 or 85 percent) appear to be Indian. At midday, the longest lines are at the food trucks serving Indian food. A row of food trucks serves up tikka masala, green and red lamb curry, chicken vindaloo, and chicken tandoori, as well as other Indian delicacies.

Implications from the Seattle and Similar Scenes

The observations about tech in Seattle highlight the shortsightedness, or tin ear, of the information technology industry. Rather than taking steps to address its obvious failing, discrimination against women in hiring and promotion, information technology companies have chosen to rely, heavily or nearly exclusively, on guest workers, mostly from India. "Even when faced with severe shortages, [IT] companies did not adopt new strategies that moved women toward parity in the IT field or increased minority participation.... [Instead] the industry worked toward raising the caps on the number of H1-B temporary visas."[1]

IT workers come to the United States from India on a visa, the H-1B visa, for three years, frequently with a follow-on extension, also for three years. Not only does the IT industry and community rely heavily on H-1B visas. Industry advocates lobby aggressively for a geometric increase in the numbers of visas that can be granted by the U.S. Citizenship and Immigration Services (USCIS), a component within the Department of Homeland Security. As far back as 2007, for instance, Bill Gates, with Paul Allen a co-founder of Microsoft, appeared before a congressional committee "warning of dangers to the U.S. economy if employers can't import more skilled workers to fill job gaps."[2] The industry's obtuseness toward its effect on women thus could project over the mid-term or even longer if the industry and its spokespersons win the day.

Tech companies are further relying on foreign nation-states and their output of male "techies," rather than training, hiring, and promoting women. Like Carrier or Ford, who wished to ship jobs to Mexico, information technology companies are shipping jobs to India. IBM has become a poster child of sorts, closing a plant in Minnesota and transferring the plant's five hundred jobs, still deemed necessary, to be carried out now in India.[3] Google and Facebook, among others, employ large support staffs in Madras or Bangalore in the south of the Indian subcontinent.

In many instances, shipping jobs overseas may merely result in a more efficient division of labor. Today, divisions of labor take place on a global rather than regional or domestic scale. Corporations situate facilities and functions where costs are low, or lowest, given an adequate supply of skilled workers and technicians, without regard to national borders. Those movements, though, usually do not impact on an additional important social issue.

This situation is different. Shipping jobs to India, similar to seeking expansion through increase in the number of H-1B visas, dims the prospects for women in information technology and, ultimately, for leadership positions. Although the industry does not often speak to the issue, many of those in it are aware of the irony, or downright hypocrisy, involved.

In 2014 Jodi Kantor of the *New York Times* did a follow-up study of the 1,700 persons in the class of 1994 from Stanford University, chronicling the utter lack of headway made by women in the class (roughly half the graduates were female) in info tech and in Silicon Valley.[4] One interviewee asked, "Why [does] the Silicon Valley celebrate some kinds of outsiders [foreign nationals from India] but not others?" She lamented the lack of progress. "The Internet was supposed to be the great equalizer. So why hasn't our generation moved the needle?"

Storm Clouds on the Horizon

As this chapter discusses below, President Trump has long been critical of the H-1B visa program, at least as USCIS administers it. His proposed executive order sets as a goal "to restore the integrity of the program." Among other things, his administration proposes to reverse earlier executive orders that permitted spouses of H-1B visa holders to work while in the United States. The order will cut back the amount of time a visa holder can work after obtaining a graduate degree in the United States.[5]

Tech firms' first response has been to throw the Indian outsourcing firms (for example, Tata Consultancy, Wipro, and Infosys) who "win a large share of the H-1B visas offered through an annual government-run lottery" under the bus. "The tech firms absolutely are going to throw the outsourcers overboard."[6] The H-1B visa lottery, in which the outsourcing firms have played a leading role, may become a thing of the past. Not giving up ground, however, the tech firms plan to take the recruitment and processing programs in-house. As they have done in the past, the tech firms have also loosed a phalanx of lobbyists upon Washington, D.C.

Thus far, the emphasis has been on opportunities for U.S. workers generally. Sources do not mention women at all. For example, the preamble to the Trump executive order states, "Our country's immigration policies should be designed and implemented to serve, first and foremost, the U.S.'s national interest. Visa programs for foreign workers . . . should be administered in a manner that protects the civil rights of American workers . . . and that prioritizes the protection of American workers."[7]

The tech industry's second response to government plans for visa program modifications has been to paint a heart-rending scenario. Undoubtedly speaking for the industry, spokesperson Gary Burtless of the Brooking Institution has stated,

> Important STEM workers have contributed an outsize share to founding new companies, getting patents, and helping build up American companies, which in turn have created . . . hundreds of thousands of jobs. Discouraging such people from applying for visas to enter the United States to work—I can't imagine how that can be considered to be in the American national interest.[8]

The Burtless response seems similarly unmindful of the crowding out of women by H-1B visa holders and other correlations between hiring and promoting women versus foreign workers.

The H-1B Visa

The visa that permits the holder to enter and work in the United States is known as the "specialty occupation" visa. The applicant must have a bachelor's degree or equivalent. They must have an offer of employment from a U.S. employer. The employment position must be one for which (a) the employer ordinarily requires a degree, and (b) the degree requirement is common for the position in the employer's industry.[9]

Critics of the specialty occupation visa program, especially labor unions, claim that industry has been sneaking in lower-cost skilled employees to achieve savings and not because of any shortages in the U.S. labor force. In response, the Department of Labor has layered another requirement on H-1B visa applications. The applicant must accompany the paperwork with a Labor Condition Application (LCA) in which the prospective employer certifies that the wage offered the prospective worker meets or exceeds the prevailing U.S. wage in the particular field of employment.

At least at first blush, current law limits the number of H-1B visas to 65,000 per year, a number that the information technology industry chafes under as patently insufficient. In lobbying efforts, the industry has sought to raise the cap from 65,000 to 180,000 or 185,000 per year. "Our nation's leaders need to fix our broken immigration system, including lifting the cap on H-1B visa. . . . [We] know the battle for talent is global. Encouraging legal, high-skilled immigration is vital for growth and prosperity."[10]

Further Wrinkles

As noted, the H-1B visa granted is for a term of three years. A further three-year extension is largely automatic. Ordinarily, under other programs, an applicant for a visa to enter the United States must overcome "the presumption of immigrant status." Visitors can do so by demonstrating that they have a job or own a house back home, that is, something that will draw them back to their country of origin. Possessions abroad or a job back home helps negate any inference that non-U.S. citizens are engaged in a plot to stay permanently in the United States. In technical terms, the house or job back home rebuts "the presumption of immigrant status."

But the H-1B visa is different from other categories of visa. The H-1B visa is what is known as a "dual intent" visa. "The H-1B holder may have legal immigration intent (apply for and obtain a green card)" while still being the holder of a visa for a temporary (albeit lengthy) stay.[11] Therefore, the visa holder may file an I-140 immigrant petition to begin the green card process and obtain landed immigrant status, which is not permitted under the guidelines for other types of visa.

Another wrinkle that lobbyists and industry spokespersons downplay, ignore, or blatantly misrepresent is the number of visas allowed, most often stating that the number is capped at 65,000. In recent years, the number if H-1B visas granted has greatly exceeded 65,000. Off the top, another 20,000 visas are available for foreign workers who have a master's or equivalent graduate degree from a U.S. university. They may immigrate to the United States on a student visa, matriculate at a U.S. university, obtain a master's degree, and then trade in their student visa for a skilled occupation (H-1B) one. Skilled workers whose prospective employment is *at* (*not necessarily for*) a university, a nonprofit research center, or a government facility are also in a category over and above the 65,000 commonly mentioned. In a representative year, the top ten universities alone bought in nearly 5,000 workers on H-1B visas via this pathway.

The number of visas granted by the U.S. Citizenship and Immigration Services thus far exceeds 65,000. For instance, in 2011, USCIS granted 129,552 H-1B visas.[12] The year following, FY 2012, USCIS granted 125,991 visas.[13] By 2014, the number had grown to 162,239, with the vast number of them (85 percent) going to prospective employees of information technology companies. The tech industry misrepresents these figures, maintaining that the H-1B visa programs allows for 65,000, or 85,000 (65,000 plus 20,000 U.S. university graduates), entrants to the United States when the actual number is double the tech industry's self-serving depiction.[14] Journalists, too, uncritically accept the industry's calculations.[15]

Criticism: Exploitation of Foreign Workers

The Department of Labor (DOL) Labor Condition Application programs, specifying a prevailing wage certification, is not policed. Knowing that, many prospective employers ignore the prevailing wage requirement. One study found that companies pay H-1B visa workers 27 percent less than they pay U.S. citizens holding equivalent or comparable jobs.[16] Another study found that IT companies pay skilled foreign workers $50,000 less than U.S. citizen engineers and programmers. H-1B opponents characterize foreign workers as "indentured servants."

Criticism: Crowding Out Qualified U.S. Workers

Employers' motive, of course, would be to achieve savings while also addressing a labor shortage. Of course, employers would not have to pay the higher salaries and wages they would have to pay American workers. Senator Chuck Grassley, chair of the Senate Judiciary Committee, elaborates on the manner in which H-1B visa workers possibly crowd out American ones:

> The program was intended to serve employers who could not find the skilled workers they needed in the United States. . . . Yet, under the law, employers are not required to prove to the Department of Labor that they tried to find an American to fill the job first. And, if there is an equally or even better qualified U.S. worker available, the employer does not have to offer him or her a job. Over the years the program has become a government-assisted way for employers to bring in cheap foreign labor, and now it appears that these foreign workers take over—rather than complement—the U.S. workforce.[17]

Railing against "rampant, widespread H-1B abuse," then presidential candidate Donald Trump was even stronger in his criticism: "The H-1B program is neither high-skilled nor immigration: these are temporary foreign workers, imported from abroad, for the explicit purpose of substituting for American workers at lower pay."[18] More centrist voices, including for instance those of the editors of the *New York Times*, echo Senator Grassley's and Mr. Trump's comments, lamenting the exploitation of both foreign workers ("indentured servants") and American workers.[19]

Criticism: Widespread Use as a Trojan Horse Used to Gain Permanent Residence

During his six-year stay, as previously mentioned, and unlike most other visa holders, a foreign worker on an H-1B visa can simultaneously pursue immigrant status, permitting him to stay for an indefinite period. The allegation is that, from the beginning of stays in the United States, or even earlier, many foreign workers' true intent is to obtain long-term status as a U.S. resident. No statistics are readily available to prove or disprove this point. Whether the argument is simply a result of xenophobia, or stands on some firmer ground, is not capable of proof one way or the other.

Criticism: A Hotbed of Immigration Fraud

Some statistics, however, are readily available. In 2008, for example, USCIS conducted an H-1B Benefit Fraud and Compliance Assessment.[20] Based on the study, USCIS concluded that 21 percent of the visas granted involved fraudulent applications. Fraud included falsification of educational backgrounds and of skill levels.[21] Much of the fraud, as well as unfair and illegal treatment of visa applicants, is attributed to brokers who, in placing foreigners with jobs in the United States, do the applications for visas on behalf of workers.[22]

Fraud levels are high in art (29 percent of applications) and highest in "accounting, human resources and advertising" (42 percent). Of thirteen categories USCIS defined, though, computer professionals came in third, with a fraud rate USCIS determined to be 27 percent. The rates in other fields are low (medicine and health at 10 percent, education at 9 percent). Moreover, indications are that fraud is nonexistent in other areas (mathematics and physical sciences or social sciences at 0 percent), although the samples of applicants in those categories are small.

Criticism: H1-B Visas as an Alternative to Integration

Early on in the women's movement, or even before it, the *New York Times* published an article bemoaning the shortage of young scientists in the United States. A subhead read "A Lady Chemist Argues the Answer Is to Tap Female Brain Power."[23] The same could be said of today's information technology industry.

The harshest criticism of IT's reliance on H1-B visas, though, has come from those whose mission is to increase the numbers of racial minorities in the industry. "There was not much heard from organized workers at the time of the H1-B visa debates."[24] The Reverend Jesse Jackson and his Rainbow/PUSH Silicon Valley Coalition strongly urged additional minority representation in the technology industry, as did the Coalition for Fair Employment in Silicon Valley. A female group did exist, the Silicon Valley Women in Human Resources, but it seems largely to have been dormant.

An Assessment

Utilization or expansion of the H-1B visa program is not a possible solution to the scarcity—indeed, dwindling number—of women in leadership and other roles in information technology. Indeed, the H-1B visa program represents the antithesis of a solution. H-1B visa applicants "crowd out" women by reducing opportunities for women in information technology.

Much of the H-1B visa debate swirls around whether or not there actually is a labor shortage, that is, a shortage of qualified workers domestically. One op-ed voices a resounding "no." The writer points to layoffs of tech workers in California alone, at Disney and Southern California Edison, among others, the American workers to be replaced by H-1B visa holders from India. The writer further cites as evidence that in 2015 Microsoft, Cisco, and Hewlett-Packard eliminated 60,000 tech jobs. Yet industry members, including the very companies that had eliminated positions, claim a labor shortage and a need to greatly expand the H-1B visa program. The writer ends with a patriotic plea: "Give Americans a fair chance. Don't continue to flood an already saturated tech labor market with more H-1B visas."[25]

It is difficult to evaluate those statements and the back and forth on the benefits versus the detriments involved. One thing that is certain, though, is that the worker shortage would be smaller if the industry devoted a portion of the resources it devotes to expansion of opportunities for foreign workers to the hiring, training, and promotion of women. From that standpoint, the H-1B visa hullabaloo actually is an indictment of the industry.

More Winds of Change

During the first few weeks of President Trump's term, a preview of his 2017 executive order restricting the H-1B visa program was leaked, foretelling "sweeping changes" in the H-1B visa program. Immediately, tech companies stated that the proposed order would "hurt their ability to tap the technical talent they need to stay competitive."[26] Tech company representatives continued to beat this drum as the new year progressed: "Many tech executives worry . . . not the least because of Mr. Trump's frequent criticism of U.S. companies that employ foreign workers. Indeed, a draft executive order proposes re-examining how the government issues H-1B visas for skilled workers, a system frequently used by tech firms."[27]

According to Microsoft officials, "Changes in U.S. immigration policies that restrain the flow of technical and professional talent may inhibit our ability to adequately staff our research and development efforts." Brad Smith, Microsoft's president, analogized the H-1B visa program to the Dreamers initiative, "a reference to young people who entered the country illegally as children but were allowed to remain by President Obama." The company "believes in a strong and balanced high-skilled immigration system and in broader opportunities for talented and law-abiding young people."[28]

Along similarly dramatic lines, Facebook CEO Mark Zuckerberg wrote, "We are a nation of immigrants. . . . I hope we find the courage and compassion to bring people together and make this world a better place."[29]

Robert Atkinson, president of the Technology and Innovation Research Group, an organization underwritten by several large tech firms, forecast another doomsday scenario: "The effect would end up being exactly the opposite of what Trump wants. Companies would go offshore like Microsoft did with Vancouver, Canada."[30] Mr. Atkinson continued: "Microsoft is hardly alone. Apple, Google, Facebook, Cisco and dozens of other large U.S. tech companies have established offices in Canada for the same reason," namely, the easier path to obtaining visas for foreign workers.[31] A Microsoft spokesperson has eased off that position, saying that "while immigration laws haven't been a primary driver of the company's investment in Canada, they've certainly been a contributing factor."[32]

The tech industry representatives' statements appear to be overemphatic. They may in fact signal an overdependence on the H-1B visa program to the detriment of other sources such as women and minorities.

The Other Side Is Heard

As the issues surrounding the program have attracted more attention, Main Street opponents of the tech industry campaign have come forward. A young American electrical engineer, an MIT graduate no less, writes to the *Wall Street Journal*,

If there is any program that has been more abused to the detriment of American workers, it is the H-1B visa program. Tech companies use it to bring in foreign workers at the expense of American Stem graduates. . . .

There are currently about 90 million people between the ages of 18 and 65 unemployed in the U.S. What efforts are being made to train the workers that are needed? . . . It is close to the truth that [tech] corporate leadership has abdicated its responsibility to the country and its workers.[33]

The young engineer concludes, "There's not a greater need for H-1B visas. What is needed is more responsible corporate leadership."

At the *Wall Street Journal*, as at other newspapers, the usual practice is to select and publish letters to the editor that express varying points of view on an issue. In this instance, the published letters all opposed expansion of the H-1B visa program. A senior engineer wrote, "In my 40 years working on the aerospace industry, I have seen many ill effects of the [H-1B visa] program. It's being used to depress American engineering salaries. Its elimination would greatly benefit American engineers."[34] Would curtailment of the program, or at least unwillingness to expand it, benefit women in tech as well?

PART IV

SOLUTIONS THAT

MAY WORK

16

LEAVENING STEM EDUCATION

Chapter 14 finds that STEM education overtures frequently have less substance than one would believe. At the high school level, STEM still means enrollment in the "pipeline courses" (trigonometry, calculus, chemistry and physics, computer science, programming) that lead to the STEM majors at college or university.[1] At university, the majors and departments remain what they have been traditionally: science, mathematics, engineering of various stripes, and technology. Often, then, STEM is an area of emphasis, a mental outlook, or a frame of mind, perhaps backed by a STEM advisor or an advising office.

At worst, then, STEM resembles a Western movie set, with false fronts lining Main Street. The question then becomes how to "dress" the set, to give STEM programs and offerings backbone and better equip STEM graduates for the job market and success beyond that. What can be added to the current array to give women in particular an increased chance for hiring, promotion, and further promotion in information technology?

The current array has not produced the results sometimes forecast for it.[2] "Many graduates in science, technology, engineering, and mathematics—the so-called STEM subjects, which receive so much official encouragement—are having a tough time getting the jobs they'd like."[3] As first visited in chapter 14, in *Will College Pay Off?*, Professor Peter Cappelli reports that only about a fifth of recent STEM graduates got jobs that made use of their training. "The evidence for recent grads suggests clearly that there is no overall shortage of STEM grads," Professor Cappelli writes.[4]

Etiology of the Idea

The idea that STEM programs might need some leavening does not originate with Professor Cappelli, although his findings support it. A germ of the idea comes from a book published in 2010 entitled *The Last Male Bastion: Gender and the CEO Suite in America's Public Companies.*[5] In that book, I examined the educational backgrounds and careers of the twenty-two women who, at that point, had become CEOs of Fortune 500 companies, of whom fifteen were still in office as *The Last Male Bastion* went to press.[6] A goal was to find out what courses and career paths these women had followed, rather than rehash the guidance and shoot-from-the-hip tips offered by the business advice books for women.

That exercise led to a number of findings, some of them more counterintuitive than others.[7] One unsurprising finding was that education matters, more so for women than for men. All twenty-two women in my CEO sample had bachelor's degrees. These included degrees from elite colleges and universities (Stanford, Princeton, Columbia, Georgetown, Rice; Wellesley, with three CEO graduates, was the leader). The list also included degrees from lesser-known or regional institutions (Queens College; University of Florida; Augustana, Illinois; Maryhurst, Oregon; Marymount, New York).

Beyond that, the sample had to be truncated, albeit slightly. One CEO and her company, Carol Meyrowitz and TJX, refused to release information about Ms. Meyrowitz. The sample of twenty-two became a sample of twenty-one.

Sixteen of the remaining twenty-one women CEOs had advanced degrees. There were twelve MBAs and one law degree (Angela Braly, CEO of Wellpoint, JD, Southern Methodist University). Carol Bartz, Yahoo! CEO at the time, had an advanced degree in computer science (PhD, University of Wisconsin). Irene Rosenfeld, then Kraft Foods CEO, had a PhD in marketing and statistics (Cornell) as well as an MBA (also Cornell). Ursula Burns, Xerox CEO, had a master's degree in electrical engineering (Columbia University). Only five in the twenty-one-member CEO group had not progressed beyond a bachelor's degree, at least in a formal educational setting.[8]

Because so many of the female CEOs had advanced degrees in business, a question that arose was, Where did the MBAs come from? More than half the MBAs came from elite schools (Harvard [three], Yale, Columbia, MIT, New York University, Northwestern) and less than half but still a significant number from less well-known or regional schools (Bellarmine, in Louisville, Kentucky; Loyola, in Chicago; University of Maryland).

Three Lessons Learned Examining CEO Career Patterns

The examination of these CEOs' career patterns produces three major lessons for women executives.

Don't be lopsided. The women with broader skills and backgrounds, even if they had a technical specialty, advanced to senior management and then the corner suite. Very often they had an advanced degree, especially a master's degree in business administration (MBA).

By contrast, though the sample is small, we may observe that the women who primarily had only a technical specialty had a short tenure in the CEO's office. For example, Jill Barad's short tenure at Mattel highlights her fixation with marketing and, more specifically, marketing the Barbie line of dolls. Mary Sammons, whose exclusive background was retailing, was unable to lift Rite Aid from the doldrums. A CEO or a senior manager must know about operations, distribution, markets, strategy, revenues, profits, share prices and finance, and a host of other topics beyond her specialty.

The direct implication of the survey was that, at a minimum, boards of directors regard women with an MBA degree as possessing the "right stuff," or some of it, to qualify for senior management positions.

Go get an MBA. This has long been the advice for young men and women in business.[9] After working three, four, or five years in an entry-level position, followed by a few years in the job after the first promotion, go back to school. In fact, many of the leading business schools regard practical seasoning as a de facto requirement for admission.

The market reflects and reinforces both the advice and the empirical evidence from examining female CEO career patterns. Over the last decade, "the number of applicants seeking admission to M.B.A. programs grew at 57% of schools world-wide offering full-time, two year programs."[10] Between 2014 and 2015, MBA applications increased 15 percent at Harvard School of Business, to approximately 9,900 applications. Other MBA schools experienced greater gains: Yale School of Management, 25.1 percent; University of North Carolina Kenan-Flagler School of Business, 23.2 percent; and Georgetown University McDonough School of Business, 16.4 percent.[11]

Broaden STEM tracks. Specifically, universities and advisors should point STEM majors toward a mini-track, a course sequence, that gives them some idea of the milieu in which, hopefully, they will function in the world beyond college. A mini track would not replicate an MBA but would give STEM majors an idea how product markets and supply and demand work. Down the line, material about finance (stocks and bonds, mutual and hedge funds, analysts and financial advisors) may aid students in managing their personal financial affairs as well as better understanding corporate financial matters. A dose of managerial accounting would tell students what financial statements are, what they tell the reader, more importantly what financial statements do not tell you, how books may be cooked, and the ubiquity of financial reporting among units, divisions, subsidiaries, layers of subsidiaries, and publicly traded corporations.

A few universities have already implemented this sort of course selection through joint programs. For example, Carnegie Mellon University, an academic leader in information technology, offers a master of science degree in computational finance, which draws upon offerings and faculty from the Department of Computer Science, the Heinz School of Public Administration, and the Tepper School of Business.[12]

A Second CEO Study

The Last Male Bastion's study was in 2010. Since that time, other women have succeeded to Fortune 500 CEO seats, still others have stepped down or retired, and members of a further group have, effectively, received pink slips. The number of female CEOs stood at fifteen in 2010, rose to twenty-four in ensuing years, and settled back to twenty-two as this book was being written.

Eliminating the duplicates with the 2010 study (there are only three holdovers from the 2010 women CEO group)[13] leaves nineteen of twenty-two female CEOs of Fortune 500 companies. Seventeen of the nineteen have advanced university degrees. Three have advanced degrees in electrical engineering (two master's and one PhD). Two have law degrees, one from the University of Pennsylvania and one from the University of Texas.

Again, though, the most noteworthy finding is that twelve of nineteen female CEOs have MBAs. The balance seems to be tipped a bit more in favor of elite colleges and universities: Columbia and Stanford, with two each, and Pennsylvania's Wharton School, with one. Lesser-known and regional universities, though, are still represented: Bellarmine University (Louisville, Kentucky) once again, Webster University (Webster Groves, Missouri), and Baylor (Waco, Texas) (a major university but one not particularly known for its MBA program). The results in 2016 seem not dissimilar from those in 2010.

Meta-Study

Is a study based upon two other studies a "meta-study"? Probably not, but academics are enamored of throwing around that "meta" modifier. Be that as it may, combining the two studies yields thirty-nine women who have held Fortune 500 CEO chairs since Jill Barad, at least in the modern era, became the first in 1997 (twenty-one from the 2010 study, plus twenty-two from the 2016 study, minus duplicates and nonparticipants equals thirty-nine). All thirty-nine have bachelor's degrees from known universities. Thirty-two of those women hold advanced degrees, including two who hold PhDs.

There are five female CEOs who hold STEM-type advanced degrees: three engineering (all by chance in electrical engineering) and two computer science (Carol Bartz and Melissa Mayer). Three female CEOs hold law degrees, all from well-known law schools (Southern Methodist University, University of Pennsylvania, and University of Texas). The most dominant finding, though, seems to be that twenty-four of the thirty-nine women hold master's degrees in business administration, or MBAs.

A case may be made for adding three to the number twenty-four, representing law degrees in the CEO group. A law school business law curriculum can and often does replicate much of what an MBA course of study would contain. Courses in business organizations, agency and partnership, corporate governance, corporate finance, mergers and acquisitions, accounting for lawyers, securities regulation, income tax, and corporate income tax add up to twenty-four semester hours, equivalent to many MBA programs.

Adding back the three to the twenty-four is something of a leap of faith, albeit a small one, for the addition assumes that the female CEOs followed a business track in their law school careers. But if one makes that leap, assuming the known unknowable, the number of CEOs with business-oriented education backgrounds rises to twenty-seven.

Of the thirty-nine women who have succeeded in reaching the top positions in major corporations, then, 70 percent (69.23 percent) have MBAs or similar education backgrounds. In contrast, among those same women, five, or 12.8 percent, have STEM degrees. Below the CEO level, the evidence is scarce but some does exist. In 2015, overall, chief financial officers in public companies had average pay raises that exceeded those of CEOs. Two of those ten highest-paid CFOs were women with business backgrounds. Moreover, both were in or soon to be in information technology companies: Safra Catz at Oracle (now co-CEO) and Ruth Porat at Morgan Stanley (who soon left for Google).

Tempering and Leavening Instrumentalist Approaches

A criticism of the STEM appellation and emphasis is that, as a result, "students don't get a quality, well-rounded education."[14] Thomas Friedman of the *New York Times* predicts that "the best jobs in the future are going to be STEMpathy [rather than STEM] jobs—jobs that blend STEM skills (science, technology, engineering, and math) with human empathy. We don't know what many of them will look like yet."[15] He laments the headlong swing toward deep immersion in STEM fields and STEM alone.

Others have offered similar critiques of the wholly instrumentalist approach taken by education programs in the United States. Longwood University president W. Taylor Reveley IV has pointed out that many high school and university curricula no longer contain the civics courses and civics exposure that once were mandatory:

> Over the past two generations, the idea of education being about teaching people how to engage in public affairs has been lost. At one point, the core curriculum at the college level was focused on: How do you get ready to be an active citizen in America? How do we make democracy endure? Today, education is thought of almost exclusively in terms of career preparation. That is what we have lost.[16]

While astute observers may apply those observations to many educational pursuits, the comments ring especially true of the STEM phenomenon.

But isn't a near-total dedication to STEM necessary because, without it, the United States would fall increasingly behind other countries in technical subjects and later in job skills and efficiency? Information technology's felt need to import more and more workers from India and other nations because increasingly the United States is unable to provide the workforce needed (see chapter 15) provides support for the proposition.

"Much of this fear stems from the biennial findings of the Program for International Student Assessment, an organization that issues a test to fifteen year olds all over the world to rank their competency in reading, math and science."[17] The statistics are "scary": out of sixty-five educational programs surveyed, the assessments ranked U.S. students twenty-seventh in math and twentieth in science. "US teens lag in global education ranking as Asian countries rise to the top," headlined an MSNBC story.

As in many things, all is not what it may seem. Looking deeper, Michael Teitelbaum of the Harvard Law School found that while the statistics did not lie, they failed to give a complete picture. "I found that the U.S. has always been in the middle, we've never been at the top."[18] He elaborates: "I'm not saying that [other countries'] performance is irrelevant but the comparison shouldn't be considered a direct one. Many of the countries above the U.S. in the rankings are much smaller and homogenous, places such as Singapore and Hong Kong." He concludes, "If you take a national average across the U.S.," as the studies do, "you have a huge disparity in educational performance across the country, even down to the local level. So you have a higher variety of educational outcomes. [Ergo] it makes sense that Americans' average is not as high as smaller education systems." Dr. Teitelbaum concludes, "We're not falling back, [it's that] some other [mostly smaller] countries are just rising."

The alarm bells about educational outcomes, therefore, should be the one-alarm rather than the three- or four-alarm varieties that have sounded more often. The implication of that conclusion is that there is more room than previously thought for tempering or leavening the onslaught of STEM programs and STEM proposals. In turn, that finding buttresses the idea that women who aspire to leadership levels and positions in information technology should delve into business subjects and attain a more well-rounded educational background.

Leavings

The empirical finding seems impressive but is subject to a number of reservations. First, the sample is small—thirty-nine women in leadership positions in business.

Second, based upon the finding, the contention would be that a STEM degree is best to equip a young woman to seek a position with an information technology firm and to obtain her first or even second promotion within the company. But to advance into management and leadership roles, an employee needs something additional that would give her a sense of perspective and some degree of depth in the issues that she will encounter.

Third, the further contention is that some sort of business and economics grounding suits that purpose better than heavy or straight-line STEM course sequences or majors a young man or woman could pursue.

The fourth reservation is that the sample is especially small on the STEM side. Not that many women have gone through STEM as corporations and universities presently conceive and emphasize it, and further few have matured and advanced to become eligible for leadership positions. We simply do not have sufficient raw material to postulate how a STEM background helps, or does not help, a young woman as she progresses in her career.[19]

Given the research, though, simplistic as it is, I believe that a very good case may be made that STEM needs some liberalization or tempering and that the direction to be taken is toward business, economics, and perhaps a dose or two of accounting and finance. Someone far above my pay grade, Larry Page, founder and now CEO of Google, also advises this:

> I think that we are not educating people in a general way. You should have a pretty broad engineering or scientific background. You should have . . . MBA training of how to run things, organize stuff, and raise money. I don't think most people are doing that and it's a big problem. Engineers [and scientists] are usually trained in a very fixed area. When you are able to think about all these disciplines together, you kind of think differently. . . . That's really an important thing for the world. That's how we make progress.[20]

17

PAYING CLOSE ATTENTION TO THE POOL PROBLEM

Examining the underrepresentation of women, as directors or as senior executives, one has to look not merely at the present but also the future. The question one should then ask is, How sufficient will the pool be, that is, the pool of candidates from which companies and their boards will choose future female directors and future senior managers? The pool is not about the present but about the future—about five years and ten years from now. That is the pool. What is the problem?

The problem is that evidence such as we have indicates that the pool in the future will not be much better, and could be worse, than the pool is at present, from women's point of view. Three pieces of evidence support that outlook:

> Forty percent of the women on corporate boards of directors have not percolated up through corporate organizations the way male directors have.[1] Instead, a plurality of women directors "sidestep" onto corporate boards after having recorded achievements in academe, government, or the not-for-profit-sector. If the pool were larger, we would expect to see more women coming up through corporations' ranks and senior executive positions rather than "sidestepping."[2]

> Many boards begin "by pursuing the same high profile people—the same people who are already over-recruited and over committed."[3] Corporations tend to choose the same women over and over. The term "trophy directors" applies to individuals who serve on four or more boards; the number of female trophy directors has shown robust growth while the number of male trophy directors has declined.[4] If the pool from which female directors and senior managers were larger, we would expect the number of women trophy directors to level off and then decline. A better pool would produce more candidates, reducing the need to choose the same women over and over again.

> Nominations and elections of women to boards of directors have
stalled in the United States, leveling off at around 14 percent, at least
according to one organization's computations (20.2 percent according
to Catalyst).[5] The plateau effect indicates that, despite pressure to add
more women to their boards, publicly held companies are having difficulty finding suitable women candidates for board vacancies. They are
having difficulty because the pool from which companies would choose
such candidates is inadequate.

The truth be known, however, the evidence we do have is for the most
part from analyses of selection of directors. We make somewhat a leap
of faith (probably a small leap) in hypothesizing that similar conditions
prevail in the selection of women for senior management positions.

Adequacy of the Pool in Information Technology

Some evidence does exist, though, and, lo and behold, it relates to
information technology. Chapter 1 and appendix A indicate that only 5
percent of upper-level managers in information technology are women,
the worst, by far, of any American industry. Taken from the compensation tables in SEC filings, the evidence is not the best. The best evidence
would give us a picture of the pool as it exists deeper down in corporations, that is, the proportion of senior middle managers and lower-level
senior managers who are female. They will populate the pool ten years
from now, or even sooner.

Nonetheless, the evidence we do have points to the inadequacy of
the pool in information technology. Together with a research assistant,
I was able to identify twenty-seven female executives, past and present,
of publicly held information technology companies, as of the spring of
2017, as I list in appendix B. So presently the pool is only 27 out of 575,
or 4.6 percent.

Before we examine the details, it is worth noting that the pool of
senior-most female executives in information technology is tiny. Critics might state that the sample is so small as to be unrepresentative,
statistically insignificant. But the pool's small size may be the principal
message. In other words, the rejoinder to critics is that "that's all there
are," a subset of 27 females in the set of 575 IT executives. The sample's

minuscule size illustrates well the puny size of the pool, boding poorly for the future.

In turn, the extremely small size of the pool indicates that, unless matters take a radical turn, the number of female CEOs in IT is unlikely ever again to reach the heights, such as they are, that chapter 2 outlines (twelve women CEOs of large cap information technology companies). It further bodes ill for ascension of women to other senior posts.

Characteristics of the Pool

Of the twenty-seven women, only two had STEM degrees. Mary Beth Westmoreland, chief technology officer, Blackbaud (BKLB), has a degree in mathematics and physics from Immaculata University (Malvern, PA). Debora Shoquist, executive vice president of operations, Nvidia (NVDA), has a degree in electrical engineering from Kansas State University (Manhattan, KS).

There were twenty-five women remaining (twenty-seven minus two who have STEM backgrounds). Five of those remaining women had law degrees. Four had juris doctor degrees (JDs) from elite universities (University of California at Berkeley, New York University, Georgetown University, and University of Virginia) and one from a regional university's law school (Cleveland State University).

Of the twenty-five women, six had bachelor's degrees only, but all were in business or closely related fields: two in accounting, two in marketing and merchandising, one in business administration, and one in economics.

That accounts for thirteen of the twenty-seven women in the pool overall (two STEM, five law, and six business bachelor's degrees). Paralleling the information in the previous chapter on where female CEOs come from, all of the fourteen remaining senior executive women in information technology had master's degrees in business administration (MBAs). The balance was tipped heavily in favor of prestigious colleges and universities: two from Harvard, two from Santa Clara University, followed by one each from Southern Methodist, Pennsylvania, Columbia, and California at Berkeley. Regional schools included Bentley University (Waltham, MA) and the University of St. Thomas (Houston, TX). One MBA was foreign, from the University of New South Wales in Sydney, Australia.[6]

Reading the Tea Leaves Again

Mimicking the add-back-ins of the previous chapter, one could fold the law degrees back in with the MBAs. Doing so increases the number of women in the pool with advanced business-type degrees to nineteen of twenty-seven, or 70 percent.

Doing a second add-back-in, folding the six business-oriented bachelor's degrees into the mix yields twenty-five of twenty-seven women with business rather than STEM educational backgrounds. Ninety-two percent (92.5 percent) of the women who have advanced to senior leadership positions in information technology companies have law or business degrees, not STEM backgrounds.

That number, twenty-five out of twenty-seven, yields an antidote to the swirl and push behind the STEM movement, particularly as it relates to young women. But, again, we must linger here for a moment. The first thing to take into consideration is that the pool is exceedingly small. A larger pool might reveal a different outcome.

Second, one can read the evidence in other ways. Contrary to this book's intimations, the evidence may reveal that a declining population of women has been pursuing STEM fields in their academic pursuits. Once the current STEM emphasis gains traction, more women will pursue STEM majors and eventually the pool will even out, or move toward a more even balance between STEM and business/law backgrounds.

Third, taking the opposite viewpoint, one can contend that the STEM anchor has been dragging the bottom for some time now. The evidence reveals that the best way to succeed to a leadership position in information technology is not a STEM degree but a business background or, better yet perhaps, a STEM undergraduate degree coupled with an MBA or similar advanced degree in business.

Fourth, given the pool in IT and the characteristics of the women in it, STEM emphasis should include filling the lacunae with some elemental business and economics courses, or creating and making that option available to students. Those courses or a recommended mini-track of them might be the flowers rather than the seeds of the STEM movement, advertised as such. The additional course offerings would complement the STEM platform nicely.

Fifth, to repeat the caveat set out earlier, this analysis pertains only to those who aspire to leadership positions in information technology companies. For young women who relish STEM subjects exclusively, or for young women whose horizon stretches only to the first or second promotion, analysis of the pool is irrelevant. At most, counselors and young women should view the evidence regarding business backgrounds reservedly.

Stars in the Ranks

Certain of the women who are senior executives in information technology have achieved star status despite not being corporate CEOs. First on any list would be Sheryl Sandberg, COO of Facebook. She has written a highly publicized book, *Lean In*, that this book critiques in chapter 8. Her portrait has been on the cover of *Time*.[7] She has received honorary degrees from several universities.[8] She received additional press, the unwelcome kind, when her husband, David Goldberg, CEO of Survey Monkey, died in a treadmill accident while he and Ms. Sandberg were vacationing in Mexico.[9]

Another recipient of fanfare and star status has been Ruth Porat, CFO of Google. She left Morgan Stanley, lured to Google by a $70 million "hello package," to be followed by one of the highest salaries for anyone, male or female, in the industry.[10]

The Silicon Valley rumor mill opines that it is only a matter of time before Catherine Lesjak, CFO at Hewlett -Packard, becomes CEO of a major company.[11] Safra Catz, an M&A (mergers and acquisitions) attorney by training, did become a CEO, at Oracle, after serving as CFO and, pre-Porat, was the highest-paid woman executive in IT ($44.3 million in 2013).[12] Everyone's list is different, but most star lists would also include Renee James, who was president at Intel, and Marie Myers, also a high executive at Hewlett-Packard, now at Hewlett Packard Enterprises.

Critical Mass Theory

Sociologists tell us that the number of minorities (female, African American, Asian American, Latino), say, in a work group or at an equivalent rank, is important not only in overcoming discrimination but also in achieving proper recognition for achievements. The first academic to flesh out this critical mass theory was Rosabeth Moss Kanter, a sociologist on the Harvard Business School faculty. She deduced the theory from an in-depth examination of men and women in the workplace, published in 1977 as *Men and Women of the Corporation*, also summarized in chapter 8.[13]

Professor Kanter theorized that a sole minority person is a token, not perceived by the work group's "dominants" as a particular threat. Indeed, any threat the token poses is ameliorated when the person makes a voluntary retreat into a stereotype or has a stereotypical label applied to him or her. Thus a token may take on the mascot, mother figure, class clown, or similar properties or appearances (stereotypes) to lessen the sting associated with being the only one.[14]

Increasing the number of minorities in a work group, say, to two, would further defuse the situation, one would think. Exactly the opposite occurs. Now feeling a threat, often imagined, the dominants engage in an exercise Professor Kanter terms "boundary heightening." For example, when the new entrants to the workplace are women, the dominant males will ratchet up their discussion of "male subjects" such as cars, hunting, fishing, or sports. The dominants may greet the minority group members with rough, inhospitable, or exclusionary treatment. The pinup photos go back up on the firehouse wall.

Building on Professor Kanter's findings, feminists began urging that three is the magic number, meaning that three or more minorities in a work group, or with a similar title or at an equivalent rank, would represent a breakthrough.[15] The minority would experience less rough handling by the dominants. They would feel free to speak out, including objecting to proposed courses of conduct. The compunction to retreat into a protective stereotype would lessen. The minority group members' comfort level would rise dramatically.

Three female consultants then attempted to apply Professor Kanter's theories, which are not about boards of directors at all, to corporate boards and corporate governance. In an advocacy piece, management consultant Vicki Kramer, along with Alison Konrad and Sumru Erkut, published *Critical Mass on Corporate Boards: Why Three or More Women Enhance Corporate Governance*. The piece applied Professor Kanter's theories and findings to corporate boards of directors and female directors' presence on boards.[16]

The Naysayers

One coterie that has done much damage to women's hoped-for role in corporate leadership consists of three academics from North Carolina. In an article entitled "Does Critical Mass Matter?," the naysayers wrote, "Critical mass is hot. But is it real?"[17] The coauthors found that "women and racial or ethnic minorities are unlikely to have an impact in the boardroom as they grow from a few tokens into a considerable minority of the board." They concluded that one should "counsel skepticism that any different outcomes" such as "enhanced opportunities for collaboration and support" or "improved [comfort levels] . . . emerge from a critical mass of female directors."[18]

The study was ill-conceived from its inception. But it did much damage to the cause of increasing female representation, not only on corporate boards, but in expansion of the pool beneath the director and senior executive ranks.[19]

First, the proponents begin by asking the wrong questions from their sample of forty corporate directors, of whom twenty-four were female and ten were nonwhite. What they were seeking was evidence of hostile behavior or inhospitable treatment and surroundings toward minority group board members. Had the authors possessed experience with actual boards of directors, they would know that they were highly unlikely to find evidence of such behavior on any public company's board. They were looking for something that rarely if ever happens. Typical boards of directors and directors themselves are diligent about maintaining decorum. Board members strive to function as members of cohesive teams. Directors are supportive of one another. It would be extremely rare to find the type of behavior the coauthors envision, or search for, on the board level. In fact, the very last thing one would expect to find would be directors being less than fully supportive of or hostile to a new duly elected board member.[20]

Second, where critical mass does matter, serving as an antidote to rude, sexist, or other forms of discriminatory behavior, is lower down in corporate organizations, say, at the pool level or the level at which the pool is beginning to emerge: the lower ranks of senior management or middle management itself. "You walk into a meeting in one of the departments and now there is another woman. You see each other . . . and you know you're both glad to see each other there."[21] But trying to be controversial, the authors attempt to discredit the critical mass construct in all its forms and applications.

Third, the study they designed was based upon a snowballing methodology, in which the first interviewees are asked for names of further corporate directors likely to sit for an interview. Following that method of election, of course, is faulty. The first interviewees, rugged individualists for whom minority status is no obstacle, are highly likely to give up names of persons who look like themselves. In that manner, snowballing often replicates the first rank of interviewees and produces an unrepresentative sample.

Fourth, obviously those advocates who advance a critical mass rationale for increasing women in corporate leadership roles put the theory forth as aspirational as well. The aspirational nature of the critical mass advocacy is lost upon the three coauthors, who respond with what they represent as facts. They remind one of Charles Dickens's Mr. Gradgrind, who insisted on "facts, facts and more facts," and for whom fancy and aspiration were anathema.[22]

The largest harm of all, then, is the damage the three coauthors inflict upon the critical mass theory and Rosabeth Moss Kanter. Professor Kanter never said anything about corporate boards of directors or how they operate. The point at which the critical mass construct does operate is in the work group or its equivalent ranks and levels throughout the organization. Professor Kanter closely examined that setting, not the operation of corporate boards.

Critical mass theory aids immeasurably in attempts to augment the pool from which future women directors and senior executives will emerge. Given the small, indeed minuscule, size of the pool in information technology (27 actives of 575 senior executives), critical mass is even more important in that field.

Developing the Pool: A Pitfall to Avoid

According to many male business executives, "the reason the number of women in management is not increasing is the lack of executive experience" and line experience.[23] The business leaders themselves, though, are often the ones responsible for women lacking profit and loss (line) responsibility. The tradition has been to shunt women into so-called pink-collar jobs on staffs, in human resources, or at the company's captive foundation. "Decision makers see women as more well suited for jobs involving human relations than those involving high visibility project and line responsibilities for profits and losses."[24] Professor Rosabeth Moss Kanter has found that women are assigned a disproportionate share of what she terms "'housekeeping jobs'—tasks that have low visibility, status and rewards."[25]

Moreover, once they are in those positions, women frequently encounter glass walls, separating them from the glass elevator shaft. Most interested onlookers know what the glass ceiling is: the impenetrable barrier that permits women to see but not realistically contend for or attain positions in the upper ranks. But there are glass walls and elevator shafts as well. The glass wall encases women in the pink-collar world, sealing them off from the job progressions that lead to the line jobs and progressions that might lead them to senior management. Meanwhile, the women in the pink-collar world see, but cannot reach out to, their male counterparts steadily ascending along traditional and other career tracks. The glass elevator shaft encases the men but not the women.[26] The glass wall and glass elevator phenomena, where they exist, inhibit development of the pool.

Managing with an Eye on the Pool Problem

Developing the pool has advantages. Besides being a resource in the selection of directors, the pool is a resource for selection of women to fill senior management positions. Women may be in short supply, but the shortage is not as extreme as numbers in information technology would seem to indicate. "Rather it's that finding them [capable female managers] requires persistence, focus, and genuine commitment to the goal of broad diversity."[27] Development of visible pools lower down in organizations facilitates the process.

Another wrinkle is that CEOs currently in office are rarely candidates for board selection, often because their companies limit them to a single outside directorship or forbid outside board seats altogether. In 2015 only 17 percent of the directors appointed were board chairs or CEOs.[28] More viable as candidates for boards and senior positions are executives with "functional depth [such] as cyber security," international experience, finance, accounting, or strategic thinking and planning.[29] Developing the pool adds visibility to women whose experience leans toward the functional side, visibility leading to further promotions within and without the company as well as CEO and director positions.[30]

Critically important then, as part of the way forward, is that upper-level executives in information technology companies enlarge the pool of women managers lower down in their organizations. "Pay attention to the pool" is a refrain heard in education and integration as well as in gender diversity.[31]

The efforts expended by leaders in IT, of course, are not immediately conducive to the solution of the pool problem the industry faces. But those efforts will bear fruit ten or twelve years from now, when the industry will have set a course and embarked upon solving this critical societal issue.

18

ENLARGING THE POOL

Easing Off-Ramps and Enhancing On-Ramps

Very early on, in advance of a pool's formation, and after the first or second promotion, many capable young women leave the management ranks. They never reach positions from which they have the pool in sight.

Women "opt out" for a variety of reasons, such as their belief that the turbo capitalism and the 24/7 availability that U.S. bosses demand of subordinates are excessive. Further, many young women believe that those features of the workplace are incompatible with the type of family and personal life they envision. Implicit requirements for face time in the office along with demands for willingness and availability to travel on short notice are further elements of a U.S. business environment. Many younger women do not wish to work that hard or under those conditions. Another principal reason for opting out is biological. Younger women opt out to give birth to a child and then, often, a second child, and sometimes a third.

Male bosses—and many female bosses as well—regard childbirth as recreational.[1] They seem to place childbirth and maternity leave in the same category as taking time off to train for running in a race or playing in a tennis tournament. Companies, including those in information technology, need to take steps to make opting out less of a watershed, career-determinative, or career-ending event. In other words, those at the head of companies must do more to "ease the off-ramps," as author Sylvia Ann Hewlett describes them.[2]

Many of the young women who opt out do not return to the same or similar employers, or do not return to the workforce at all. Companies thus lose the institutional memory and the human capital that are associated with capable employees who leave and do not come back. Of the women who do think about a return, they are forestalled by thoughts of hostility by coworkers who have never left; the self-perceived or actual obsolescence of their knowledge and skills; and the work/life balance, including child care issues and tug-of-war (home versus job) that confront them. Thus, heads of companies must talk about and implement steps to build and then enhance the "on-ramps" too.

The less fearsome the opting-out process is, and the more facile and smooth the subsequent return, the more robust will be the stream flowing into and enlarging the pool from which future female leaders will emerge. Even after stretching a four-month maternity leave into a year, or a multiple of years, absences are statistically of little significance, leading to working lives of thirty-five or thirty-six years rather than thirty-seven, thirty-eight, or thirty-nine years.

Naysayers

Of course, a few outliers insist that, in the first place, opting out does not exist. Recently, Aaron Dhir, professor of law at Osgood Hall in Toronto, made just such an assertion:

> I am skeptical that [gender disparities] can be attributed to a shortage of qualified women. Rather than there being an insufficient "pool," or "supply," I suggest that . . . a more appropriate explanation lies in the coupling of implicit cognitive biases [sexism] with the fact that the networks of existing directors are limited in scope and restricted entry.[3]

In support of his statement, Professor Dhir "re-tweets" the Catalyst pronouncement: "Catalyst has characterized the supply problem in Canada and the United States as a 'myth.'"[4]

Professor Dhir's assessment, that a good ole boys' club is still in control ("networks of existing directors"), and that "implicit cognitive biases" among males hold women down, has far less explanatory power that it did thirty or forty years ago. More importantly, assertions about sexism as the primary cause are going to be a turnoff to dominant males, many of whom have daughters, have acted as mentors to female coworkers, and live in a world that differs markedly from the one Professor Dhir seems to have in his mind's eye.[5] The males may still be dominant, but many harbor the belief that their daughters and their coworkers live in a changed world in which women can do anything that men can do, in sports, in business, in politics, or in academe.

Rather, there are other, more cogent explanations for the leaky pipe syndrome, that is, that many capable qualified younger women enter the pipeline but few emerge at the opposite end, as senior executives. One prevalent one is the opting-out phenomenon.[6] Young women who have graduated from university and have possibly garnered an MBA obtain a management position at a company. Then, at age thirty, thirty-one, or thirty-two, they marry. They become pregnant, taking a maternity leave that stretches into a year or two. They have a second child.

Professor Dhir and Catalyst flatly deny that any of this takes place. "There is ample reason to question conclusions that women are 'opting out,'" Professor Dhir, for example, again asserts.[7] True, "little empirical evidence [indicates] that women are leaving in droves when they have children."[8] What the naysayers ignore are the reams of circumstantial evidence, strong circumstantial evidence, that validate the existence and widespread nature of the opting-out phenomenon.

First is the trophy director phenomenon. Why, if the pool of female candidates is sufficient, do corporations and their boards of directors choose the same women over and over again for board positions? No one can do a capable job holding more than two or three board seats, but in corporate America a number of women hold six, seven, or eight board seats. Part of it may be that corporations have a tin ear, or are ham-fisted, or are merely ticking the boxes, choosing only road-tested, safe female candidates for their boards of directors. But another very plausible reason for why corporations choose the same women over and over is that the pool of possible candidates, at least from corporate settings, is small and deemed insufficient. The reason: the pool has not appeared promising, and a principal reason for that has been opting out by well-educated, capable women.

Second, where do directors, especially women directors, come from? Scholars and analysts in the field assume that female directors have come up through the ranks, at the same and at other corporations. My studies show just the opposite. Forty percent or more of the female directors on U.S. Fortune 500 boards "sidestep" onto corporate boards, having spent most of their careers in government, academe, nonprofits, and similar endeavors, not in corporate settings.[9] They do not percolate up through the ranks. Why is this so? It may very well be, and probably is, due to the small size of the pool, the pool being potential female board candidates coming up through corporate hierarchies. The sidestepping phenomenon and its prevalence evince, again, the existence of a pool problem, exacerbated by opting out.

Third, if women are not opting out shortly before they reach the cusp of the eligibility range, how do you explain the leaky pipe? No doubt exists that the leaky pipe exists. I personally have heard of no explanation for the phenomenon other than that younger, qualified women are opting out, in great numbers, and not later opting back into corporate management ranks.

Easing the Off-Ramps

Women can take steps themselves that may lessen the slope of the off-ramp and, possibly, decrease the steepness of the on-ramp they may encounter in the future. Sheryl Sandberg in her book *Lean In*, discussed in chapter 8, suggests just that. With a maternity leave on the horizon, a young woman may view that as the time to cut back and relax on the job. Sandberg's point is that she should do precisely the opposite. She should "lean in," if not taking on extra tasks, putting in extra effort in carrying out the responsibilities she does have. In that way, she cements in the minds of bosses and coworkers alike her worth to the enterprise. The regard for her worth will make opting out less a fearsome process and may well carry over, easing any subsequent return.

From her lofty perch, though, Ms. Sandberg develops only one side of the issue. In contrast, a Sandberg critic chimes in from the opposing side: "Plenty of women have leaned in for all they're worth but still run up against insuperable obstacles created by the combination of unpredictable life circumstances and the rigid inequalities of our workplaces, the lack of a public infrastructure of care, and cultural attitudes that devalue them."[10]

The Opt-Out Phenomenon

As has been seen, one phenomenon that more than any other detracts from building up a pool of capable, experienced female candidates is opting out.[11] Young women who enter the employ of companies spend three to five years in entry-level positions and then, after a promotion or two, in sophomore management jobs. Most MBA programs require or prefer to see that kind of real-world experience in applicants. So, after several years in the workforce, the young female manager then takes a leave of absence to pursue an MBA or similar degree. Those programs take two years. She returns to the employer but now at the age of twenty-nine or thirty.

After two or three additional years, she and her spouse decide to have or adopt their first child. Often they earlier had delayed, and then delayed again, the decision to have children. The woman takes a maternity leave but, infused with the joy of such a blessed event, namely, the birth of a child, and preoccupied with the newborn's needs, delays returning to the workforce. Ultimately, she may decide to postpone any decision on whether to return. Adding to the aura is the special nature of giving birth to and raising a child at a later age. A Princeton graduate with a law degree from Duke who has opted out to tend to two small children states, "This is what I was meant to do. . . . I know it's very un-p.c., but I like life's rhythms when I'm nurturing my child."[12]

The woman who opts out thus never returns to her former employer or to the workforce at all. Women have received a near-majority of the law degrees and 40 percent or so of the MBA degrees since the late 1970s or early 1980s. But ten and fifteen years later, the number of women still in the workforce and moving into the pool has dwindled. For example, the Harvard Business School survey of women MBAs from the classes of 1981, 1985, and 1991 found that fifteen years after graduation, only 38 percent of the women were still working.[13]

This has been described as the "leaky pipe phenomenon": again, a robust flow exists at the intake end of the pipe, but at the pipe's outflow, or tap, end the flow has ebbed to a mere trickle.[14] "One of the misleading impressions [of] the women's movement is that it swept away women's traditional lives, like a sandstorm covering artifacts of an ancient civilization. The media constantly remind us of women and how they have become doctors, lawyers," corporate managers, and company directors.[15]

One explanation for the dearth of candidates for the pool is that there are many leaks in the pipe. A principal one of these leaks is the decision to opt out.

A Welcoming Off-Ramp: Family Leave Programs

Companies offer maternity leaves ranging from six to twelve weeks, but the time allowed is patently insufficient, especially for a first child. Some women, if they are able to arrange day-care, may be able to return to work part-time before they have used up the time off allotted them, stretching a ten-week leave to sixteen weeks, for example. But women, and men too, may need extended leaves for a variety of reasons, and not merely childbearing or child-rearing. They "may need to take time off work to care for a seriously ill child, parent, parent-in-law, grandparent, grandchild, sibling' spouse, [partner], or to bond with a new child entering the family by birth, adoption, or foster child placement."[16]

Deloitte, the Big Four accounting firm, surveyed a thousand employees of other firms, and found that 88 percent of the respondents wanted a leave program broader than merely for maternity/paternity and early childcare. A significant number, for example, cited the need to care for an elderly parent. Seventeen percent of Americans over age fourteen, numbering approximately 40 million, are providing unpaid care to another adult, according to the American Association of Retired Persons (AARP) Public Policy Institute and National Alliance for Care Giving.[17] For these reasons, to accommodate more uses, the lexicon and the concept have broadened to family leave rather than merely maternity leave.

Mandatory versus Voluntary Family Leaves

Only a few of the family leave programs are mandatory, the product of statutory enactments. Other programs are voluntary policies set in individual corporations. A third category of family leave programs are hybrids that build upon and extend the leave that statutory programs require.

In 2002 California became the first state to enact a mandatory program, effective in 2004, guaranteeing employees six weeks off at partial income. An employee may invoke her right once every twelve months, entitling her to six weeks' pay (at 55 percent of base pay and capped at $1,129 per week) during her absence from work.[18] In addition, under the California Family Rights Act, enacted later, the employee's position is protected for up to twelve weeks of unpaid leave.

New Jersey, Rhode Island, and Washington have comparable paid leave programs for working parents.[19] New York recently adopted a family leave statute.[20] The Washington, D.C., leave program would be expansive: requiring sixteen weeks of paid leave for a worker to care for a newborn or a sick family member.[21]

The federal Family and Medical Leave Act (FMLA) foreshadowed the California enactment by nine years.[22] FMLA gives certain workers the right to twelve weeks *unpaid* leave, but new workers (less than twelve months' employment), part-time workers (less than 1,250 hours per year), those deemed executives, workers in smaller enterprises (fewer than fifty employees), and others are exempt, necessitating broader state enactments in some cases.

A cluster of *voluntary* paid family leave programs exists, in of all places, many companies in the information technology industry. Amazon, Microsoft, and Facebook have formal leave programs. At Netflix, employees can have up to a year off for childcare and similar purposes. In 2015 Facebook founder Mark Zuckerberg made headlines and won plaudits after he announced that as CEO, and a new father, he would take a two-month leave to care for his newborn daughter (although the Facebook corporate program is more generous, providing for leaves of up to four months).[23]

The Facebook program took effect January 1, 2016. Lori Matloff Goler, Facebook's Global Head of People, resolutely announced that "our approach to benefits at Facebook is to support all employees."[24] IKEA, the Swedish company, adopted a similarly generous four-month paid family leave program, effective January 1, 2017.[25] Deloitte Touche's program is for sixteen weeks of "fully paid leave for a wide range of caregiving, including maternity and paternity leave, eldercare, and aid for other sick family members or partners."[26]

Corporations as well as work/life balance specialists see family leave programs as a key tool in hiring and retaining women employees. Along those lines, the financial services firm Credit Suisse Group is using data analytics to carefully track whether its formal family leave policy has had an impact when it comes to hiring and retaining women.

All of the above may mislead. To set the record straight, the U.S. Department of Labor Bureau of Labor Statistics calculates that paid family leave programs cover only 7 percent of private sector workers.[27] That statistic would include the 18 million workers covered under the California paid family leave program, thus taking a significant chunk out of the 7 percent statistic as applied outside California. Thus, few U.S. workers have access to paid family leave programs, while governments in many other nations have made paid leave, at least for mothers, mandatory.

One Prominent Counterexample

By contrast, Marissa Mayer, CEO of Yahoo!, delivered a setback to the wave of family leave enactments and adoptions. Ms. Mayer eschewed taking advantage of any corporate leave program, prominently announcing to the world that her maternity leave would be "a few weeks long and I will work right through it."[28] Ms. Mayer reiterated this anti–family leave attitude in anticipation of the birth of her twins, in December 2015: she would take only "a limited time away," she told the press.[29] She further aggravated perceptions of her attitude by causing to be built, proximate to her CEO's office suite, an in-house day care facility for her first child, in part to facilitate her quick return to the office after childbirth. Unwittingly perhaps, Ms. Mayer's actions rubbed salt in the wounds of family leave advocates and other women at Yahoo!. They, alone or with their spouses, have to scramble to find off-premises day care for their offspring.

Some On-Ramps in Aid of Building the Pool

Researching and exploring the opt-out phenomenon, as well as the entire work/life balance that particularly affects women in their careers, is beyond the scope of this work. Analysts offer many solutions, such as increased tolerance for part-time endeavor, flex-time for personnel, de-emphasis on face time and time in the office, less insistence on availability for travel, particularly for employees with younger children, encouragement of job sharing, and more.[30] "Designing effective work-family programs [must] assume higher priority. Four out of five women say they need more flexibility at work."[31] "Promising approaches include expanding the number of upper-level positions that are eligible for extended leave."[32]

The latter statement highlights an additional problem encountered by women who aspire to higher positions. Corporate employers may deem them ineligible for programs and benefits applicable to lower echelons. If employers do not formally exclude them, "those who take extended leaves or reduced work schedules appear lacking as [potential] leaders. [This] is one of several [more subtle] gender inequalities in career development."[33] Of course, there are those who pooh-pooh all of this and say so. One of the more prominent of those is Jack Welch, longtime and highly successful chief executive officer of General Electric and the acknowledged management guru of the 1990s. To Mr. Welch, "There is no such thing as work-life balance. There are work-life choices, and you make them, and they have consequences." Women who take time off "[should see] their chances of reaching the top decline."[34] Fortunately, Mr. Welch's view is becoming less popular as time goes by.

On-Ramp Initiatives

Three of the more recent overtures, "on-ramps" easing women's return to the workforce, include alumni programs, welcome back programs, and career customization.

ALUMNI PROGRAMS. Corporations keep track of employees who have taken leaves of absence or have opted out for longer periods. Companies attempt to keep their former junior managers and executives informed about matters at the company, through periodic newsletters and even telephone calls or emails.[35] It is a recognition of the value associated with institutional memories and experiences that the hopefully temporarily absentee employee may possess. Further, it is a recognition that a thirty-three- or thirty-four-year working life with a three-year hiatus and perhaps a later one-year leave (say, when the first child is beginning school) is not dissimilar from the thirty-seven-year work span that has been the norm. The former employee, kept somewhat in the fold by an alumni program, will not regard the employer as so distant and the gulf to be navigated in order to return as so vast.

WELCOME BACK PROGRAMS. Enlightened corporations have instituted these programs as well, for much the same reason. Many former employees who wish to return to the workforce, most of them women, fear resentment and opprobrium from those who have remained on the job, pursuing a linear career path, with more or less continuous service. The times have changed, though, at least in some quarters.

For many persons in the workforce, absences taken to rear children are not permanent. "It's not black and white; it's gray. You're working. Then you're not working. Then maybe you're working part time or consulting. . . . Childbearing and child rearing are merely chapters; they're not whole books."[36]

Returning to employment is a front-burner issue in the work/life debate: how liberal will employers be in permitting women to return to the workforce, especially without significant losses in seniority, job status, and salary levels? How will supervisors and coworkers regard and treat the returnees? A consortium of tech companies—IBM, Google, Apple, LinkedIn (Microsoft)—have started and funded an eight-week program for women returning to the industry. The "Reboot Career Accelerator for Women" is an eight-week course that teaches, or refreshes, skills such as design thinking, cloud applications, and personal branding.[37]

Part of the on-ramps answer also lies in the team-production and collaborative nature of work in many companies. Managers and subordinates move from team to team, with higher-ups assembling ad hoc task forces to address the matters at hand. The upward linear progression in employment is a thing of the past. "People are more likely to move from project to project, rewarded for each accomplishment, like professionals."[38] A strategy is to "design work around discrete projects and to allow people to decide how much to take on."[39] This creates a dynamic very different from the hierarchical atmospheres, with unwavering chains of command, that used to dominate in many companies.

CAREER CUSTOMIZATION INITIATIVES. One advocate argues that "more organizations should follow the lead of those that have established 'career customization' which enables individuals to dial back (or dial up) their commitments without penalty." Career customization is an important subtext to the need for organizations "to rethink expectations of 24/7 availability for everyone on the career track."[40] It is somewhat counterintuitive that accounting, "a profession scarcely indifferent to the bottom line, has led the way in allowing flexible work arrangements, largely to benefit women." In addition to career customization, "KPMG [for example] offers compressed work weeks, flexible hours, telecommuting, job sharing and reduced workloads."[41]

"Deloitte Touche's Mass Career Customization [program] allows individuals to work less, work from different places, and shoulder less responsibility to accommodate caretaking commitments."[42] In fact, the national accounting firms have implemented many steps and programs to ease the pathway, the off-ramps and the on-ramps for women and for female advancement in their organizations. In doing so, the accounting firms have come from far back in the pack, at a time and place when their treatment of women was dismal, to a position of leadership today. Chapter 19 recounts that leap forward in greater detail.[43]

The Tone at the Top

Paying close attention to the pool problem thus necessitates sensitivity toward and thoughtful actions and policies aimed at ameliorating or solving work/life balance issues. Alumni and welcome back programs, family leave, and career customization are only several of the many initiatives enlightened corporations could adopt. Attention to off-ramp and on-ramp issues must percolate upward, affecting the entire organization. Board members and senior managers should "insist upon diverse slates of candidates for any opening," including in the pool of employees who have left and then opted back into the organization.[44] Such insistence would aid in enlarging the pool and smoothing out off-ramps and on-ramps.

As Deborah Rhode puts it, "It is not enough for leaders to proclaim their [generalized] commitment to equal opportunity; they also need a corresponding commitment to the policies, programs and reward structures that will encourage it. To that end, organizations should set goals and targets to hold top management accountable in compensation and advancement."[45]

By the same token, however, in the end corporations should avoid mindless wheel spinning. Taking inspiration from Nike's advertisements, they should "Just Do It."

19

MEASURING WHAT YOU INTEND TO MANAGE AND WAYS TO MANAGE IT

Peter Drucker was a consultant-educator-scholar-author who published thirty-nine books, including two novels, an autobiography, and thirty-six management treatises. He taught in the Claremont Graduate School, a constituent college of California's Claremont Colleges. Despite lacking an affiliation with Harvard, the Wharton School, or Yale, from faraway California, Drucker became known as the "founder of modern management."[1] He was a "true polymath" who was "the world's best known business 'guru.'"[2]

Drucker, who died in 2005, explained the difference between himself and other management consultants and economists. While attending a lecture by John Maynard Keynes at Cambridge, he recalled, "I suddenly realized that . . . all the brilliant economics students in the room were interested in the behavior of commodities while I was interested in the behavior of people."[3] Drucker applied quantification techniques to measure the behavior of leaders and senior persons within an organization. In one of his famous early books, *The Practice of Management*, Drucker introduced and expanded on what he termed "management by objectives."[4] In Drucker's lexicon, "You manage what you measure" mutated into statements such as "What gets measured gets improved."[5]

A later Drucker book, *Managing for Results*, had a similar thesis.[6] Shortly before he died, Drucker hosted a *Forbes* writer at his home for a wide-ranging discussion. He repeated many times one of his mantras, that a business leader must have "yardsticks." "Effective leaders check their performance. . . . [They] check their performance against goals."[7] A good corporate leader must be "mission driven."

Drucker Applied to Diversity

An astute reader can easily foresee the direction in which the discussion is headed. An information technology company sincerely interested in making progress in hiring and promoting women must set goals and periodically measure progress toward those goals, in detail. "What gets measured gets improved."[8] "You manage what you measure." Former Catalyst CEO Irene Lang is quite passionate about it:

> Starting now, set consecutive targets for achieving gender parity on your board within nine to fifteen years. . . . If a board sets parity as a business objective, it can achieve parity by 2030. . . . And if it doesn't have a specific objective, progress will be elusive and likely unachievable.[9]

Organizations can implement those exhortations, and do so on a much wider front, by setting goals and tracing progress of women into and through middle management and then on to the lower and middle rungs of senior management.

A relevant object lesson can be found in the experiences of large multinational accounting firms and their earlier lack of progress in hiring women, promoting them, and accepting them into partnership, and how those firms, or some of them, righted the ship.

The Watershed Case

Every treatment of this subject must begin with the tale of Ann Hopkins. Ms. Hopkins rose to the level of project leader at accounting giant Price Waterhouse (PW, now Pricewaterhousecoopers, or PWC). She labored in the firm's Office of Governmental Services in Washington, D.C., where she "played a key role in PW's successful effort to win a multimillion dollar consulting contract with the Department of State." Her superiors viewed her as a "highly competent project leader who worked long hours, pushed vigorously to meet deadlines, and demanded much from the multidisciplinary staffs with which she worked."[10] But partners' comment sheets also criticized her interpersonal skills, one partner suggesting that Hopkins was "overbearing and abrasive":

> One partner described her as "macho"; another suggested that "she overcompensated for being a woman"; a third advised her "to take a course in charm school." Several partners criticized her use of profanity. Another suggested that those partners objected . . . only "because it's a

lady using foul language." Another supporter explained that Hopkins "had matured from a tough-talking somewhat masculine hard-nosed manager to an authoritative, formidable, but more appealing partnership candidate."[11]

Of course, many of those behaviors would have gone unmentioned in a male's evaluation sheets; indeed, PW's partners (662 of 665 of whom were male at the time) would have praised male accountants for certain of those characteristics.

The PW Policy Board voted not to approve Ms. Hopkins's application for partnership, even though she had billed more hours and brought in more business than any other candidate, male or female, for partnership. Ms. Hopkins was the only female of eighty-eight senior PW managers to apply for partnership that particular year.[12] The board of directors (managing partners) decided, though, that her application was not an "up or out" event for Hopkins. The board voted to hold her candidacy over with the possibility that it might reconsider the matter the following year.

Afterward, a PW partner took Hopkins aside, telling her "*to walk more femininely, talk more femininely, dress more femininely, wear makeup, have [your] hair styled, and wear jewelry.*"[13] In other words, with a woman, outstanding results did not matter: appearances did. Ultimately, though, PW made the decision *not* to re-propose Ann Hopkins for partnership. She sued under Title VII of the Civil Rights Act of 1964. It took Ms. Hopkins seven years and five levels of judicial decision making, with rulings by two trial courts, two appellate court panels, and finally the Supreme Court, the protracted nature of the defense infected with the lawyer-like zeal to defend PW "to its last dime." In the end, in 1990 the Court of Appeals took the exceptional step not only of awarding Ms. Hopkins money damages but also of affirming the trial court's order that PW admit Ms. Hopkins to partnership.

Each court along the way had agreed that "sexual stereotyping," not merits, "thoroughly infected the decision making process among Price Waterhouse's partners" when it came to considering a woman for promotion. Nonetheless, Ms. Hopkins and her attorney faced seven years of technical, nitpicking arguments by PW and its lawyers.

Fallout from the *Hopkins* Case

Some good did come from the case (aside from that for Ann Hopkins). PW's actions and the judicial gauntlet Ms. Hopkins had to run galvanized the accounting industry to do something about the industry's role in relegating women accountants to an inferior status. As one could have guessed (they were accounting firms, after all), a principal plank of the accounting firms' platform was taking to heart what Peter Drucker taught so many times: rigorous measurement of the hiring and promotion, at all junctures, of women accountants within firms.

In 1993 Deloitte Touche, one of the Big Four international accounting firms, which employs more than sixty-five thousand people worldwide, inaugurated its Women's Initiative, after noting that only 7 percent of its partners, principals, and directors were female (still better than information technology firms, but poor nonetheless). The initiative included other components centered on the firm's dedication to ameliorate work/ life barriers such as childbearing and child-rearing that put women at a disadvantage from nearly the start of their careers. For instance, the program provided that "all Deloitte employees, including senior managers, can choose to 'dial up' or 'dial down' their careers, depending upon life's circumstances."[14] Thus began Deloitte's use of career customization, as the previous chapter describes.

The firm tracked women's progress not only at the partnership stage but at other junctures as well, including progress toward manager, promotion to manager, progress toward senior manager, promotion to senior manager, director, and so on. The program, which included tracking and counseling as central components, produced results: Deloitte advanced from 7 percent of women directors and partners in 1993 to 23 percent in 2010.[15] In varying degrees, other Big Four firms have followed Deloitte's lead.[16] They have met with success.[17]

Beyond the "Big Four"

In 2010 the American Woman's Society of Certified Public Accountants (AWSCPA) kicked off a similar program (MOVE) for midsize and smaller accounting firms. The forty-seven CPA firms participating in

MOVE collectively moved from 17 percent women partners in 2010 to 22 percent in 2015.[18]

The accounting profession's progress has not been without naysayers. *Forbes* contributor Peter Reilly noted that while "public accounting got off to a good start," the profession as a whole had plateaued. He wondered whether a once retracted glass ceiling once again was extending itself. While 40 percent of the college and university accounting graduates are women and 60 percent of those passing the tough CPA exam are female, only 20 percent of the partners are female.[19] These recent numbers do give one pause, wondering whether measurement as a management tool has limits. That is not to say that companies serious about the issue should not institute rigorous regimes of tracking and management of female hiring and promotion.

In terms of promoting women executives, Deloitte & Touche again led the way. In 2015 the firm's partners elected a woman partner (Cathy Engelbert) as chief executive officer of the U.S. Deloitte, "making her the first woman to lead any of the country's big professional services firms."[20]

Other Adjuncts to and in Aid of Female Hiring and Promotion

Once upon a time, the corporation's CEO staffed the board of directors. The CEO's spouse, the joke went, played a leading part in choosing which of the CEO's golfing partners would receive board of director status. To remove the specter of CEO influence over the selection process, from an early point, good governance blueprints and governance engineers invented the board nomination committee.[21] Specifically, the committee, comprising outside (non-management—no CEOs) directors, would identify candidates and recommend their nomination. The committee may identify candidates for senior management positions as well.

The nomination committee construct has worked tolerably well. Partly as a result, many corporations have broadened the committee's functions, renaming it the "governance and nominating committee" or simply the "governance committee." The SEC has enhanced the committee's role. For example, the SEC requires publicly held companies to disclose the process the company uses to identify and nominate candidates for the board. The SEC also requires companies periodically to disclose to shareholders the entirety of the nomination committee's charter.[22]

With that prelude out of the way, the recommendation is that corporations include on the governance committee a director, or directors, dedicated to or particularly interested in the advancement of women in the organization. "Every public corporation should put a woman on the Governance and Nominating Committee. . . . Those women directors would take it as part of their mission to increase . . . diversity" on the board and among senior managers.[23] Further, the board and senior management would be informed, in no uncertain terms, that the director's role included overseeing cultivation for and promotion of women for senior-level management positions. Most often, the director would be female, thus tending to assure a longer-term interest in the specific role.

Cautions against Queen Bee Women Directors

Directors should assure themselves that the woman director on the governance or nomination committee is neither a "queen bee" nor an "iron maiden."[24] A queen bee director or senior executive relishes being the only woman on a board or at a high level within the corporation. She may take covert steps to see that things remain that way. Queen bee directors obviously would be unfit for the nominating or governance committee role.

The iron maiden is a bit different. She takes steps to disguise and even repress her femininity. In an earlier era, she might resort to wearing masculine-style suits and severe hairstyles. One "wardrobe engineer" determined that for women "the best route to the top was [the] 'uniform'; different variations of the same [masculine-like] look every day." For women clients, he recommended a "feminine fedora," "shoulder length hair," and "a scarf tied around the neck somewhat like a necktie."[25] The iron maiden is a shade or two beyond what wags of that time termed "shoulder pad" feminism. At the 1985 fall fashion show in Paris, "designers were featuring clothes with shoulders so massive that the models appeared to have emerged from locker rooms rather than dressing rooms." "Shoulders forever" became a motto.[26] Needless to say, an iron maiden director may not fit well with the governance committee role, but her appearance may only be an appearance that should not necessarily disqualify her.

Diversity Committees and Diversity Officers

These are more intrusive devices recommended from time to time. Indeed, another element of the Deloitte Women's Initiative is the appointment of a national managing director for retention and advancement of women—in other words, a diversity officer.[27] Moreover, Deloitte went that one better, appointing women managers division-by-division directors of "diversity and inclusion" programs.[28]

Beyond charging diversity officers with maintenance of records as to recruitment, hiring, and promotion, corporations and senior managers would task diversity officers with analyzing acts and practices within the organization that constitute subtle and not-so-subtle forms of discrimination. Diversity officers would then recommend how the company and its managers might rearrange the conduct of the corporation's business to eliminate forms of second-generation discrimination. Conceivably, an organization might form a subcommittee of its board nominating or governance committee to undertake some of those functions and to underline the emphasis the company wishes to place on hiring and advancement of women.

On the other side of the ledger, though, the Sarbanes-Oxley and Dodd-Frank legislative enactments add a myriad of other responsibilities such as audit and compensation committee functions placed upon directors' heads. It may not be in furtherance of good governance to add significantly to directors' burdens, especially as to those demanding hands-on management versus oversight. Under the U.S. scheme of corporate governance, of course, directors still are part-time functionaries. They can undertake only so many responsibilities.

The Need for a Focal Point

Chapter 10, which examines the British Davies Committee and its pledge program, and chapter 12, which examines the Australian Institute of Company Directors mentoring and sponsorship program, express reservations about the ability to transplant similar programs to the United

States. Those British and Australian programs assign an important role to the corporate board chair in conducting, overseeing, and evaluating the progress of the programs to increase female representation on boards of directors.

By contrast, in the United States, the board chair position has considerably less status and heft. In the United States, the second most common phenomenon is to regard the board chair position largely as a ceremonial or honorary one, frequently awarded to the ex-CEO, whom the board of directors has kicked upstairs for a few additional years' service prior to complete retirement. The most common phenomenon, though, by far, is for the CEO also to wear the board chair hat. The question is whether two-fisted, extremely busy CEOs can give the requisite attention to their role in such programs, especially if the programs are extended to increasing women among the ranks of senior executives. Despite the best of intentions, as their plates fill up and fires flame that must be extinguished, corporate CEOs may not be able to give programs the attention they require.

The principal question then is not "yes" or "no." You manage what you measure. Today, the principal questions are, Who measures? Who manages?

20

ADOPTING A VERSION OF THE ROONEY RULE

From 2009 to 2012, Dan Rooney served as the U.S. ambassador to the Republic of Ireland. Americans, though, may have known Mr. Rooney, who passed away in the late spring of 2017, as the lead owner and public face of the National Football League's Pittsburgh Steelers, a position he inherited from his father.[1] So the Rooney Rule is not about setting quotas for bringing Irish to America's shores. It's not about the Irish at all and it's not about quotas, although casual observers may think the latter rings true.

Instead of quotas, the Rooney Rule is about process. To human resources professionals, the Rooney Rule mandates "a structured search," one that begins with an analysis of the entity's needs and then identifies and includes female and minority candidates for the position.[2] The process rule mandates that the thirty-two teams in the National Football League (NFL) have as an objective an effort to increase the number of minorities serving as head coaches and general managers of NFL teams and organizations. But the rule does not require that in the end any at all be hired. Each team, though, must include a minority member on the short list of candidates for every open upper-level position. The teams must give those on that short list an in-person interview, or what students refer to as a "callback." Neither will a telephone or drive-by live interview suffice: the call-back extended to the minority candidate must be plenary, in-depth, and at least as extensive as interviews the teams arrange for other finalists for the head coach or general manager position.

To the teams, the latter requirement constitutes a drawback created by compliance with the rule. In what is often a fast-paced, competitive hiring situation, the rule and the evolutions it requires slow down the search and hiring processes, sometimes considerably so. The advantage is that following the rule's adoption, teams' implementation immediately produced the result the rule was designed to achieve, namely, increasing the number of minority (primarily African American and Latino) coaches in professional football. Prior to the owners' adoption of the rule, from 1992 to 2002, minorities filled seven of ninety-two head coaching vacancies, or 10 percent. In the decade following implementation of the rule, from 2003 to 2013, minorities filled seventeen of seventy-five head coaching vacancies, or 20 percent. In 2011, eight of the thirty-two NFL head coaches, or 25 percent, were minority persons.[3]

Due to its success, the Rooney Rule and its nearly immediate results are popular topics. The NFL has also extended the rule's coverage so that teams would have to interview female candidates for administrative posts in their front offices.[4] Former secretary of defense Carter Ash ordered that subordinates examine the rule, or an approximation of it, with a view to increasing the number of minorities holding more senior positions at the Department of Defense and in the armed services.[5] Several of the prominent IT companies have adopted approximations of the Rooney Rule to increase the chances for women to move into senior positions. Notable among these has been Facebook, whose early hiring appeared misogynic until CEO Mark Zuckerberg had an epiphany of sorts.[6] Last of all, at least one prominent scholar advocates widespread adoption of a Rooney Rule that "would obligate organizations to consider a woman as a finalist for an open leadership position."[7] This chapter explores the history of the Rooney Rule, its mechanics, and its use in information technology.

Before and After

In 2002, 70 percent of the players in the NFL were African American, while only 6 percent of the head coaches were (two of thirty-two). In addition, while the cries for increasing diversity were loud, and teams were paying lip service to those calls, there was a plethora of window dressing. Teams "would release to the press that you [a minority person] were on their list of potential guys but you didn't get an interview," said Herman Edwards, New York Jets head coach from 2001 to 2005. "If you got one, it was over the phone."[8]

The NFL owners ordered that member teams form a committee to study the problem, namely, the disconnect between the player population's makeup and the lack of diversity among head coaches and general managers. The committee included one of the few minority persons in NFL front offices, Ozzie Newsome, former Cleveland Browns tight end and Baltimore Ravens vice president in charge of player personnel. A spark plug on the committee was Tampa Bay Buccaneers GM Rich McKay, son of famed University of Southern California football coach John McKay. Others included Baltimore Colts executive Bill Polian and Atlanta Falcons executive Ray Anderson. Dan Rooney chaired the committee. Mr. McKay reviewed the background for the committee's handiwork: "We created a system that requires a process for hiring. . . . There were too many times in the past when the hiring was done based upon whom someone knew from the past or upon one recommendation. There was not enough process."

As recounted, the rule has had a number of imitators. New ones spring up from time to time. For example, in 2015 University of Texas chancellor William McRaven announced the adoption of a version of the Rooney Rule applicable to the hiring of University of Texas administrators. His reasoning, which could be equally applicable to the information technology industry as well as the NFL, was as follows:

> The slide [the increasing racial gap between students and administrators] makes it very clear that we are not doing the job we ought to be doing in driving equal opportunity and fairness in our hiring and promotion processes. This is particularly disappointing because education is all about opportunity. Making sure our faculty and staff reflect the changing look of Texas is not just about fairness. We need faculty [and] administrators who understand the people they are serving, who come from the same kinds of places.[9]

The Bloom Off the Rose

In 2013 there were an extraordinary number of head coaching and general manager vacancies in the NFL, with fifteen openings on thirty-two teams. Despite the Rooney Rule, not a single team filled one of those openings with a minority person.[10] One close observer concluded that "the NFL's initiative to increase racial diversity in the coaching ranks appears to have stalled, . . . stuck at six or [fewer minority head coaches] for the past five years."[11]

Early on, a few teams ignored the rule, at their peril. In 2003, for instance, the Detroit Lions hired former San Francisco head coach Steve Mariucci, without interviewing any minority candidates or interviewing anybody at all. The NFL promptly fined the Lions $200,000. Responses to the rule's more recent shortcomings have been urgings that the NFL not only retain the rule but expand it to the hiring of offensive and defensive coordinators. As a result of expansion, the number of minority persons in the highest-ranked assistant coaching positions would increase. In turn, such a development would increase the number of credible minority candidates in the pool of candidates for head coaching slots.[12]

"Can the NFL do better? Absolutely. But the rule has made a positive impact."[13] Reacting to the nadir of 2013, Rich McKay, then GM of the Atlanta Falcons, said, "It was a surprise. I think it brings back the idea that we need to continue to work on career development."[14]

Not surprisingly, the ubiquitous Reverend Jesse Jackson stepped in, taking an equally longer-term view: "The Rooney Rule is a first step, not a final step."[15]

Rooney Rule Inroads in Information Technology

At its annual meeting in 2014, prompted by Jesse Jackson, who was in attendance, IT giant Microsoft announced that it "may consider adopting a Rooney Rule." Apparently, however, Microsoft would consider adoption of the rule for board of director seats only.[16] Openings on the board, of course, are relatively rare occurrences. Mandating that a diverse slate of candidates be considered for each such opening would represent only the tiniest part of any solution to the lack of diversity endemic in information technology.

Closer to the Rooney Rule mark are the Pinterest initiatives. Pinterest announced three prongs to its program. The first is to set goals and keep tabs on progress toward those goals (see chapter 18). "We think one reason it's been so hard to get numbers to change is that companies have not set specific goals," co-founder Evan Sharp opined.[17] Pinterest set goals in three categories:

> Increase hiring rates for full-time engineering roles to 30% female.
> Increase hiring rates for full-time engineers to 8% underrepresented ethnic backgrounds.
> Increase hiring rates for non-engineering roles to 12% underrepresented ethnic background.[18]

Second, those goals represent only a first portion of Pinterest's version of a Rooney Rule. "In Pinterest's version, the company commits to interviewing one . . . female candidate for every open leadership position."[19] Third, to be the point person on diversity issues, Pinterest hired Candice Morgan, a longtime Catalyst analyst, as diversity director. Yet another social networking company, Twitter, announced a plan to adopt initiatives in the diversity area, including possibly adoption of a Rooney Rule. "Little is known about how Twitter plans to address the lack of women or people of color at the social network."[20]

Seemingly along Rooney Rule lines, Twitter then set and announced diversity goals for 2016:

> Increase women [employees] overall to 33%.
> Increase women in tech roles to 16%.
> Increase women in leadership roles to 25%.
> Increase underrepresented minorities overall to 11%.
> Increase underrepresented minorities in tech roles to 9%.
> Increase underrepresented minorities in leadership roles to 6%.[21]

Twitter was criticized for the vagueness of its description, and on other grounds as well. "Twitter was called out for announcing that it has hired a white guy to head up its diversity efforts."[22]

Facebook's Adoption and Implementation of a Rooney Rule

In her book *The Boy Kings*, Katherine Losse notes that of the first fifty employees hired at Facebook, she was one of only two women.[23] As Facebook grew, apparently its male-dominated atmosphere and demographics did not change. As of 2014, of ten thousand employees, 94 percent were white or Asian; 85 percent were male.[24]

Shortly before that time, however, an important event took place. On May 19, 2012, Facebook's founder and controlling shareholder, Mark Zuckerberg, married another Harvard College graduate, Priscilla Chan.[25] Ms. Chan, however, was not another run-of-the-mill Harvard graduate, if indeed there is such a thing. She is a two-fisted advocate for women's rights, including in the workforce and in leadership positions. She took her new spouse to task for his blind eye toward diversity issues.

Facebook renamed the Rooney Rule initiative that it adopted "a diverse slate approach," a more descriptive label for the program.[26] Facebook released its first annual diversity report at the end of 2014, establishing baselines for evaluation of subsequent efforts. The second report, however, showed basically the same demographics as the first, which critics had panned, perhaps unfairly, or at least precipitously, as "pathetic" and "dismal."[27] Facebook pledged to continue its efforts and the program. "Essentially, what something we call a diversity-based approach does is build muscle in people," said Maxine Williams, Facebook's global head of diversity. "It builds the habit of looking longer, looking harder."

Much like crews of ships at anchor in the fog, the information technology industry and some of the companies within it have had a vague notion that something is out there, namely, that they should be undertaking efforts to introduce diversity into their hiring and promotion. To galvanize them to further action, in 2015 the White House invited representatives of leading information technology companies to a summit on the subject of diversity in hiring. Fourteen firms attended. Seven of the fourteen firms, including Intel, Xerox, and Amazon, followed Facebook's lead in implementing a Rooney Rule, or stated that as firms they intended to do so.[28]

Other Diversity Initiatives in Silicon Valley

The other seven firms attending the White House summit have not let grass grow under their feet. They have adopted approaches to diversity different from or in addition to the Rooney Rule, or diverse slate, approach. For instance, Google has embedded software engineers at traditionally black colleges and universities, including Howard University,

Hampton University, Fisk University, and Spelman and Morehouse Colleges.[29]

In its public disclosures, Intel devoted an entire brochure to its myriad efforts, pledging $300 million in aid of those programs. Intel "set an ambitious goal to reach full representation of women and underrepresented minorities in our U.S. workforce by 2020."[30] Representative Intel efforts include $4 million for scholarships for Latinos in tech studies; $5 million to Oakland, California, public schools to enhance computer-based and information technology laboratories and programs; and $5 million to Georgia Tech University for similar labs and programs. In addition, Intel has implemented its version of the Rooney Rule and hired a full-time chief diversity officer.[31] "More than nearly any other company in Silicon Valley, Intel appears to be making a genuine effort to improve."[32]

An Assessment: A Rooney Rule for Everyone?

Among the various programs in existence, including, for instance, pledge and certificate programs, quota laws, mentorship/sponsorship programs, comply or explain requirements, disclosure regimes, and so on, the diverse slate approach seems to offer the best fit for information technology. There are several reasons for this. One is that the diverse slate approach is benevolent: it tends to produce some or much of the quantity desired without imposing mandatory regulations or commands, likely to "get backs up." Second, as the longer-term picture emerging from the National Football League demonstrates, it is not perfect, but there is a track record and improvements in diversity have resulted, at least in the NFL, since its adoption of the rule. Third, the Rooney Rule approach seems to have won the most acceptances of any of the alternatives out there, at least by the larger players in the industry.

On the other hand, universal imposition of a Rooney Rule would also bring about perceived disadvantages. In effect, the Rooney Rule is a comply or explain rule (chapter 11) with consequences (sanctions by the NFL) following an inadequate explanation or no explanation for noncompliance, that is, a "hard" comply or explain regulation. In an industry as diverse and widespread as information technology, there is no master or supervising body like the league commissioner's office in the NFL. The discipline of a Rooney Rule would at best be self-imposed.

Violations of the rule or failure to abide by it in the first place could be shrugged off or minimized. No consequence would follow. At best, a Rooney Rule for IT would be a soft rather than hard comply or explain requirement.

Another disadvantage, for smaller firms at least, is that competition for the qualified individuals would increase, perhaps dramatically. In that milieu, smaller firms might become convinced that they would come off as second or third best in the competition, and they would not be wrong in reaching those conclusions. So the most that might be said of a Rooney Rule is that it is a good tool for information technology firms to increase prospects for enhancing diversity in hiring and promotion—but also that a Rooney Rule may not be the best approach for everybody.

21

THEORETICAL FEMINIST VIEWS

As the introduction notes, there are several perspectives on the status of women in information technology. First is the individualist view, exemplified by the myriad how-to and advice books on the shelves, ready to advise women how to succeed (*Going to the Top*; *Same Game, Different Rules*; *Breaking the Glass Ceiling*; *Lean In*; *Hardball for Women*).[1] These books include exhortations for women to acquire mentors, engage in networking, modulate and lower their voices, and even watch *Monday Night Football* so as to be able to discuss it with male colleagues on Tuesday morning.

A second perspective is found in journal articles and books that analyze institutions such as secondary schools, colleges, and universities. A third perspective, also incorporating an institutionalist viewpoint, is offered in the articles and books, if any, that direct themselves toward the industry and companies within it. Curiously, very little fills that space: no one has closely examined the positions the industry takes and what courses of action it should consider, as this book attempts to do.

A fourth perspective, possibly informing all the others, utilizes a collectivist viewpoint. These theories and schools approach the status of women generally rather than the status of individual women, as do the "how-to" and advice books. The feminist literature predominates in this "space," as MBAs refer to areas of endeavor. The question here is, What do collective viewpoints offer that will inform institutionalist approaches? Rephrased, Do the schools of feminist thought help tell those in control of corporations and influential in the information technology industry what can or might be done?

Schools of Collectivist Thought

One knowledgeable source adumbrates no fewer than nine theories or schools of feminist thought.[2] The "relevant features of nine feminist theories" may be "directed toward improving the position of women in science (and, by extension, engineering and technology)." Theorists recognize the problem as a significant one because, "from the perspective of women's studies, technology and engineering represent one of the last bastions of male domination and appear impervious to gender change."[3] In its short existence, the IT industry has been characterized as representing "technological somnambulism," with companies controlled by persons "willing to sleepwalk through the process of reconstituting the conditions of human existence."[4]

The framework of feminist theory is useful for an examination of three issues involving the relationship of gender to information technology: women in the workforce, women as users of technology, and women and technology design. The primary emphasis of this book is, of course, on the first of those three issues, that is, women in the workforce, especially those in or who aspire to senior management or governance positions.

LIBERAL FEMINISM. Much like our current Supreme Court, which regards everyone including corporations as equal before the law, no more and no less,[5] liberal feminism deals with woman questions the same way. That is, "liberal feminists seek no special privileges for women and simply demand that everyone receive equal consideration without discrimination on the basis of sex."[6]

Most of the organizations that attempt to advance women in the workplace and in corporate governance, such as Catalyst, the Association of University Women, the Women's Engineering Program Advocates, or the Society of Women in Engineering, espouse this view. Either implicitly or explicitly, most women's organizations and advocates urge equality between the sexes and no more.

SOCIALIST FEMINISM. As the label implies, this approach is imbued with Marxist theory. Women form another element in the means of production, the members of which are engaged in an upward struggle to overcome past discrimination and untoward treatment ("workers unite"). "Socialist feminists . . . place gender on an equal footing with class in shaping technology."[7]

Middle- and upper-class men create and design new technology. They also serve as the sources of capital for design and creation. Incorporating women as designers in, as well as the potential users of, technology "suggests that more technologies might meet the needs of women," reducing the "white [male], upper-middle-class, suburban" element that currently dominates in the industry.[8] The foregoing is one example of what socialist feminist critiques emphasize as sources of oppression that combine with gender in shaping information technology.

ESSENTIALIST FEMINISM. According to an essentialist view, what most unites women is their biology. Women are different from men not only because of their reproductive systems but also because of their secondary sex characteristics. Essentialist feminism may also extend to other alleged gender differences such as visuospatial and verbal ability, aggression and other behavioral differences, and mental and physical traits based on hormone levels.[9]

Higher aggression levels in males have been attributed to higher levels of testosterone. The same is true for larger physical size and increased muscle mass.[10] An essentialist approach implies that men, because of their biology and inability to conceive, develop technology to dominate, control, and exploit the natural world, including women and nonwhite peoples. By contrast, women give birth, leading to a proclivity to nurture life in all its forms rather than dominating and exploiting others.[11]

EXISTENTIALIST FEMINISM. In contrast to essentialist feminism, existentialist feminism maintains that it is not the biological differences themselves but the values the society assigns to them that lead us to believe that men and women are more different than they really are.[12]

Women serve as the predominant caregivers to children, perhaps because they give birth to and nurse them. But to consign to women a permanence, or an exclusivity, in those roles does not necessarily follow. Rather than biology, those characteristics (permanence and exclusivity) result from the viewpoints and resulting values the surrounding society takes on, based upon historical precedents. But even those precedents are changing rapidly as the society evolves. The stereotypical roles assigned to men and women have been breaking down for some time, in some geographical areas more than others and in certain roles nearly altogether (sharing childcare, for example).

PSYCHOANALYTIC FEMINISM. Sigmund Freud famously stated that anatomy is destiny. Boys and girls resolve differently the Oedipus and castration complexes that arise in the stage of normal sexual development. This has been called "biological determinism."

Later in life, encouraged to be independent, autonomous, and distant, male engineers, programmers, and computer scientists adopt the "hard systems" approach to computer systems development that follows a positivist, linear, and technicist roadmap. By contrast, women, because of their different psychoanalytic background and makeup, are socialized to value connections and relationships. Women tend to feel uncomfortable with the hard-systems approach many males use. Women bring "caring values" to research and design in computer science. Caring values include empathy, an other-oriented relationship to people, and a more holistic and less hierarchical worldview. Women have a less competitive way of relating to colleagues and a greater affinity to users.[13]

RADICAL FEMINISM. Radical feminists reject altogether nearly all scientific theories, collections of data, and experiments testing various hypotheses. They reject studies that exclude women as well as those that include them. The only approaches palatable to radical feminists are those that are "women-centered."[14] Legal scholar Catharine MacKinnon adds a further element to radical feminism. She suggests that a consciousness-raising feminist group methodology form part of the doctrine.[15] "Using their personal experiences as a basis, women meet together in communal, nonhierarchical groups to examine their experiences."[16]

Early on (1983), radical feminist Cynthia Cockburn applied the idea to information technology:

> In my view, by far the most effective principle evolved to date is [the call for] separate, women-only organizations. It enables us to learn (teach each other) without being put down. Provide schoolgirls with separate facilities and the boys won't be able to grab the computer and bully the girls off the console. Provide young women with all-women courses so that they can gain the experience to make an informed choice about an engineering career. . . . Autonomy works wonders for our feelings and our strength. We need, before all else, a great expansion of the autonomous sphere in technology.[17]

Of course, imagining technology from a women-centered perspective in the absence of male influence and control is not only extremely difficult;

at this late date, it is impossible, with the exception of smaller pockets of endeavor (computer clubs, computer labs, single-sex education perhaps).

POSTMODERN FEMINISM. "Postmodern" has become a buzzword that professors and sophisticates like to throw into their analyses. In this context, according to postmodern feminists, across a broad spectrum, women differ in their national, class, and cultural identities. So viewed, women "can no longer be regarded as smooth, uniform and homogeneous."[18] These postmodernist theories imply that no universal research agenda, technologies, or approaches will be appropriate. Various women will have different reactions to technologies or approaches depending upon their class, race, sexuality, country, region, and other factors. There are limitations to perceiving women as a universal group. The views and approaches historically advocated are thus simplistic.

CYBERFEMINISM. Yes, there is such a field or subcategory of feminism.[19] The theory overtly fuses technology with gender. Modern information technologies are "inherently liberatory. . . . Their development will lead to an end to male superiority because women are uniquely suited to life in the digital age."[20] Sexism, racism, tyranny, and oppression will have much less of a presence in cyberspace, serving "as a major contrast between the virtual world and the real world."[21]

Some question whether cyberfeminism is a feminist theory at all. For example, "the Internet becomes a tool for making women more vulnerable to men using it for [soliciting] . . . prostitution, cybersex, assumption of false identities, and pornography."[22]

Omissions

The list of feminist schools of thought goes on. Other important theories are the African American and racial/ethnic feminism schools. Treating racial diversity combined with gender diversity is simply beyond the scope of this work, deserving of volumes and more on its own.[23]

Certain other feminists also maintain that patriarchal views dominate everyday life in postcolonial and in neocolonial nations and regions much the same as they did in colonial days. Moreover, postcolonial feminism separates out and examines more closely those phenomena.[24] Postcolonial feminism also is beyond the scope of this chapter.

Discards

For a variety of reasons, this work will address only some of the feminist theories listed above. Radical feminism, for example, seems too militant to offer many insights into issues of gender, information technology, and business. Alternatively, a radical feminist theorist rather than a male law professor should argue for the theory's application.

Marxist philosophies have been decidedly on the wane over the last several decades. Only four traditional socialist countries remain: Cuba, North Korea, Vietnam, and the People's Republic of China (PRC). The latter two (Vietnam and the PRC) have basically capitalist economies; only the political side can lay claim to being socialist. Yet on the economic side, state-owned enterprises (SOEs) still operate in many fields in Vietnam and the PRC. Those nations first corporatized many SOEs, then further privatized many of the corporations, in whole or substantial part. Given that background, socialist feminism seems to be able to bring little to the table these days.

Postmodern feminism, which holds that women differ greatly across a wide spectrum and that therefore no universal or broad-based theories or reforms are possible, is antithetical to the fiber of this book and will be discussed no further.

This work will also not engage with psychoanalytic feminism, which argues that many differences exist between males and females, owing in part to their sexual development, as Sigmund Freud first espoused.

As will be developed later, to make any inroads on the significant lack of gender diversity in IT, or in any other industry, we need to take as our starting point the assumption that, aside from inescapable biological differences, no differences or disparities exist, or at least should be recognized, in the treatment of men and women. For too long now, those in control of corporations, employment, promotion, and governance have chosen the path of least resistance, able to get away with the throwaway line, "After all, she is a woman," implying or explicitly stating that women are different—too emotional, not analytical, and so on.

A last rationale for not covering this ground in depth comes from Winston Churchill, who observed that "what the mind can absorb is limited by what the rear end can endure."

Relevant Theories

So, on to three theories that may have relevance here: liberal feminism, essentialist feminism, and existential feminism. Of the three, essentialist feminism has to go out the window as well, for much the same reason as psychoanalytic theories. Little or no progress, or at least progress across the board, can be achieved if those with power to influence the advancement of women can tune out, or sign off on half-hearted measures, on the grounds that women are different.

Boards of directors and senior managers should tell everyone in their corporations that

> the organization will bend over backward to treat all employees fairly and equally . . . with one exception. Equality gives way when there exists a universal and defined biological trait that requires equality to assume a secondary role. And there is only one such trait—child bearing. . . . Any woman who goes on the "mommy track" for any reason (more lengthy maternity leave, part-time when children are entering school, Fridays off when children are young) . . . nevertheless is entitled to equal treatment. No adverse inferences will be drawn. No negative or neutral ("damning by faint praise") evaluation practices will be tolerated. The exception, as well as the rule [of equality across the board] are to become part of [this] organization's very fabric.[25]

Thinking or voicing that women otherwise are different in any other respect, whether supported by evidence or not, does nothing to advance women in corporate management and leadership positions. In fact, voicing such beliefs has had a decidedly negative effect in certain milieus.

In January 2005 Lawrence Summers, a PhD in economics, former cabinet secretary (Treasury) and former World Bank president, spoke to the Harvard University faculty. Summers by then was the president of Harvard. Addressing the question of why women had such a poor record in tenure and promotion as faculty in the sciences and in mathematics at Harvard, Summers wondered whether there were "innate" or "biological" differences between women and men and whether those differences accounted for differing tenure and promotion rates. Summers questioned women's desire and ability to work the late nights and weekends necessary to do the research and write the articles and books that bring tenure and promotion. In reaction, one female Harvard professor felt so ill at Summer's pronouncements that she had to leave the room while Summers held the floor.[26]

Ultimately, as a result of the incident and the unrelenting furor that ensued, Summers resigned as president of Harvard. Nonetheless, leading U.S. business publications, as well as Summers himself, later wondered what the furor had been about.[27] They believed it demonstrable that women do not compare to men in visuospatial skills and in interests in math and science. Why should there have been a reaction? Why the fuss?

Any such view, whether inherent in any theory of feminism or in male chauvinists' declarations, has to be rejected as anathema to what we are attempting to achieve and maintain in our society, namely, fairness and equality for all, and not some subgroup of our population.

On a lighter note, it seems as though the advocates of certain of the radical, Marxist, and other types of feminism are akin to headmistresses "at a re-education camp, typing with one hand and sharpening their machetes with the other."[28] Neither extreme, willful blindness (or at least tone deafness) by those in business on the one hand, or militancy by certain theorists and feminists on the other, will contribute to an understanding of the problem and possible approaches to solve it.

From a collectivist standpoint, the views of the liberal feminists as modified by those of the existentialists seem most relevant to a discussion of female leadership in information technology. Explaining and attempting to apply other views and schools of thought would be akin to trekking down a rabbit hole, beyond the scope of a work such as this. The intent of this chapter has been modest, to alert readers to the existence and variety of perspectives that inhabit a universe ordinarily regarded as separate and apart from business leadership and corporate governance topics.

PART V

NEEDED FIXES—NOW

22

REFORMING THE GAMING INDUSTRY

About half of U.S. adults (49 percent) now report that they play video games on a computer, game console (an Xbox, for example), mobile device (Android or other mobile telephone), or a combination of the foregoing.[1] By mid-2012, the gaming industry's annual revenues had grown to $78 billion, while the worldwide motion picture industry recorded revenues of $86.7 billion.[2] One venerated ninety-year-old film studio, ranked third in global box office, has video game revenue exceeding that of films.[3] Two and a half years after the 2012 industry-wide report, in December 2014, *CBS Evening News* reported that the video and computer gaming industry's revenues had exceeded *twice* those of the motion picture industry.[4]

Individual successes have been stunning. *Pokémon Go*, which Nintendo introduced in the summer of 2016, was the latest evolution in the *Pokémon* series. Nintendo initiated the series for play on Game Boy devices of the 1990s. Marketers estimated that the newest *Pokémon* will bring Nintendo and its partners $5 billion in annual revenue.[5] Nintendo's share price doubled in the first two weeks after the game's North American release, adding $9 billion in market capitalization.[6] Nintendo's introduction of the game in Japan was "treated as a national event, with widespread news coverage and a cautious endorsement from the government."[7]

Pokémon Go's predecessor as a hot release, *Candy Crush Saga*, produced $2 billion in revenue for Irish company King Digital Entertainment.[8] *Grand Theft Auto V* produced $1 billion in annual revenue, spiking a 77 percent rise in share price for Take-Two Interactive Software.[9] *Call of Duty* is a line of best-selling games produced by Activision Blizzard. A recent iteration, *Call of Duty: Infinite Warfare*, although panned by the reviewers and other critics, makes the thirteenth sequel to the original, following predecessors such as *Call of Duty: Constant Warfare*.[10]

Why All This Success?

One observer believes that computer games have become "crack cocaine" for youth, highly addictive and likely to produce significant revenues and profits for developers/publishers.[11] In addition to the content of the games, as an industry, gaming is more male-dominated than even information technology as a whole. Virtually no women occupy leadership positions. As to content, the games the industry produces are characterized by violence and cruelty, designed to appeal to adolescent males. The games feature women mainly as objects of sex or violence.

The industry derisively terms the games and software it does produce for girls and young women as "pink ware." It accounts for less than 5 percent of the industry's output. Pink ware developers' designs are crude, unsophisticated, cheaply produced, and force-fed to retailers at bargain prices, with little or no marketing to accompany them.[12] Another pejorative term for cheaply produced software of that ilk is "shovel ware": products made for a quick profit with little concern for quality.[13] Examples include games such as *Barbie, Groom and Glam Pups, Disney Sing It*, and *High School Musical*.

To market their products, gaming company marketing and sales executives rely upon the objectification and demeaning of women just as much as game designers do in the games' content. Gaming companies hire professional models, outfit them in scanty attire, and use sex to introduce and sell products. The trade refers to these scantily clad models as "booth babes."

All the foregoing takes on triple or quadruple significance because gaming is, if not crack cocaine, the gateway drug, so to speak, for young men and women who later on follow up on nascent interests developed through computer and video gaming. The through-and-through misogynistic soul of the gaming industry is a principal reason for females' reduced presence in information technology. Gaming industry reform is a *sine qua non* for increasing the number of women in the information technology field.

The Industry: Developers

The developers include Atari, Nintendo (*Super Mario Brothers, Super Mario Run*), Activision Blizzard (number one producer by market capitalization), Take-Two Interactive, Electronic Arts (*Battlefield I*, *Titanfall II*, *Heroes of the Galaxy*), Ubisoft, and Niantic (spun off from Google), to name a few. Others include foreign firms such as Rovio Entertainment (Finland). Many users find Rovio's principal product, *Angry Birds*, to be addictive.[14] The foregoing is, however, misleading. Smaller developers and producers dominate the industry, many of whom hope "to catch lightning in a bottle," as Rovio did with *Angry Birds* or King Digital Entertainment (Ireland) with *Candy Crush*.[15]

Eighty-eight percent of the personnel in these organizations are white males.[16] The developers' group makeup contrasts with the makeup of the user group: 57 percent of young African Americans and 66 percent of Asian Americans play video games, as contrasted with whites, of whom 53 percent play. The group in which women do have a significant presence is the group over age forty, in casual games, defined as quick and simple games that do not require long periods of play.[17] *Solitaire* and *Angry Birds* are examples. By contrast, female representation in complex games is very low.

For example, Riot Games is the creator of one of the world's most heavily played computer games, *League of Legends*. The company has also created, as an adjunct to the game, a global professional gaming league called the League Championship Series. There are sixteen teams in North America and Europe. Not a single member of any of those teams is female.[18]

With regard to gender diversity, from within the industry, an anonymous British computer game developer observes that "marginalization is happening in the very fabric of the design process and this is just as damaging to the health of the industry and its ability to hold our attention— both as developers and as gamers."[19] The marginalization within the industry extends beyond the marginalization of women or other ethnicities to the marginalization of large numbers of white males as well.

> The mainstream industry is preoccupied with adolescent power trips and gritty revenge sagas. . . . The lack of gender diversity doesn't just affect players, it affects employees within the industry, especially women . . . outside of the shooter-killer wavelength. . . . Eventually the industry will feel like it's just not a place for people who aren't interested in heavy weaponry [which will exclude large numbers of white males as well].[20]

For its part, when the industry does speak, which given its disper-
sal and atomization appears to be rarely, it avoids the pithier problems.
For instance, the Entertainment Software Association blames the lack
of diversity squarely on the paucity of women and African Americans
with STEM backgrounds. "University graduates with STEM degrees
were highly likely to be white or perhaps Asian males. This has created a
widespread and prejudicial expectation [with the industry] about people
who [would be] good at STEM subjects and would like to pursue careers
in gaming."[21] The industry's response to the problem is thus a shrug of
the shoulders, a "whatya-gonna-do" expression. The gaming industry's
diagnosis of the problem accepts the status quo, foreseeing an industry
makeup that replicates itself. Gaming's developers appear prepared to be
inclusive only in words and not in deeds. It seems the gaming industry
could not find a proper path to achieving diversity even with GPS route
guidance and a seeing-eye dog.

The Industry Landscape

Reform may be difficult. For the most part, larger producers such as
Nintendo, Activision Blizzard, Electronic Arts, or Atari were predominant early on and still loom large today. Midsize producers such as
Take-Two Interactive or Rovio are publicly held and visible.[22] We know
their addresses. But, as seen, there are a myriad of small developers who
pop up here and there, have a hit or quasi-hit (again, as seen, to "catch
lightning in a bottle"), and disappear.[23] They will be much more difficult
to reach or reform. Their visibility is ephemeral.

A principal reason for the predominance of smaller developers is the
absence of significant barriers to entry. Opening a software shop entails
far less cost than, say, building a steel mill or producing electric cars
(Tesla). Rovio developed *Angry Birds* for $140,000. A team of fewer than
ten developed *Candy Crush* for King Digital.[24] The downside of that is
that smaller producers may have far less concern for diversity either in
their leadership and staffing within their firms, or in the games they produce, both as to content and as to projected audience, and the manner in
which they market their games.

Another change affecting the industry is the movement from desk
and laptop computers and game consoles to mobile devices:

Technology companies have increasingly turned to mobile as their customers give up their desktop computers and shift . . . to smartphones and
tablets. But mobile has proved to be a difficult area to make money, in
part because smaller screens do not offer as much space for advertising.[25]

Be that as it may, the treatment of gender diversity, or the lack thereof,
in the gaming industry must return to the fore.

A Significant Change in the Landscape: Distribution

Changes in the way producers and retailers market and sell games
support the trend toward survival of, or even increase in, the number
of smaller producers. In days gone by, producers sold games through
specialized retailers located in shopping and strip malls. The industry
leader was GameStop, with 20,000 employees and 7,117 stores in the
United States, Australia, Canada, and Europe.[26]

Taking a cue from the video store industry's demise, along with Netflix's ascendancy and the rapid rise of streaming direct to end users,
analysts predicted that GameStop would quickly dwindle and perhaps
disappear. "Comparisons are rife between the video-game retailer[s] and
defunct video-rental giant Blockbuster."[27] The computer game retailers,
however, have not gone the way of Blockbuster, which disappeared rapidly. One reason is that a principal portion of GameStop's and its rivals'
businesses has been trade in used games, for which the markup ranges
from 42 percent to 48 percent.[28] Further, hands-on browsing is much
more prevalent in used as opposed to new games. Stores and inventory
within them are conducive to browsing and used game sales.

Nonetheless, the introduction and evolution of new games have
moved from retail stores to the cloud and direct streaming to gamers. In
that milieu, barriers to entry that may have existed in the days of brick-
and-mortar retailers, principally in marketing and sales, have become
lower. Marketing muscle is not so important. The opening for smaller
producers has expanded.

Content: Excessive Violence, Sex, and Objectification of Women

"Ubisoft technical director James Therien told the *Video Gamer* about the decision not to include female characters in" *Assassins Creed: Unity*. He noted in 2013 that there had been a significant backlash from gamers to the predecessor game (*Assassins Creed III: Liberation*) that had depicted "Ellie [a woman] as a strong female character."[29] A 2009 study by researchers at Michigan State University and the University of Cambridge "found that depictions of women in video games [when they exist] are skewed toward emphasizing sex characteristics."[30]

Within the industry, one critic notes, is "a central notion that games are best for shooting or killing things—or scoring goals—and that all other intricacies are subservient" at best.[31] In the last several years, games include *Call of Duty* (thirteen or fourteen iterations total), *Black Ops 3*, *War Halo*, *Fallout 4*, *Mobile Strike*, *Mortal Kombat X*, *World of War*, *Battlefield*, *Titanfall*, *Grand Theft Auto V*, and *Gears of War*, in addition to the previously mentioned *Assassins Creed* games.[32] "Narrative games, multidirectional platforms, strategy [simulations], and casual puzzle apps aren't weird outliers: they are all part of games that have been completely jettisoned in the race toward the perfect shoot-'em-up mono-experience."[33]

As one financial columnist observes, "Here, in a 100 billion dollar industry that is bigger than Hollywood, violence toward women is integral to the product itself. Games in which near-naked female characters are degraded or mutilated rake in billions of dollars for game publishers."[34]

Near pornography appears frequently. In *Revenge*, the goal of a naked General George Custer is to reach a nude Native American woman tied to the stake. If Custer reaches the woman, the game then depicts Custer's rape of her. *Dead or Alive* and *Soul Caliber* are well known for their scantily clad female characters. Multiple spin-off games from *Dead or Alive* feature buxom women characters playing in beach volleyball tournaments.[35]

Pink Software and Girly Games

What, though, of the claim that games potentially attractive to female players, especially games that are "too girly," do not sell? Game producers' decreased or minimal revenues do not lie. Yet there is a chicken-and-egg problem here. The argument goes that the egg must come first, the egg being more games attractive to young women. In turn, that introduction and use of those games will increase the flow of girls and young women into computer subjects, the computer lab, and, ultimately, into STEM subjects and majors. Then, so educated, certain of those women will matriculate to the entertainment software industry. A difficulty is that this particular scenario, as a solution to increasing diversity, may take fifteen years or longer to play out, with no guarantee that measurable improvements will follow.

A subsidiary problem is that those who have been critical of games' content and have blogged or otherwise gone public with their observations and criticisms "have been hacked and cyber-bullied by some in the gaming community. . . . Some members of the gaming community have responded with threats of rape and death against" one critical blogger and her family.[36]

The troll fraternity is responsible for many of the defamatory and threatening actions. A troll is a gamer who in games or on gaming forums devotes time primarily to harassing others.[37] Thought to consist mainly of teenage males, the troll fraternity tends to focus its ire on women, minorities, and gay, lesbian, and transgender members of the population. Among other things, trolls' behavior has a chilling effect on female participation in online games or gaming forums.[38] As a result, young women tend to have more negative gaming experiences than males do. In turn, observers hypothesize that young women's negative gaming experiences play a significant role in discouraging them from pursuing information technology and game development careers.[39]

A subsidiary of Alphabet (Google's parent company), Jigsaw has developed an algorithmic filter that uses artificial intelligence to determine which comments and threats are toxic.[40] Both Facebook and Twitter have their own systems "for flagging abusive behavior and an escalating ladder of punishments for those who commit it."[41] The systems are nascent, not yet fully developed.

Additional Sexism in How Games Are Marketed and Sold

Within the computer gaming industry, the needle seems not to have moved at all. In fact, anecdotal evidence may point in the opposite direction, to the prevalence of the "bro culture." Not long ago, Microsoft's Xbox division held a "Women in Gaming" luncheon. As entertainment, the Xbox division leadership "hired scantily clad female go-go dancers" to perform at the after party following the luncheon.[42]

Game publishers continue to hire "booth babes," attractive women attired in bikinis, who know little or nothing of the publishers' products. The women's principal role is to be highly visible at conventions and shows to lure customers to displays and booths.[43] Booth babes are, for example, highly in evidence at the annual Consumer Electronics Show, held each January in Las Vegas, hosted by the Consumer Technology Association. The CES is considered a must-attend event for many of those who work in the information technology industry.[44]

Solutions for the Chicken-and-Egg Problem

The importance of remedying, at least in some degree, the female-male imbalance in all aspects of the computer gaming industry looms much larger than the gaming development and publishing business itself. It affects the entire future of gender diversity in information technology, lying as it does at the commencement of the pathway that would lead to computer courses, STEM majors, and jobs in systems analysis, artificial intelligence, big data analytics, and robotics, to name a few. In short, gaming development, content, distribution, and sales will play a major role as the first stepping-stone to the future. Reform of the gaming industry, with an eye toward increasing gender diversity, is essential.

In this regard, no one silver bullet may be chambered that will fix or ameliorate all the problems. The need to generate revenue and profits likewise militates against any quick fix. But several policies would be important steps toward a solution:

> Continuing the crackdown on the trolls, the troll gangs, and cyber-bullying. The authorities, aided significantly by the IT industry, could use existing defamation and assault laws as well as formulating new statutory approaches to deter the troll fraternity. The statute and common law regulations and prohibitions would only be as effective as the policing of them. The industry could contribute there as well.

> Adopting voluntary quotas. Gaming developers, distributors, and retailers could set objectives for themselves such as making sure that 20 percent of games do not involve scoring goals or shooting bad guys. Parity is not the goal here: a significant increase in the space attractive to girls and young women is the objective.

> Reducing the violence and eliminating sex and the objectification of women. The large and middle-size developers can easily achieve this by adopting voluntary standards. Smaller producers will continue to come forward with games that are objectionable on this count, but that would not put the major players at a significant competitive disadvantage.

> Adopting an industry code of conduct addressed to certain of these problems. Such a code would aim at curtailment of use of booth babes and other unseemly sales and promotion practices.

> Leaning on the producers. The entire information technology industry, including particularly the major producers within it, and not merely the gaming component, can lean on gaming developers to curb the practices that have had such a negative effect on diversity in the industry.

A real impediment to all of this is the First Amendment to the U.S. Constitution. That amendment, of course, guarantees to citizens the right of free speech ("Congress shall make no law . . . abridging the freedom of speech"). The amendment pertains to abridgments by the federal government, by state governments, and by private actors if "state action" is involved in their dealings.

But our culture is such that acts by wholly private parties that impinge upon freedom of speech will be condemned. Going overboard in policing or attempting to police the output of game developers would run afoul of our free speech culture. Regulation and policing could certainly reach conduct by trolls that is equivalent to "shouting fire in a crowed theater," or that defames other persons, or that puts objects of their actions in reasonable fear of an imminent battery (a harmful or offensive touching). But there are First Amendment considerations here, especially if instruments of government (courts, for example) are asked to enforce sanctions and thereby curb harmful behavior and if standards and sanctions go too far.

So the problems associated with achieving reform within the computer game industry are not simple. That is not to deny, however, that achievement of significant reform is essential to the entire information technology business and its legitimacy. Reform of the software entertainment industry, mainly including the gaming industry, has to be one of the very first steps.

23

FINAL OBSERVATIONS

This book has not been about black-and-white or binary choices, although it may have seemed so. In treating these subjects, though falling short, the author's intent has been to paint in shades of gray.

Take the subject of the H-1B visa program (chapter 15). The tenor of the discussion is to raise questions. Has the information technology industry relied too extensively on the H-1B visa program? Has sole reliance, or overreliance, on the H-1B program resulted in a failure to think about and increase gender and other forms of diversity in senior management?

Emphasis on STEM education is similar. A healthy dose of it, especially for girls and young women, is long overdue. But remember H. L. Menken's aphorism: "For every complex problem, there is an answer that is clean, simple, and wrong." The emphasis on STEM is not wrong, but an overemphasis on STEM may be. An analysis of the career paths of women who actually have reached senior positions (CEOs and senior executives), though, does give one pause. That may be because the sample is small, but it may also may be because the headlong rush to reliance on STEM should be tempered by emphasis on other subjects as well, such as business subjects and certain of the liberal arts (government, economics), as chapter 14 suggests and the small sample available demonstrates.

For the most part, mentoring (chapter 12) is to the good, but it has become clear that the experts have placed too many eggs in that basket. Properly done, mentoring is valuable. Gone even slightly awry, mentoring may have several drawbacks, potential deficiencies the self-styled experts ignore. The emerging *zeitgeist* is that mentoring combined with sponsorship is much better, as a few observers have begun to recognize.[1]

Overall, early advocates for increased business opportunities for women were simplistic. They theorized that attacking the problems of women's underrepresentation in business was similar to a game of golf:

"you just had to whack it," that is, get a mentor, network, and the like. Time has shown that there is not a single locus but many loci. Solving the multiple issues involved resembles "solving a multilevel Rubik's Cube."[2] Resolving the work/life imbalance, for example, requires much more prolonged and diverse efforts than merely "whacking at it."

There is a potential for backlash. "Among those who opposed the efforts of [early women's rights advocates] were the leaders of the civil rights movement themselves. They thought that women's-rights advocates were trying to piggyback on the movement for rights for African-Americans, and that the load will kill the piggy."[3] Civil rights activists often had emphatic reactions to the women's movement.[4] So, too, with staunch advocates of STEM and STEM programs. From those advocates, negative reactions will emerge in supposed or real revulsion over certain of the courses of action this book suggests, or samples of data that purport to support them. Proponents of the H-1B visa program and of its expansion will take strong exception as well.

Others, opposed to the advancement of women in business and to the devotion of resources to that cause overall, will have arrows in their quiver other than competition with the causes they espouse, for example, on behalf of African Americans or Native Americans, on the one hand, or profit maximization advocates, on the other. A significant number of individuals, including some leaders, within those groups claim that women lack competence, at least outside of areas such as marketing or fashion, or at least they make those claims *sotto voce*, inhibited from more vocal assessments by considerations of political correctness,

According to the Pew Research Center's 2015 study, a large majority of the public sees men and women as equivalent on key leadership traits such as intelligence, honesty, ambition, and innovation.[5] The main differences perceived between men and women "were compassion and organization, and on these traits women were rated as superior to men. Women are also more likely than men to engage in 'transformational leadership.'"[6]

Another objection raised to expenditures on behalf of increasing female representation is that "women don't want it," or "don't want it badly enough." Sheryl Sandberg gives some credence to this view with her thesis that not enough women "lean in" (see chapter 8).[7] Lisa Belkin wrote in her seminal *New York Times* piece that women's underrepresentation is not only because "the workplace has failed women. It is also that women are rejecting the workplace." "Why don't women run the world?," she asks. "Maybe because they don't want to."[8]

One hears this or similar refrains quite often. "Work at the top of the greasy pole takes time, saps energy, and is time-consuming. . . . Maybe the tradeoffs [that] high positions entail are ones that women do not want to make."[9] Women occupy 50 percent of the positions at U.S. businesses, similarly constituting 50 percent of the middle managers. In part, those statistics belie the claims that women "don't want it." Women's desires, of course, are not monolithic. It's impossible to group all women together and conclude that "they don't want it."

There are a number of reasons to encourage diligent efforts to include more females on promotion ladders and in senior positions. The preface to this books sets out a few of them. I have attempted to respond to the "Why women" question, as have other authors. There are at least fourteen or fifteen organizations whose stated goal is to increase the number of women in business and on boards of directors especially.[10] A partial list would include the following:

1. Boardroom Bound
2. Boardroom Boot Camp
3. Board Ready Women's Initiative
4. Catalyst, Inc.
5. Clayton Institute for Gender (Stanford University)
6. Direct Women (American Bar Association)
7. Forte Foundation Women's Program
8. Lean In (with McKinsey & Company)
9. Men as Allies (Forte Foundation)
10. Paradigm for Parity
11. Thirty Percent Coalition
12. WomenCorporateDirectors Foundation
13. 2020 Women on Boards

There are a few specialized organizations such as Women in Technology (Washington, D.C.) and Women in Technology International (Los Angeles), although the latter seems suspect, organized as it is as a for-profit entity and selling T-shirts on its website.

Be that as it may, these organizations tiptoe around the barriers rather than confronting them. Moreover, for the most part they muddle on in the same old vein, urging women to do this or try that (again, lean in, find a mentor, network, be assertive, smile in job interviews, use "we" instead of "I"). What seems to be needed are organizations on the corporate side, either nationally or at least in Silicon Valley, spearheading efforts to increase opportunities for women in information technology.

In fact, elsewhere and overall, quests for women's equality long predate the National Organization for Women (NOW) or Germaine Greer's or Betty Friedan's writings. The U.S. suffrage movement began in 1848 with the Seneca Falls (New York) convention. As long ago as 1895 Mark Twain wrote, "One of the signs of savagery is a civilization where equality between man and woman is furthest apart. . . . No civilization can be perfect until exact equality between man and woman is included."[11]

Exact equality (parity) is not the goal, for this book at least. A significant self-examination, thought, analysis, and devotion of resources by the information technology industry are objectives for which the industry and companies within it must strive. Progress toward them is long overdue.

APPENDIX A

Publicly Held Information Technology Companies*

Name	Stock Ticker	Female Executive(s)	Business and Location
1. Activision Blizzard, Inc.	ATVI	None	Graphic software (games), Santa Monica, CA
2. Adobe Systems, Inc.	ADBE	None	Application software, San Jose, CA
3. Aecom Tech, Inc.	ACM	None	Technology consulting and support, Los Angeles, CA
4. Aerohive Networks	HIVE	None	Communications technology, Sunnyvale, CA
5. Akamai, Inc.	AKAM	Melanie Haratunian, General Counsel	Content and business applications cloud services, Cambridge, MA
6. Align Technology, Inc.	ALGN	None	CAD/CAM for dentistry, San Jose, CA
7. Alliance Data Systems Corp.	ADS	Melisa Miller, VP, Marketing & Loyalty Solutions	Retail credit, Plano, TX
8. Alliance Fiber Optics	AFOP	Anita Ho, CFO	Diversified electronics, Sunnyvale, CA
9. Amazon.com, Inc.	AMZN	None	Internet retail, Seattle, WA
10. Analog Drivers, Inc.	ADI	Eileen Wynne, Chief Accountant	Semiconductors, Norwood, MA
11. Apple, Inc.	AAPL	Angela Ahrendts, VP, Retail	Electronic products, retail and online stores, Cupertino, CA
12. Applied Materials, Inc.	AMAT	None	Semiconductors, Santa Clara, CA
13. Applied Micro Inc.	AMCC	None	Circuits, Silicon solutions, Sunnyvale, CA

* Appendix A (2015) and appendix B (2017) were compiled at different points in time and therefore do not correspond perfectly. For example, women listed in appendix A may have left their companies or moved to other positions within the same company by the time the author compiled appendix B. On the other hand, women listed in appendix B, compiled later, may not have reached their senior positions at the earlier time when the author compiled appendix A.

Name	Stock Ticker	Female Executive(s)	Business and Location
14. Apptio, Inc.	APTI	Susanna Morgan, VP, Finance	Cloud-based management solutions, Bellevue, WA
15. Aspen Technology, Inc.	AZPN	None	Software engineering and supply, Bedford, MA
16. Autodesk, Inc.	ADSK	Jan Becker, HR & Real Estate	CAD software, San Rafael, CA
17. Blackbaud, Inc.	BLKB	Mary Beth Westmoreland, CTO	Software, Charleston, SC
18. Black Box Corp.	BBOX	None	IT infrastructure, Lawrence, PA
19. Box, Inc.	BOX	None	Cloud-based collaboration software, Redwood City, CA
20. BroadCom, Inc.	BRCM	None	Semiconductors, Irvine, CA
21. BroadSoft, Inc.	BSFT	None	Software, Gaithersburg, MD
22. CA, Inc.	CA	Lauren P. Flaherty, CMO	Business software, New York, NY
23. Cadence Design Systems, Inc.	CDNS	None	Automation software, San Jose, CA
24. Cavium, Inc.	CAVM	None	Semiconductors, San Jose, CA
25. Check Point Software	CHKP	None	Hardware/software, San Carlos, CA
26. Cirrus Logic, Inc.	CRUS	None	Integrated circuits, Austin, TX
27. Citrix Systems, Inc.	CTXS	None	Business software, Fort Lauderdale, FL
28. Cisco Systems, Inc.	CSCO	Rebecca Jacoby, COO	Networking systems, San Jose, CA
29. Cognizant Technology	CTSH	Karen McLaughlin, CFO	Business and technology services, Teaneck, NJ
30. Computer Programs & Systems	CPSI	None	Healthcare IT, Mobile, AL
31. Computer Services Corp.	CSC	None	Global IT services, Falls Church, VA
32. Concurrent Computer Corp.	CCUR	Davina Furnish, General Counsel	Software, Duluth, GA
33. Cypress Semiconductor Corp.	CY	None	Semiconductors, San Jose, CA
34. DTS, Inc.	DTSI	None	Audio/electronic solutions, Calabasas, CA
35. eBay, Inc.	EBAY	None	Internet retail, San Jose, CA
36. Electronic Arts, Inc.	EA	None	Multimedia and graphics software, Redwood City, CA
37. EMC Corp.	EMC	None	Data storage, Hopkinton, MA

Name	Stock Ticker	Female Executive(s)	Business and Location
38. Expedia, Inc.	EXPE	None	Internet travel booking, Bellevue, WA
39. Facebook, Inc.	FB	Sheryl Sandberg, COO	Social media provider, Menlo Park, CA
40. Fact Set Research Systems, Inc.	FDS	None	Financial analytics, Norwalk, CT
41. FireEye, Inc.	FEY	Alexa King, General Counsel	Application software, Milpitas, CS
42. FisServ, Inc.	FISV	None	Financial services technology, Brookfield, WI
43. 1-800-Flowers.com, Inc.	FLWS	None	Internet flowers and gifts, Carle Place, NY
44. Fortinet, Inc.	FTNT	None	Internet security, Sunnyvale, CA
45. F-5 Networks	FFIV	None	Business software, Seattle, WA
46. Gamestop, Inc.	GME	None	Computer gaming, Grapevine, TX
47. Gigamon, Inc.	GIMO	None	Network traffic control, Santa Clara, CA
48. GigPeak, Inc.	GIG	None	ICs and software, San Jose, CA
49. GoDaddy Inc.	GDDY	Eliza Murphy, CTO	Cloud-based small business solutions, Scottsdale, AZ
50. Google/Alphabet	GOOG	Ruth Porat, CFO	Internet information providers, Mountain View, CA
51. Hewlett-Packard Enterprises	HPE	None	Software solutions, Palo Alto, CA
52. H-P, Inc.	HP	Catherine A. Lesjak, CFO; Marie Myers, CAO	Computer hardware, Palo Alto, CA
53. Interactive Corp.	AC	None	Internet services, New York, NY
54. IHS, Inc.	HIS	None	Information/analytics provider, Englewood, CO
55. Ingram Micro, Inc.	IM	None	Technology peripherals, Irvine, CA
56. Intel Corp.	INTC	Renee James, President	Semiconductors, Santa Clara, CA
57. International Business Machines Corp.	IBM	None	Information technology, Armonk, NY
58. Intuit Inc.	INTU	None	Management software, Mountain View, CA
59. Juniper Networks, Inc.	JNPR	Robyn Denholm, CFO	Networking devices, Sunnyvale, CA
60. Liberty Interactive Inc.	LUNTB	None	Health and fitness ecommerce, Englewood, CO

Name	Stock Ticker	Female Executive(s)	Business and Location
61. LinkedIn Corp.	LNKD	None	Internet information providers, Mountain View, CA
62. Maxim Integrated Products Inc.	MXIM	None	Integrated circuits, San Jose, CA
63. Mentor Graphics, Inc.	MENT	None	Tech consulting and support, Wilsonville, OR
64. Microchip Technology, Inc.	MCHP	None	Semiconductors, Chandler, AZ
65. Micron Technology, Inc.	MU	None	Semiconductors, Boise, ID
66. Microsoft Corp.	MFST	Amy Hood, CFO	Business and personal software, Redmond, WA
67. Net App, Inc.	NTAP	None	Data storage devices, Sunnyvale, CA
68. Netflix, Inc.	NFLX	None	Internet entertainment, Los Gatos, CA
69. Nvidia Corp.	NVDA	Colette Kress, CFO; Debora Shoquist, VP, Operations	Visual software, Santa Clara, CA
70. Oracle Corp.	ORCL	None	Application software, Redwood City, CA
71. Palo Alto Networks, Inc.	PANW	None	Networking and communications, Santa Clara, CA
72. Paychex, Inc.	PAYX	None	Internet payroll, Rochester, NY
73. PayPal, Inc.	PYPL	None	Internet credit services, San Jose, CA
74. Priceline Group, Inc.	PCLN	None	Internet travel and dining reservations, Norwalk, CT
75. Proofpoint, Inc.	PFPT	Tracey Newell, VP, Worldwide Sales	Regulatory compliance, Sunnyvale, CA
76. Qlik Technologies, Inc.	QLIK	None	Business software, Radnor, PA
77. Qualcom, Inc.	QCOM	None	Communications equipment, San Diego, CA
78. Qualsys, Inc.	QLYS	None	Application software, Redwood City, CA
79. Quantum Corp.	QTM	Linda Breard, CFO	Data storage and protection, San Jose, CA
80. Quick Logic, Inc.	QUIK	None	Low-power semiconductors, Sunnyvale, CA
81. Rackspace Hosting, Inc.	RAX	None	Information technology, San Antonio, TX
82. Red Hat, Inc.	RHT	None	Application software, Raleigh, NC
83. Root 9B Technologies	RTNB	None	Security and risk management, Charlotte, NC
84. Salesforce.com, Inc.	CRM	None	Cloud logistic solutions, San Francisco, CA

Name	Stock Ticker	Female Executive(s)	Business and Location
85. SanDisk Corp.	SNDE	Judy Bruner, CFO	Disk drives, Milipitas, CA
86. Semtech, Inc.	SMTC	None	Semiconductor products, Camarillo, CA
87. Shopify, Inc.	SHOP	None	B to C commerce, Ontario, CA
88. Skyworks Solutions, Inc.	SWKS	None	Semiconductors, Woburn, MA
89. Sonus Networks, Inc.	SONS	None	Communications equipment, Westford, MA
90. Super Micro Computer, Inc.	SMCI	None	Performance server solutions, San Jose, CA
91. Symantec Corp.	SYMC	None	Security software, Mountain View, CA
92. Take-Two Interactive Software, Inc.	TTWO	None	Entertainment solutions, New York, NY
93. TD Ameritrade Holding Corp.	AMTD	None	Internet financial services, Omaha, NE
94. Teradyne, Inc.	TER	None	Semiconductor test equipment, North Reading, MA
95. Texas Instruments, Inc.	TXN	None	Semiconductors, Dallas, TX
96. TriNet Group, Inc.	TNET	None	Internet human resources, San Leandro, CA
97. TripAdvisor, Inc.	TRP	None	Travel information and booking, Newton, MA
98. Twitter, Inc.	TWT	Vijaya Gadde, General Counsel	Internet information provider, San Francisco, CA
99. Ultimate Software Group, Inc.	ULTI	None	Cloud-based HR software, Weston, FL
100. Unisys Corp.	UIS	None	Information technology and services, Blue Bell, PA
101. Upland Software, Inc.	UPLD	None	Cloud-based software, Austin, TX
102. Verisign, Inc.	VRSN	None	Internet security, Reston, VA
103. VMWare, Inc.	VMW	None	Technical and system software, Palo Alto, CA
104. Web.com Group, Inc.	WEB	Roseann Duran, Executive VP	Internet information providers, Jacksonville, FL
105. Xilinx, Inc.	XLNX	None	Semiconductors, San Jose, CA
106. Yahoo! Inc.	YHOO	None	Internet service provider, Sunnyvale, CA
107. Zebra Technologies Corp.	ZBRA	None	Printing and computer hardware, Lincolnshire, IL

Name	Stock Ticker	Female Executive(s)	Business and Location
108. Zebra Technologies Inc.	ZEB	None	Peripherals and related software, Lincolnshire, IL
109. Zendesk, Inc.	ZEN	Amanda Kleha, Senior VP	Software, San Francisco, CA
110. Zynga, Inc.	ZNGA	Jennifer Nuckles, CMO	Online social services, San Francisco, CA

Foreign IT Companies with U.S. Share Listings

Name	Stock Ticker	Female Executive(s)	Business and Location
111. Alibaba	BABA	Wei Wu, CFO	Internet shopping, Hangzhou, China
112. Avago Technologies, Ltd.	AVGO	Patricia McCall, General Counsel	Semiconductors, Singapore
113. Baidu, Inc.	BIDU	Xinzhe Li, CFO	Internet services, Beijing, China
114. CyberArk Software, Ltd.	CYBR	None	Internet security, Petach Tikva, Israel
115. DragonWave, Inc.	DRWI	None	Internet communications, Ottawa, Ontario, Canada
116. Garmin Ltd.	GRMN	None	Navigation devices, Schaffhausen, Switzerland
117. Infosys, Inc.	INFY	None	System software, Begaluru, India
118. International Game	IGT	None	Technology Internet gaming, London, England
119. Jiayuan.com. Int'l	DATE	Shirley Zhang, Investor Relations	Internet dating service, Beijing, China
120. Lenovo Group Ltd.	LNGVY	None	Computer hardware, Beijing, China
121. Marvell Technology Group	MRVL	Maya Strelar-Migotti, VP, Business Group	Semiconductors, Hamilton, Bermuda
122. NXP Semiconductors NV	NXPI	None	Semiconductors, Einhaven, Netherlands
123. SAP, Inc.	SAP	None	Applications and analytics software, Walldorf, Germany
124. Seagate Technology, PLC	STX	None	Electronic storage, Dublin, Ireland
125. Taiwan Semiconductor	TSM	Li Mei He Ho, CFO	Integrated circuits, Hsinchu, Taiwan
126. Tencent Holdings Ltd.	TCTZF	None	Online advertising, Shenzhen, China
127. Ubisoft, SA	UBI.PA	None	Entertainment software, Montreuil, France

APPENDIX B

Women Senior Executives in Publicly Held Information Technology Companies

Company	Name	Position	Terminal Degree
1. Akami	Melanie Haratunian	Exec. VP	JD, Georgetown
2. Alliance Fiber	Anita Ho	CFO	BA (Accounting), Soochow Univ.
3. Analog	Eileen Wynne	Controller	MA (BS, Accounting), Bentley Univ.
4. Apple	Angela Ahrendts	VP, Retail	BA (Marketing), Ball State
5. Apptio	Susanna Morgan	CFO	MBA, Harvard
6. Autodesk	Jan Becker	Human Resources	BS (Business Administration), San Jose Univ.
7. Blackbaud	Mary Beth Westmoreland	CTO	BS, Immaculata
8. Broadcom	Patricia McCall	Gen. Counsel	JD, Virginia
9. CA	Lauren Flaherty	CMO	BA (Marketing), Syracuse
10. Cisco	Rebecca Jacoby	VP, Operations	MBA, Santa Clara
11. Cognizant	Karen McLoughlin	CFO	MBA, Columbia
12. Concurrent	Davina Furnish	Gen. Counsel	JD, Cleveland State
13. Facebook	Sheryl Sandberg	COO	MBA, Harvard
14. Fireeye	Alexa King	Gen. Counsel	JD, Cal Berkeley
15. Google	Ruth Porat	CFO	MBA, Pennsylvania
16. H-P	Catherine Lesjak	CFO	MBA, Cal Berkeley
17. H-P	Marie Myers	Controller	MBA, St. Thomas
18. Intel	Paula Tolliver	CIO	MBA, Babson
19. Juniper Networks	Robyn Denholm	CFO	MBA, New South Wales
20. Microsoft	Amy Hood	CFO	MBA, Harvard
21 Nvidia	Colette Kress	CFO	MBA, SMU
22. Nvidia	Debora Shoquist	VP, Operations	BS EE, Kansas State
23. Proofpoint	Tracey Newell	VP, Sales	BA (Economics), Santa Barbara
24. SanDisk	Judy Bruner	CFO	MBA, Santa Clara
25. Square	Sarah Friar	CFO	MBA, Stanford
26. Twitter	Vijaya Gadde	Gen. Counsel	JD, NYU
27. Zendesk	Amanda Kleha	Senior VP	MBA, Yale

NOTES

Preface

1. *NBC Nightly News with Brian Williams*, September 30, 2014.
2. Jason Zwieg, "Three New ETF Ideas That Really Make Sense," *Wall Street Journal*, August 20, 2016, at B-1.
3. *See* Bureau of Economic Research, U.S. Department of Commerce, press release, January 27, 2017 (GDP of $18,861 trillion), www.bea.gov (visited February 7, 2017). As of February 7, 2017, statisticians estimated market capitalization as 127.2 percent of gross domestic product, or $23.99 trillion. See www.ycharts.com (visited February 7, 2017).
4. *See* "List of Countries by Projected GDP," *Statistics Times*, April 23, 2017, www.statisticstimes.com (data source: International Monetary Fund World Economic Outlook , April 2017, www.imf.org). The GDPs of France, Germany, and the United Kingdom are $2.4 trillion, $2.85 trillion, and $3.4 trillion, respectively. The GDPs of Japan and China are $4.8 trillion, and $11.8 trillion, respectively.
5. Farhad Manjoo, "In Defeat, a Woman Disrupts How Silicon Valley Does Business," *Pittsburgh Post-Gazette*, March 29, 2015, at A-8 (*New York Times* analysis).
6. Jessica Guynn, "Women in Computing to Decline Even More," *USA Today*, October 21, 2016, at B-1 (statistics jointly published by consulting firm Accenture and not-for-profit Girls Who Code).
7. *New York Times*, December 23, 2014.
8. Rhode, *Women and Leadership*, at 2.
9. Sandberg, *Lean In*.
10. An exception is Professor Deborah Rhode of Stanford University School of Law. In her newest book, *Women and Leadership*, she devotes subsections of most chapters to recommendations for what organizations might do or should consider.
11. Friedan, *The Feminine Mystique*.
12. Greer, *The Female Eunuch*.
13. "The test for whether or not you can hold a job should not be the arrangement of your chromosomes."
14. Christine LaGarde, "Women, Power and the Challenge of the Financial Crisis," *New York Times*, November 12, 2010, at A-4.
15. A leading piece is Marleen O'Connor, "The Enron Board: The Perils of Groupthink," 71 *U. Cincinnati L. Rev.* 1323 (2003).

16. *See, e.g.*, Kristof and WuDunn, *Half the Sky*, at 238; the authors also compare Pakistan and Bangladesh: "One reason that Bangladesh is more stable today is that it invested enormously in women and girls, so that a girl in Bangladesh is far more likely to go to school than a Pakistani girl, and afterward far more likely to hold a job."

17. *See generally* Branson, *The Last Male Bastion*, chap. 10, "Why Women?," at 121–27.

18. Branson, *Corporate Governance* (with annual supplements).

19. *See, e.g.*, Clarke & Branson, *The Sage Handbook of Corporate Governance*; Branson, Heminway et al., *Business Enterprises*; Pinto & Branson, *Understanding Corporate Law*; Branson, *Problems in Corporate Governance*.

20. Branson, *No Seat at the Table*.

21. Branson, *The Last Male Bastion*.

22. Rhode, *Women and Leadership*, at 2.

Chapter 1. Industries That Do Not Hire or Promote

1. *See, e.g.*, Shayndi Raice & Joann Lublin, "New Face Atop Facebook," *Wall Street Journal*, June 26, 2012, at B-1 (Sheryl Sandberg appointed COO but no female board appointments; Anne Sheehan, California State Teachers' Retirement System, comments, "We are disappointed that the Facebook board will not have any women").

2. Losse, *The Boy Kings*.

3. Ken Auletta, "A Woman's Place: Can Sheryl Sandberg Upend Silicon Valley's Male-Dominated Culture?," *New Yorker*, July 11, 2011.

4. *See, e.g.*, Yoree Koh, "Twitter Adds Its First Female Directors," *Wall Street Journal*, December 6, 2013, at B-5 (former *New York Times* reporter Marjorie Scardino). *See also* Yoree Koh, "Twitter Swaps Two New Board Members," *Wall Street Journal*, April 10, 2016, at B-3 ("investors have long criticized Twitter for having a board of nearly all white males"; Twitter adds second female director).

5. Claire Cain Miller, "Curtain Is Rising on a Tech Premier with (as Usual) a Mostly Male Cast," *New York Times*, October 4, 2013.

6. John Bussey, "Gender Wage Gap Reflects 'Ask' Gap," *Wall Street Journal*, October 11, 2014, at B-4.

7. Mike Snyder & Elizabeth Weise, "Clamor Continues over Microsoft CEO's Women's Pay Comments," *USA Today*, October 14, 2014. The industry's tin ear perpetuates itself. Recently, after a 2016 investigation, the Department of Labor found that both Google and Oracle discriminated against women by paying them less than men for comparable work. For one, Oracle said that "the complaint was politically motivated, based on false allegations, and without merit." Jack Nicas, "Women at Google Are Paid Less Than Men, Investigation Finds," *Wall Street Journal*, April 10, 2017, at B-4.

8. Jack Nicas & Yoree Koh, "Gender Pay Ruling Looms for Google," *Wall Street Journal*, June 26, 2017 (Google and Facebook also refuse to produce any pay data).

9. Rhode, *Women and Leadership*, at 126.

10. Catalyst, *Missing Pieces Report: The 2016 Board Diversity Census of Women and Minorities*, at 9 & 10, Table 4 (July 7, 2016). *Compare* Pew Research Center, Social and Demographic Trends (female board membership at 9.6 percent in 1995), www.pewsocialtrends.org (visited August 26, 2015) *with* Catalyst, "Catalyst Census," January 13, 2015, at 1 (board membership at 19.2 percent women), www.catalyst.org (visited August 26, 2015).

11. Catalyst, *Missing Pieces Report*, at 10. *See* also Catalyst, "Women in S&P Corporations," November 18, 2015.

12. Joyce Gannon, "CMU Conference Targets Women Aspiring to Leadership," *Pittsburgh Post-Gazette*, February 17, 2016, at D-1.

13. Reported in Sheryl Sandberg, "Women Are Leaning In—But They Face Pushback," *Wall Street Journal*, September 27, 2016, at R-2.

14. Joyce Gannon, "Who Says It's a Man's World?," *Pittsburgh Post-Gazette*, February 3, 2013, at D-1 (statistics by Board Source, Washington, D.C.).

15. See, e.g., Branson, *No Seat at the Table*, at 96 & 106.

16. *See* Branson, *No Seat at the Table*, at 106.

17. Branson, *No Seat at the Table*, at 107.

18. Branson, *No Seat at the Table*, at 106.

19. For example, Anne Mulcahy, who later became CEO of Xerox, took her first sales manager job in Maine, a position others of her rank avoided. The decision turned out to be a fortuitous one. *See* "Women CEOs Recall Bad Jobs, Bad Bosses," *Wall Street Journal*, October 17, 2016, at B-1, excerpting Lublin, *Earning It*.

20. *See generally* Branson, *The Last Male Bastion*, chap. 6, "Going Where They Aren't," at 78–90; also 105–7.

21. Francesco Guerrera, "Gender Gap in Finance Is Wide," *Wall Street Journal*, December 17, 2013, at C-1 (12.4 percent executives and 18.3 percent directors).

22. Census dated January 15, 2016, on file with the author. The companies were CSX, Union Pacific, Norfolk Southern, Kansas City Southern, Canadian National, Canadian Pacific, United Air, Delta Air, Southwest Air, American Air, Alaska Air Group, Jet Blue, CH Robinson Worldwide, JB Hunt Trucking, Landstar, Federal Express, and United Parcel Service.

23. Census dated January 15, 2016, on file with the author.

24. Census dated January 15, 2016, on file with the author (excluding Meg Whitman at H-P, Marissa Mayer at Yahoo!, Virginia Rometty at IBM, and Safra Catz at Oracle).

25. An earlier and very similar finding to my own was made by Andrea Matwyshyn in 2003. She found that women held fewer than 8 percent of the engineering positions and fewer than 5 percent of the management jobs at information technology companies. Matwyshyn, "Silicon Ceilings: Information Technology Entities, the Digital Divide, and the Gender Gap among Information Technology Professionals," 2 *Northwestern J. Tech & Intellectual Property* 2, 31 (2003).

26. *See, e.g.*, Clayton Institute for Gender Research, Statistics, Women in Technology Factsheet, www.gender.stanford.edu (visited November 15, 2016).

27. In 2010 the Clayman Institute for Gender Research at Stanford did host a conference on the subject, entitled "Silicon Valley Leadership Greenhouse."

28. Koh, "Twitter Adds Its First Female Directors."

29. Jeff Elder, "John Doerr Testifies as Kleiner Trial Continues," *Wall Street Journal*, March 6, 2015, at B-4.

30. Losse, *The Boy Kings*, at 20.

31. *See* Jeff Elder, "Accuser in Kleiner Perkins Case Testifies of Sex Discrimination," *Wall Street Journal*, March 10, 2015, at B-3.

32. Todd S. Frankel & Andrea Peterson, "Jury Finds No Gender Discrimination in Case That Captivated Silicon Valley," *Pittsburgh Post-Gazette*, March 28, 2015, at A-8 (*Washington Post* News Service).

33. *See, e.g.,* Stross, *eBoys*, at xix (Benchmark Capital partner served as director of eBay), and at 116 (Benchmark partner would not go on board of portfolio company, an unusual exception to the normal practice of having a venture capital firm rep holding a board seat). Professor Stross's firsthand experiences in two years at Benchmark Capital and his writing about them are a must-read for anyone interested in information technology and "B to C" (business to consumer) and "B to B" commerce's early days.

34. *See* Deborah Gage & Jeff Elder, "Sex-Bias Trial Takes Big Toll on Kleiner," *Wall Street Journal*, March 25, 2015, at B-1.

35. *See* Jeff Elder, "Silicon Valley Venture Firm Prevails in Sex-Bias Suit," *Wall Street Journal*, March 28, 2015, at A-1.

36. *See generally* Manjoo, "In Defeat, a Woman Disrupts How Silicon Valley Does Business"; Margaret Carlson, "Ellen Pao Leaned In," *Pittsburgh Post-Gazette*, March 31, 2015, at B-5 (Bloomberg).

37. Christina Passariello, "Silicon Valley Gets Agitated: Venture Capitalist Shames Industry's Shortage of Women and Minorities, Making Enemies," *Wall Street Journal*, April 23, 2016, at A-1 (survey by Social Capital, Inc., and CEO Chamath Palihapitiya).

38. Vivek Wadhwa, "Six Myths about Tech Entrepreneurs," *Pittsburgh Post-Gazette*, May 11, 2014, at B-1 (statistics from the National Center for Women and Information Technology).

39. Heather MacDonald, "Meritocracies Care about Profits, Not Gender," *Wall Street Journal*, March 31, 2015, at A-17.

40. Manjoo, "In Defeat, a Woman Disrupts How Silicon Valley Does Business," quoting Karen Catlin, former vice president, Adobe Systems.

41. *See, e.g.,* Martin J. Lawler & Margaret Stock, "Saying 'No Thanks' to 87,500 Skilled Workers," *Wall Street Journal*, May 8, 2014, at A-17 (the problem with the labor shortage in IT: "There aren't nearly enough [H-1B] visas. . . . On April 1 [there were] 172,500 applications for H-1B visas. . . . Congress allows only 85,000 of the three-year visas to be issued annually") (actually approximately 130,000 H-1B visas are granted each year, a statistic the IT industry consistently understates, as

chapter 15 discusses); Jeffrey Handal, "A Green Solution to the H-1B Problem," *Wall Street Journal*, November 19, 2014, at A–12 "Green cards [for imported IT workers] are real solution").

42. Reported in Hirshman, *Sisters in Law*, at 56.

Chapter 2. The Paradox

1. Manjoo, "In Defeat, a Woman Disrupts How Silicon Valley Does Business."
2. Black, *The Power of Knowledge*, at 1 and at 366:

    The Internet presents a new form of oral as well as written culture. . . . New words have emerged, such as the noun and the verb "podcast," referring to programs for downloading onto iPods, or similar portable devices. Software languages have also become part of the linguistic mix. . . . Information and practices linked to the new technology are affecting communications to an unprecedented extent.

3. Harking back seventy-five years, to the integration of Major League Baseball, it was the players from California who not only rejected any notion of a boycott but welcomed the first black players (Jackie Robinson of the Brooklyn Dodgers and Larry Doby of the Cleveland Indians) to the big leagues. Those California players, who might be thought to represent more enlightened opinions, included Ted Williams (from San Diego), Bob Lemon (Long Beach), Duke Snider (Compton), Ralph Kiner (Alhambra), and Dominic DiMaggio (San Francisco). *See, e.g.*, Branson, *Greatness in the Shadows*, at 278, n. 19. An uneducated guess might be that, similarly, enlightened attitudes prevailed in information technology—but that guess would be wrong.
4. Losse, *The Boy Kings*, at xxi (memoir of early Facebook employee as the fifty-first employee and the second woman hired).
5. Hap Klop, "Silicon Valley Boards Think and Act Differently," *Directors & Boards*, 4th Quarter, 2015, at 21.
6. On its websites, Hewlett-Packard is inconsistent, hyphenating the corporate name sometimes and not hyphenating it at others. I adopt the hyphenated version as more in keeping with the founders' visions of a cooperative venture. By contrast, the company does not hyphenate abbreviations for the corporate name (HP) and subsequent spin-offs (*e.g.*, Hewlett Packard Enterprises, or HPE).
7. *See, e.g.*, Fairfax, "The Bottom Line on Boards," 810–20.
8. Rhode, *Women and Leadership*, at 133.
9. Pew Research Center, "Women and Leadership" (Philadelphia, 2015), cited in Rhode, *Women and Leadership*, at 6.
10. Quoted in Rhode, *Women and Leadership*, at 137.
11. Branson, *The Last Male Bastion*, at 123.
12. Joann Lublin, "Female CEOs Make Room for Female Directors," *Wall Street Journal*, November 12, 2014, at B-7.
13. *See, e.g.*, Linda Bell, *Women-Led Firms and the Gender Gap in Top Executive Positions*, www.papers.ssrn.com (visited February 23, 2016).

14. "Susan Ivey Made It Happen for Women," *Director & Officer*, Third Quarter, 2011, at 26. *See* also Branson, *Last Male Bastion*, at 123.

15. Earlier support for a trickle-down hypothesis came from political science studies in which it was demonstrated that greater female presence in legislatures and in politics translated into greater support for policy positions important for women (maternity benefits, family leave, etc.). *See, e.g.,* E. Ghani, A. Mani, & S. D. O'Connell, "Can Political Empowerment Help Economic Empowerment? Women Leaders and Female Labor Force Participation," World Bank Research Paper WPS6675 (2010); R. Chattopadhyay & E. Duflo, "Women as Policy Makers: Evidence from a Policy Experiment in India," 72 *Econometrica* 1409 (2004).

16. *Today Show*, November 5, 1999 ("One-on-One with HP CEO Carleton Fiorina," interview with James Gangrell).

17. Patricia Sellers, "The Fifty Most Powerful Women on American Business," *Fortune*, October 12, 1998, 76, at 94. *See also* Michael Meyer, "In a League of Her Own: There's No Such Thing as the Glass Ceiling for Carleton Fiorina, Now the Nation's Highest Ranking Female Executive," *Newsweek*, August 2, 1999.

18. John Markoff, "Hewlett-Packard Picks a Rising Star at Lucent as Its Chief Executive," *New York Times*, July 20, 1999, at C-1.

19. Perhaps evincing a tendency toward hypocrisy, after the HP board removed Ms. Fiorina as CEO, she attributed every slight she suffered as well as her removal to rampant sexism within the industry and within the company. Her post-CEO comments in her tell-all autobiography stand in marked contrast to statements she made while she was in office. *See, e.g.,* Fiorina, *Tough Choices*, at 249, 266, and at 173: "After striving my entire career to be judged by results and accomplishments, the coverage of my gender [and] my appearance . . . would outweigh anything else."

20. Hanna Rosin, "Why Doesn't Marissa Mayer Care about Sexism?," *Slate*, July 16, 2012.

21. Rivers & Barnett, *The New Soft War on Women*, at 236–37.

22. "Susan Ivey Made It Happen," at 27.

23. Losse, *The Boy Kings*, at 33.

24. Katherine Losse, "The Woman in the Facebook Frat House," *Wall Street Journal*, June 23, 2012, at C-3.

25. Losse, *The Boy Kings*, at 5.

Chapter 3. Qualifications and Reservations

1. Including foreign firms that have a U.S. presence (stock exchange listings) the numbers rise slightly: 27 women of 575 positions at 115 firms. *See* chapter 1.

2. Steven Sinofsky, "Inside the Plex," *Wall Street Journal*, October 4, 2014, at D-6 (review of Schmidt & Rosenberg, *How Google Works*).

3. *See, e.g.,* Mark Henderson, "Women Who Break through the Glass Ceiling Face a Cliffhanger," *London Times*, September 7, 2004, at 3.

4. Haslam & Ryan, "The Glass Cliff." *See also* Barnard, "At the Top of the Pyramid."

5. See Branson, *The Last Male Bastion*, at 73.

6. Branson, *The Last Male Bastion*, at 66.

7. *See, e.g.*, Julie Jargon, "High Costs Put Sara Lee CEO in a Bind," *Wall Street Journal*, July 23, 2008, at B-1; John Schmeltzer, "Sara Lee's Brenda Barnes Set to Add Chairman's Title," *Chicago Tribune*, October 25, 2005, at C-3; John Schmeltzer, "Brenda Barnes: Focus on Education Started Journey to Top Spot at Sara Lee," *Chicago Tribune*, October 28, 2005, at C-1.

8. *See, e.g.*, Branson, *The Last Male Bastion*, at 100-101.

9. *See* Jenna Goudreau, "New Avon CEO Vows to Restore the 126-Year-Old Beauty Company to Its Former Glory," *Fortune*, February 27, 2013. *See also* Joann Lublin, Joe Palazzolo, & Serena Ng, "Avon Near Settling U.S. Probe of Bribery," *Wall Street Journal*, February 13, 2014, at B-4. Ms. McCoy later presided over the sale of Avon's North American operation to a private equity firm. Serena Ng & Joann Lublin, "Deal Gives Avon CEO Chance to Revamp," *Wall Street Journal*, December 17, 2015.

10. *See generally* Branson, *The Last Male Bastion*, at 1–117.

11. *See generally* Rana Foroohar, "Mary Barra's Bumpy Ride," *Time*, October 6, 2014, 32, at 34; "General Motors CEO Barra to Earn \$14.4 million in 2014," Reuters, February 10, 2010, www.finance.yahoo.com (visited February 10, 2014).

12. Jeff Bennett & Siobhan Hughes, "GM's Troubled Legacy Weighs on CEO in Capitol Hill Grilling," *Wall Street Journal*, April 2, 2014, at A-1 ("GM waited nearly a decade to recall 2.6 million Chevrolet Cobalts, Saturn Ions, and other vehicles over an ignition switch issue"). *See also* Jeff Bennett, "GM Recall Costs Rise to \$1.7 Billion," *Wall Street Journal*, May 21, 2014, at B-1; Siobhan Hughes & Jeff Bennett, "Size, Cost of GM's Recall Mount," *Wall Street Journal*, April 1, 2014, at B-1.

13. "'I certainly never expected to be in a situation like this,' GM's Mary Barra told staffers . . . after she described an internal probe's harsh findings about failures involving a defective ignition switch." Joann Lublin, "Rookie CEOs Face a Steep Learning Curve," *Wall Street Journal*, June 25, 2014, at B-7.

14. Ms. Barra passed the tests facing her as a new CEO so well that the GM board made her board chair, "a move that reflects fellow directors' confidence in her leadership of the nation's largest auto dealer." Joann Lublin, "GM Names CEO Barra Chairman of Its Board," *Wall Street Journal*, January 5, 2016, at B-2. "Ms. Barra . . . has steered GM through a crisis involving defective cars and pressure from activist hedge funds."

15. Amir Efrati, "Yahoo to Pay Mayer \$100 Million over Five Years," *Wall Street Journal*, July 20, 2012, at B-3 (by contrast, Ms. Mayer's predecessor, Scott Thompson, had received a \$27 million hello package; Mr. Thompson's predecessor as Yahoo! CEO, Carol Bartz, had received a \$44.6 million hello package). *See also* Amir Efrati & John Leitzing, "Google's Mayer Takes Over as Yahoo Chief," *Wall Street Journal*, July 17, 2012, at B-1 ("Ms. Mayer will try to orchestrate one of the most notable turnarounds in corporate America").

16. Efrati & Leitzing, "Google's Mayer Takes Over."

17. Rolfe Winkler, "Yahoo's New CEO Must Fire," *Wall Street Journal*, July 19, 2012, at C-12.

18. Joann Lublin & Leslie Kwoh, "For Yahoo CEO, Two New Roles," *Wall Street Journal*, July 18, 2012, at B-1 (CEO and expectant mother).

19. *See, e.g.*, Lisa Beilfuss, "Mayer Pregnant with Twins," *Wall Street Journal*, September 2, 2015, at B-5.

20. Melinda Henneberger, "Woo Hoo to Yahoo: Some Women Really Do Have It All, or at Least Most of It," *Pittsburgh Post-Gazette*, July 19, 2012, at B-5.

21. Winni Wintermeyer, "From Koogle to Google," *Wall Street Journal*, July 17, 2012, at A-1 (photographs of all six Yahoo! CEOs). *See also* Amir Efrati & Greg Bensinger, "Ousted Yahoo Chief Lands New CEO Role," *Wall Street Journal*, July 24, 2012, at B-3 (Mayer predecessor Scott Thompson, removed from office by Yahoo! board after only two months in office, obtains new CEO position); Jessi Hempel, "Marissa's Moment of Truth," *Fortune*, May 19, 2014, 80, at 83 (seven predecessor CEOs pictured).

22. Rolfe Winkler, "Yahoo Drinks from a Tumblr of Opportunity," *Wall Street Journal*, May 20, 2013, at C-6 (derisively termed a "navel gazing" website that enables "teens, twenty-somethings and others to create and share photos, links or blogs"); Amir Efrati, Spencer Ante, & Evelyn M. Rusli, "Hazards of a Buzzy Startup," *Wall Street Journal*, May 21, 2013, at B-1 ("Yahoo's Purchase of Tumblr Puts Spotlight on Highfliers Like Pinterest and Quora with Little Revenue").

23. Ryan Knutson & Deepa Seetharaman, "Verizon to Pay $4.8 Billion for Yahoo," *Wall Street Journal*, June 25, 2016, at B-1 ("a remarkable fall for the Silicon Valley pioneer that once had a market capitalization of more than $125 billion").

24. Jack Nicas, "Yahoo's Tale Is One of Missed Chances," *Wall Street Journal*, July 27, 2016, at B-1.

25. Deepa Seetharaman, "Mayer Stands at Career Crossroads," *Wall Street Journal*, July 27, 2016, at B-1.

26. Ben Worthen, "What's Gone Wrong with H-P?," *Wall Street Journal*, November 7, 2012, at B-1.

27. Worthen, "What's Gone Wrong with H-P?"

28. Aaron Ricadela, "Why Hewlett-Packard's Impulse Buy Didn't Pay Off," *Business Week*, December 3, 2012, 35, at 36.

29. *See, e.g.*, Ben Worthen, Paul Sonne, & Justin Scheck, "Long before H-P Deal, Autonomy's Red Flags," *Wall Street Journal*, November 27, 2012, at A-1; Rolfe Winkler, "At H-P, Judgment Goes by the Board," *Wall Street Journal*, November 27, 2012, at C-10.

30. Ben Worthen, "H-P Tries to Put the Worst behind It," *Wall Street Journal*, February 22, 2013, at B-1 (photo of new H-P CEO Meg Whitman).

31. Worthen, "What's Gone Wrong with H-P?" (graphic).

32. *See, e.g.*, Ben Worthen, "H-P Chief May Cut 30,000 Workers," *Wall Street Journal*, May 18, 2012, at B-1.

33. Rolfe Winkler, "H-P Faces a Long, Hard Grind," *Wall Street Journal*, August 28, 2012, at C-10.
34. Spencer Ante, "IBM's Chief to Employees: Think Fast, Move Faster," *Wall Street Journal*, April 25, 2013, at B-1.
35. Watson, *Father, Son & Co.*, at 303, 308 ("supreme sales and service" for customers and inculcation of a "proprietary interest in the company" for employees).
36. Gerstner, *Who Says Elephants Can't Dance?*
37. Ante, "IBM's Chief to Employees."
38. Ted Greenwald, "IBM Revenue Declines Again as Strategy Shifts," *Wall Street Journal*, January 20, 2017, at B-3.
39. Rachel King, "IBM CEO Offers Advice to Trump," *Wall Street Journal*, November 17, 2016, at B-7.
40. Jena McGregor, "Here's Why Women CEOs Are More Likely to Get Sacked from Their Jobs," *Washington Post*, May 2, 2014, www.washingtonpost.com (visited January 1, 2016).
41. Branson, *The Last Male Bastion*, at 108, and generally at 107–12.
42. "Bartz: No Time to Change for Others," *Forbes ASAP*, December 1997, at 140.
43. McGregor, "Here's Why Women CEOs Are More Likely to Get Sacked."
44. Shira Ovide, "Once Again, Oracle Must Reinvent Itself," *Wall Street Journal*, September 20, 2014, at B-1 (quoting Drew Johnson of Aeris Communications).
45. James Willhite, "CEO Pay: Two Women Crack Top 10," *Wall Street Journal*, June 24, 2014, at B-6 (the other was Pamela Craig, CEO at Accenture, who clocked in as number 8, earning $12.8 million).
46. Quentin Hardy, "The Cult of Carly," *Forbes*, December 13, 1999.
47. Branson, *The Last Male Bastion*, at 14.
48. Booz Hamilton & Co., "14th Annual Chief Executive Summary" (2014).

Chapter 4. Poor Performances by Female CEOs

1. "Fiorina's H-P Tenure: A Disputed Legacy," *Wall Street Journal*, October 7, 2015, at A-1 (during the same period Dell fell 5 percent, IBM 31 percent, and Cisco 45 percent. HP fell 55 percent).
2. "Fiorina's H-P Tenure."
3. *See* Packard, *The HP Way*; Collins & Porras, *Built to Last*.
4. Quoted in Branson, *The Last Male Bastion*, at 13.
5. *See also* Vance, *Elon Musk*, at 173 (Musk put a stop to the work-anywhere culture at SpaceX); John Simmons, "IBM Says No to Home Work," *Wall Street Journal*, May 19, 2017, at A-1 ("40% of employees spent their workdays outside of traditional company offices").
6. *See generally* Rachel E. Silverman & Quentin Fottrell, "The Home Office in the Spotlight: Yahoo CEO's Move Shows Tension between Workers' Desire for Flexibility and the Need for Visibility," *Wall Street Journal*, February 27, 2013, at B-6 ("The outcry surrounding Yahoo Inc's decision to end work-from-home

arrangements has shown just how strongly many companies and employees have embraced remote work").

7. Hempel, "Marissa's Moment of Truth," at 84. *See also* Noah Rayman, "The Mayer Event: It's Crunch Time for Yahoo's Turnaround Strategy," *Time*, February 17, 2014, at 16 ("The honeymoon is over: Yahoo's fourth quarter revenue was down and its sales are struggling").

8. Douglas MacMillan, "Yahoo Chief's Next Task: Woo Madison Avenue," *Wall Street Journal*, January 17, 2013, at B-1.

9. Douglas MacMillan, "Is Yahoo Chief's Time in the Sun Ending?," *Wall Street Journal*, May 19, 2014, at B-1.

10. Douglas MacMillan, "Yahoo CEO Set to Refresh Turnaround Plan," *Wall Street Journal*, October 20, 2014, at B-6.

11. The course of events may be tracked in the following articles: Douglas MacMillan, "Yahoo's Alibaba Spinoff Faces IRS Setback," *Wall Street Journal*, September 9, 2015, at B-1 (dashing "investors' growing enthusiasm for its Alibaba stake and the CEO's commitment to return billions of dollars to shareholders"); Mariam Gottfried, "For Yahoo, Moment of Truth Approaches," *Wall Street Journal*, October 26, 2015, at C-6; and Douglas MacMillan & Liz Hoffman, "Yahoo Shelves Alibaba Plan," *Wall Street Journal*, December 10, 2015, at B-1.

12. Douglas MacMillan, "Yahoo to Unveil Cost Cuts," *Wall Street Journal*, February 2, 2016, at B-1.

13. *See, e.g.*, Vindu Goel, "Yahoo Ends Expensive Magazine Experiment," *New York Times*, February 18, 2016, at B-3.

14. Mariam Gottfried, "Yahoo Still a Portal to Nowhere," *Wall Street Journal*, September 10, 2015, at C-10.

15. Gottfried, "For Yahoo, Moment of Truth Approaches."

16. Douglas MacMillan, "Yahoo CEO Faces a Morale Challenge," *Wall Street Journal*, November 24, 2015, at B-1.

17. *See* Vindu Goel & Leslie Picker, "Yahoo Takes Formal Step toward a Possible Sale," *New York Times*, February 20, 2016, at B-2; Douglas MacMillan & Dana Mattioli, "Yahoo Review to Exclude CEO," *Wall Street Journal*, February 20, 2016, at B-1 (Yahoo! stock price declined 30 percent and revenues were basically flat in 2015).

18. *See, e.g.*, Mike Snider, "9 Potential Suitors for Yahoo," *USA Today*, February 5, 2016, at 2B.

19. Douglas MacMillan & David Benoit, "Starboard Calls for Yahoo CEO's Ouster," *Wall Street Journal*, January 7, 2016, at B-1 ("Forget turning around Yahoo. Ms. Mayer likely will spend 2016 trying to keep her job and resolve the crisis gripping the company").

20. Robert McMillan, "Executives to Watch in 2016," *Wall Street Journal*, January 4, 2016, at A-10.

21. Vindu Goel & Michael de la Merced, "Yahoo's Sale to Verizon Ends an Era for a Tech Pioneer," *New York Times*, July 25, 2016.

22. Brian Solomon, "Yahoo Sells to Verizon in the Saddest $5 Billion Deal in Tech History," *Forbes*, July 25, 2016, www.forbes.com (visited November 9, 2016).

23. *See* Deepa Seetharaman & Robert McMillan, "Yahoo Probe Prompts Cut in CEO's Pay," *Wall Street Journal*, March 2, 2017, at B-4.

24. McMillan, "Executives to Watch in 2016."

25. Spencer Ante, "IBM's Rometty Gets Blunt with Workers," *Wall Street Journal*, April 25, 2013, at B-1.

26. Ante, "IBM's Rometty Gets Blunt."

27. Spencer E. Ante, "As IBM Disappoints, Rometty Feels the Heat," *Wall Street Journal*, April 17, 2014, at B-4.

28. Robert McMillan & Nathan Becker, "IBM's Revenue Falls but New Products Pick Up," *Wall Street Journal*, January 20, 2016, at B-5 (comments by CFO Martin Schroeter).

29. Robert McMillan, "IBM Profit, Income Slide," *Wall Street Journal*, April 19, 2016, at B-3.

30. Even at the time of her appointment, in April 2009, Carol Bartz's chances for success were next to nil. Ms. Bartz faced a daunting glass cliff, succeeding Yahoo! founder Jerry Yang as the CEO. Mr. Yang, effectively, had painted a target on Ms. Bartz's chest. Nearly singlehandedly, Mr. Yang had caused Yahoo! to spurn an all-cash takeover offer from Microsoft, at $45 billion representing more than twice Yahoo!'s market capitalization, an unheard-of super-premium bid. Yahoo! investors were infuriated that Mr. Yang and his board had blocked the Microsoft offer. *See generally* Jon Fortt, "Yahoo's Taskmaster," *Fortune*, April 16, 2009.

31. Amir Efrati & Joann S. Lublin, "Yahoo Ousts Carol Bartz as CEO," *Wall Street Journal*, September 11, 2011.

32. Shira Ovide & Rachael King, "HP: Will Slimmer Make Stronger?," *Wall Street Journal*, October 7, 2014, at B-1.

33. Dan Gallagher, "Printing Out a New Deal for Hewett-Packard," *Wall Street Journal*, October 7, 2014, at C-10.

34. Rolfe Winkler, "H-P Suffering Separation Anxiety," *Wall Street Journal*, August 23, 2013, at C-8.

35. *See, e.g.*, Drew Fitzgerald & Joshua Jamerson, "Xerox Settles with Shareholder," *Wall Street Journal*, October 29, 2016, at B-3 (spin-off of Conduent, Inc., from Xerox planned for January 2017).

36. Ovide & King, "HP: Will Slimmer Make Stronger?"

37. Don Clark & Tess Stynes, "Hewlett Packard Spinoff to Split Again," *Wall Street Journal*, May 25, 2016, at A-1.

38. Joann Lublin & Ben Worthen, "H-P to Meet Restive Investors," *Wall Street Journal*, February 25, 2015, at B-1 (share price down 62 percent).

39. Gallagher, "Printing Out a New Deal."

40. Robert McMillan, "H-P Makes Breakup Plan Official," *Wall Street Journal*, July 2, 2015, at B-3.

41. Robert McMillan, "H-P to Slash Jobs ahead of the Breakup," *Wall Street Journal*, September 16, 2015, A-1.

42. Rachel King, "Whitman to Exit HPE after Big Overhaul," *Wall Street Journal*, November 27, 2017, at B-1.

43. *See* Dana Mattioli, David Benoit, & Drew FitzGerald, "Xerox to Split, Reversing Strategy," *Wall Street Journal*, January 29, 2016, at A-1; Drew FitzGerald & David Benoit, "Xerox Chief Defends Split," *Wall Street Journal*, January 30, 2016, at B-1.

44. Drew Fitzgerald & Joshua Jamerson, "Xerox's Burns to Drop CEO Role after Split," *Wall Street Journal*, May 21, 2016, at B-1.

Chapter 5. Once upon a Time

1. "Women hold up half of the sky" is an ancient Chinese proverb. *See* Kristof and WuDunn, *Half the Sky*, title page; Caroline Clarke Hayes, "Computer Science: The Incredible Shrinking Woman," in Misa, *Gender Codes*, at 28.

2. *See generally* Beyer, *Grace Hopper*; Marx, *Grace Hopper*; and Williams, *Grace Hopper*.

3. *See* https://awards.acm.org (visited February 6, 2016). The Association of Computing Machinery (ACM) originated the award in the 1970s.

4. Thomas J. Misa, "Gender Codes: Defining the Problems," in Misa, *Gender Codes*, at 4.

5. Hayes, "Computer Science: The Incredible Shrinking Woman," at 32.

6. Thomas Haigh, "Masculinity and the Machine Man: Gender in the History of Data Processing," in Misa, *Gender Codes*, at 64.

7. *See, e.g.*, Strom, *Beyond the Typewriter*.

8. Haigh, "Masculinity and the Machine Man," at 56.

9. Misa, "Gender Codes: Defining the Problems," at 5.

10. Haigh, "Masculinity and the Machine Man," at 53.

11. Haigh, "Masculinity and the Machine Man," at 54.

12. Corinna Schlombs, "A Gendered Job Carousel: The Employment Effects of Computer Automation," in Misa, *Gender Codes*, at 83.

13. Schlombs, "A Gendered Job Carousel," at 79.

14. Nathan Ensmenger, "Making Programming Masculine," in Misa, *Gender Codes*, at 130–31.

15. Ensmenger, "Making Programming Masculine," at 131.

16. Haigh, "Masculinity and the Machine Man," at 56.

17. Haigh, "Masculinity and the Machine Man," at 67.

18. Kanter, *Men and Women of the Corporation*, at 210–16. *See also* Branson, *No Seat at the Table*, chap. 9, "Women and Minorities in Organizations: The Legacy of Tokenism," at 109–23.

19. Kanter, *Men and Women of the Corporation*, at 210.

20. Novelist Chimamanda Ngozi Adichie, *New Republic*, quoted in *Week*, February 12, 2016, at 17, www.theweek.com.

21. *See* Branson, *No Seat at the Table*, at 121.

22. Kanter, *Men and Women of the Corporation*, at 223.
23. Kanter, *Men and Women of the Corporation*, at 316.
24. *See, e.g.*, Branson, *No Seat at the Table*, at 117.
25. Misa, "Gender Codes: Defining the Problems," at 11.
26. Margolis & Fisher, *Unlocking the Clubhouse*, at 4.
27. Margolis & Fisher, *Unlocking the Clubhouse*, at 104.
28. Ensmenger, "Making Programming Masculine," at 137.
29. Branson, *The Last Male Bastion*, at 123.
30. *See, e.g.*, Bell, *Women-Led Firms and the Gender Gap*.
31. After the H-P board dismissed her, Ms. Fiorina sang the opposite tune: every slight she suffered was because she was a woman.
32. Hayes, "Computer Science: The Incredible Shrinking Woman," at 45–46.
33. Margolis & Fisher, *Unlocking the Clubhouse*, at 65.
34. Eric S. Raymond, *The New Hacker's Dictionary*, 3rd ed., at 629 (Cambridge: MIT Press, 1996).
35. Margolis & Fisher, *Unlocking the Clubhouse*, at 70.
36. Ensmenger, "Making Programming Masculine," at 128.
37. Ensmenger, "Making Programming Masculine," at 129.
38. Jane Abate, "The Pleasure Paradox: Bridging the Gap between Popular Images of Computing and Women's Historical Experiences," in Misa, *Gender Codes*, at 215.
39. Thomas J. Misa, "Gender Codes: Lessons from History," in Misa, *Gender Codes*, at 258.
40. Losse, *The Boy Kings*, at 4–5.
41. Losse, *The Boy Kings*, at 5.
42. Haigh, "Masculinity and the Machine Man," at 61.
43. Recounted by Ensmenger, "Making Programming Masculine," at 115.
44. Ensmenger, "Making Programming Masculine," at 116.
45. Schlombs, "A Gendered Job Carousel," at 115.
46. Losse, *The Boy Kings*, at 42.
47. Jeffrey Yost, "Programming Enterprise: Women Entrepreneurs in Software and Computer Services," in Misa, *Gender Codes*, at 232.
48. Margolis & Fisher, *Unlocking the Clubhouse*, at 6 (Carnegie Mellon University).
49. Margolis & Fisher, *Unlocking the Clubhouse*, at 73.
50. Margolis & Fisher, *Unlocking the Clubhouse*, at 2.

Chapter 6. Basic Education

1. Hayes, "Computer Science: The Incredible Shrinking Woman," at 25. By way of comparison, as of 2010, in mathematics women had achieved near parity (45 percent). Hayes, "Computer Science," at 32.
2. Kiesler & Sproull, *Computing and Change on Campus*, at 194.
3. Margolis & Fisher, *Unlocking the Clubhouse*, at 17.
4. Margolis & Fisher, *Unlocking the Clubhouse*, at 17–18.
5. Margolis & Fisher, *Unlocking the Clubhouse*, at 19.

6. Ensmenger, "Making Programming Masculine," at 137.
7. Margolis & Fisher, *Unlocking the Clubhouse*, at 49, 55.
8. Margolis & Fisher, *Unlocking the Clubhouse*, at 59.
9. American Association of University Women, *Tech Savvy*, at 10.
10. Margolis & Fisher, *Unlocking the Clubhouse*, at 19.
11. AAUW, *Tech Savvy*, at 42.
12. Margolis & Fisher, *Unlocking the Clubhouse*, at 22, 26.
13. AAUW, *Tech Savvy*, at 30.
14. Margolis & Fisher, *Unlocking the Clubhouse*, at 25.
15. AAUW, *Tech Savvy*, at 34.
16. Margolis & Fisher, *Unlocking the Clubhouse*, at 20, quoting Professor Sherry Turkle.
17. Vance, *Elon Musk*, at 60; Margolis & Fisher, *Unlocking the Clubhouse*, at 20, quoting Professor Sherry Turkle.
18. Margolis & Fisher, *Unlocking the Clubhouse*, at 33.
19. Margolis & Fisher, *Unlocking the Clubhouse*, at 34.
20. Columbia Pictures, *A League of Their Own* (1992) (starring Tom Hanks and Geena Davis).
21. AAUW, *Tech Savvy*, at 7.
22. AAUW, *Tech Savvy*, at 25.
23. AAUW, *Tech Savvy*, at 23.
24. *See also* chapter 5.
25. Kathryn Bartol & William Aspray, "The Transition from the Academic World to the Workplace: A Review of the Relevant Research," in Cohoon & Aspray, *Women and Information Technology*, 337, at 385.
26. AAUW, *Tech Savvy*, at 53 ("Consider single-sex after school and other extracurricular activities for girls").
27. Lindsay Gelman, "Harvard B-School Targets Recruitment from Women's Colleges," *Wall Street Journal*, April 8, 2015, at B-6.
28. Lecia Barker & William Aspray, "The State of Research on Girls and IT," in Cohoon & Aspray, *Women and Information Technology*, 3, at 25.
29. Misa, "Gender Codes: Defining the Problem," at 10.
30. Margolis & Fisher, *Unlocking the Clubhouse*, at 3.
31. Margolis & Fisher, *Unlocking the Clubhouse*, at 130.
32. *See generally* Seymour & Hewitt, *Talking about Leaving*, at 38–40 ("Weed-out classes also have the unintended effect of driving out some highly talented students").
33. Margolis & Fisher, *Unlocking the Clubhouse*, at 91.
34. Margolis & Fisher, *Unlocking the Clubhouse*, at 92.
35. AAUW, *Tech Savvy*, at 16.
36. AAUW, *Tech Savvy*, at 14.
37. AAUW, *Tech Savvy*, at 14–15.
38. *See generally* Lin & Hiss, *Teachers and Peers*.

39. *See* Robin Wilson, "Scholarly Education's Publishing Gap," *Chronicle of Higher Education,* October 22, 2012, at A-3 (female faculty account for only 30 percent of the scholarly articles published).

40. Hayes, "Computer Science: The Incredible Shrinking Woman," at 25.

41. Margolis & Fisher, *Unlocking the Clubhouse,* at 63 (Carnegie Mellon University Department of Computer Science).

42. Margolis & Fisher, *Unlocking the Clubhouse,* at 134.

43. AAUW, *Tech Savvy,* at 59.

44. AAUW, *Tech Savvy,* at 18–19.

45. AAUW, *Tech Savvy,* at 19 (teachers must move from being the "sage on the stage" to the "guide by your side").

46. AAUW, *Tech Savvy,* at 21.

47. Margolis & Fisher, *Unlocking the Clubhouse,* at 51.

48. AAUW, *Tech Savvy,* at 29.

49. AAUW, *Tech Savvy,* at 30.

50. Susan Pinker, "Can Students Have Too Much Tech?," *New York Times,* January 30, 2015, at A-21.

51. Pinker, "Can Students Have Too Much Tech?," reviewing studies by Duke University economics professors Jacob Vigdor and Helen Ladd, who tracked the academic progress of one million middle school children.

52. Pinker, "Can Students Have Too Much Tech?"

53. Abate, "The Pleasure Paradox," at 220.

54. Margolis & Fisher, *Unlocking the Clubhouse,* at 37.

55. Margolis & Fisher, *Unlocking the Clubhouse,* at 71–72.

56. Margolis & Fisher, *Unlocking the Clubhouse,* at 132 (recommendation #2).

Chapter 7. The Distant Past and Near Future

1. Seymour & Hewitt, *Talking about Leaving,* at 15.

2. Seymour & Hewitt, *Talking about Leaving,* at 3. The volume, published in 1997, predates use of the term STEM (science, technology, engineering, mathematics), instead using the precursor term, SME (science, mathematics, engineering), which includes and frequently refers to computer science and IT subjects.

3. Seymour & Hewitt, *Talking about Leaving,* at 19. These statistics were provided to the authors by the Higher Education Research Institute at UCLA. Seymour & Hewitt, *Talking about Leaving,* at 24.

4. Seymour & Hewitt, *Talking about Leaving,* at 39.

5. Seymour & Hewitt, *Talking about Leaving,* at 12.

6. Seymour & Hewitt, *Talking about Leaving,* at 7, 9.

7. Seymour & Hewitt, *Talking about Leaving,* at 236.

8. Seymour & Hewitt, *Talking about Leaving,* at 256–57.

9. Seymour & Hewitt, *Talking about Leaving,* at 239.

10. Seymour & Hewitt, *Talking about Leaving,* at 17.

11. *See, e.g.,* O'Brien, *Albert Camus.*

12. Strom, *Beyond the Typewriter*, at 4, 6.
13. The Nineteenth Amendment to the U.S. Constitution, prohibiting U.S. citizens from being denied the right to vote on account of sex, was ratified and became effective in 1920.
14. Eaton & Stevens, *Commercial Work and Training for Girls*, at 198–99.
15. Strom, *Beyond the Typewriter*, at 67.
16. Taylor, *The Principles of Scientific Management*.
17. Strom, *Beyond the Typewriter*, at 73.
18. Solomon, *In the Company of Educated Women*, at 60.
19. Strom, *Beyond the Typewriter*, at 69.
20. Harrington Emerson, "The Twelve Principles of Efficiency," 41 *Engineering Magazine*, at 811–12 (August 1911).
21. Strom, *Beyond the Typewriter*, at 76–77.
22. Bureau of the Census, "Occupational Trends Data," cited in Strom, *Beyond the Typewriter*, at 83.
23. Strom, *Beyond the Typewriter*, at 93–94.
24. A leading work is Wellington, *Be Your Own Mentor*, published at a time when Ms. Wellington was president and CEO of Catalyst. *See, e.g.*, *Be Your Own Mentor*, at 3: "The single most important reason why . . . the equally talented men tend to rise higher than the equally talented women is that most men have mentors and women do not." *See also* G. E. Clements, F. J. Lunding, & D. S. Perkins, "Everyone Who Makes It Has a 'Mentor,'" *Harvard Bus. Rev.*, July–August 1978, at 89.
25. *See, e.g.*, Branson, *No Seat at the Table*, at 82–85.
26. Strom, *Beyond the Typewriter*, at 284.
27. Losse, *The Boy Kings*, at 43.
28. Rebecca Mead, "Learning Different: Silicon Valley Disrupts Education," *New Yorker*, March 7, 2016, 36, at 38 (quoting AltSchool founder Max Ventilla).
29. Mead, "Learning Different," at 39.

Chapter 8. Women to Try Harder

1. Sandberg, *Lean In*.
2. Sandberg, *Lean In*, at 148.
3. Belinda Luscombe, "Confidence Woman: Facebook's Sheryl Sandberg and Her Mission to Reboot Feminism," *Time*, March 18, 2013, 34, at 37 (cover story).
4. Sheryl Sandberg, quoted in Luscombe, "Confidence Woman," at 37.
5. Sandberg, *Lean In*, at 8.
6. Anna Holmes, "Maybe You Should Read the Book: The Sheryl Sandberg Backlash," *New Yorker*, March 2, 2013 (concluding paragraph, penultimate sentence).
7. Maureen Dowd, "Pompom Girl for Feminism," op-ed, *New York Times*, March 23, 2013 ("[Sandberg] has a grandiose plan to become the PowerPoint Piper in Prada ankle boots reigniting the women's revolution. Betty Friedan for the digital age").
8. Sandberg, *Lean In*, at 9.

9. *Cf.* Dowd, "Pompom Girl for Feminism": "Sandberg has co-opted the vocabulary and romance of a social movement not to sell a cause, but herself."

10. Ann Belser, "Sheryl Sandberg's Privileged Manifesto . . . 'Lean In' Seems Ignorant of the Reality of a Less Than Privileged Life," *Pittsburgh Post-Gazette*, March 17, 2013, at B-5.

11. Sandberg, *Lean In*, at 28.

12. Charlotte Allen, "Do as I Do, Not as I Say," *Wall Street Journal*, March 13, 2013, at A-13.

13. *See* Allied Freightways v. Cholfin, 91 N.E. 2d 765 (Mass. 1950).

14. Branson, *No Seat at the Table*, at 183.

15. Branson, *No Seat at the Table*, at 183. There should be, however, one exception to the disregard of feminine stereotypes, as discussed in the following note.

16. Branson, *No Seat at the Table*, at 183–84.

> Equality gives way when there exists a universal and defined biological trait that requires equality to assume a secondary role. And there is only one such trait—child bearing. . . . Any woman who goes on the "mummy track" for any reason (more lengthy maternity leave, part-time employment when children are entering school, Fridays off when children are younger). . . . No adverse inferences are to be drawn. No negative or neutral ("Damning with faint praise") evaluation practices will be tolerated.

17. *See, e.g.*, Khurana, *Searching for the Corporate Savior.*

18. Sandberg, *Lean In*, chap. 4, "It's a Jungle Gym, Not a Ladder," at 52.

19. Sandberg, *Lean In*, at 53.

20. "Don't Leave before You Leave" is the title of the book's chapter 7. Sandberg, *Lean In*, at 92.

21. Sandberg, *Lean In*, at 95.

22. Sandberg, *Lean In*, chap. 5, "Are You My Mentor?," at 64.

23. Wellington, *Be Your Own Mentor*, at 3 ("The single most important reason why . . . the equally talented men tend to rise higher than women is that most men have mentors and most women do not").

24. *See, e.g.*, Branson, *No Seat at the Table*, at 82:

> Mentors can provide many of the same things that members of an informal network may provide. They may advise on how to close a deal, handle a particular personnel problem, or put out this or that brush fire. They may also provide broader strategic advice or information: suggesting possible steps for the woman executive ultimately to reach her goal or examining the political landscape within the company and advising the woman executive how to deal with it to move through and beyond the ranks of middle management.

25. Sandberg, *Lean In*, at 65.

26. Sandberg, *Lean In*, at 53. On women as mentors, *see, e.g.*, Peggy Drexler, "The Tyranny of the Queen Bee," *Wall Street Journal*, March 2, 2014, at C-1 ("Women who reached positions of power were supposed to be mentors to those who followed—

but something is amiss in the professional sisterhood"; "80% of bullying by female bosses is directed at other women"). *See also* Hollands, *Same Game, Different Rules*, at 5–19.

27. Sandberg, *Lean In*, at 58.
28. Sandberg, *Lean In*, at 62.
29. Branson, *The Last Male Bastion*.
30. *Cf.* Rhode, *Women and Leadership*, at 25: "Popular how-to books for women give contradictory advice. Some counsel women to act like men."
31. Lean In & McKinsey & Co., "Women in the Workplace," September 2016.
32. Sandberg, "Women Are Leaning In."
33. Sandberg, "Women Are Leaning In."
34. *See, e.g.*, bibliography in Branson, *No Seat at the Table*, at 225–31.
35. Jody Greenstone Miller, "The Real Women's Issue: Time," *Wall Street Journal*, March 9, 2013, at C-3.
36. *See* Deepa Seetharaman, "Entrepreneur Who Headed Web Survey Firm Dies at 47," *Wall Street Journal*, May 4, 2015, at B-6.
37. *See generally* Deepa Seetharaman, "Sandberg Rethinks Parts of 'Lean In,'" *Wall Street Journal*, July 21, 2016, at B-1.

Chapter 9. Mandatory Quota Laws

1. Michael D. Goldhaber, "Bye-Bye Boys' Club," *American Lawyer*, June 14, 2015, at 23; Rhode & Packel, "Diversity on Corporate Boards."
2. *See, e.g.*, Ulrike Dauer, "Germany Adopts Quotas to End All-Male Boards," *Wall Street Journal*, December 12, 2014, at B-1 (7.4 percent women on supervisory boards, "very low by international standards," and "top female executives are even rarer").
3. James Quinn, "EU Quota for Women on Boards Moves Step Closer after Vote," *Daily Telegraph* (London), November 15, 2013, at B-3 (twenty-seven nations after Brexit).
4. Laurence Norman & Matina Stevis, "European Union Shelves Women Board Quotas," *Wall Street Journal*, November 24, 2012, at B-2 (proposal was for a quota of 40 percent women directors by 2020).
5. *See, e.g.*, R. Shambaugh, "Should U.S. Follow Europe's Lead for Quotas on Boards?," *Huffington Post*, March 19, 2015; Jane Goodhew, New Zealand Minister for Women's Affairs, "Report to the United Nations Committee on Convention on the Elimination of All Forms of Discrimination against Women (CEDAW)," July 18, 2012 (describing firm New Zealand opposition to quota laws or regulations); G. O'Brien, "Women in the Boardroom: Should the U.S. Have Quotas?," *Business Ethics*, August 3, 2011.
6. G20/OECD, *Principles of Corporate Governance*, Article VI, Section E, Subsection 4.
7. Dhir, *Challenging Boardroom Homogeneity*.
8. *See, e.g.*, Rosenblum, "Feminizing Capital," at 61–67.

9. S. Terjesen, R. V. Aguilera, & R. Lorenz, "Legislating a Woman's Seat on the Board: Institutional Factors Driving Gender Quotas for Boards of Directors," 128 *Journal of Business Ethics* 233 (2015). *See also* L. Senden, "The Multiplicity of Regulatory Responses to Remedy the Gender Imbalance on Corporate Boards," 10 *University of Utrecht Law Rev.* 51 (2014) (charting variations in European legislative and regulatory regimes).

10. Rhode, *Women and Leadership*, at 124 & notes 155–56 (citing studies).

11. *See* Bryce Covert, "It's Time to Fix the Very Pale, Very Male Boardroom," *New Republic*, July 8, 2014; John D. Stoll, "Norway's Exemplary Gender Quotas? Just Don't Ask about CEOs," *Wall Street Journal*, May 22, 2014, cited in Rhode, *Women and Leadership*, at 124 & n. 142.

12. Jon Swartz, "USA Today Interview: Facebook's Sheryl Sandberg," *USA Today*, March 12, 2003, at 1.

13. For example, in Canada, the proportion of board seats held by women has risen to approximately 20.8 percent. "One in Five Directors in Canada Are Women," *Toronto Star*, January 13, 2015, www.thestar.com (visited August 26, 2015); Catalyst, "Catalyst Census," at 1 (board membership at 19.2 percent women in United States, 20.8 percent in Canada).

14. *Compare* Pew Research Center, Social and Demographic Trends (female board membership at 9.6 percent in 1995), *with* Catalyst, "Catalyst Census," at 1 (board membership at 19.2 percent women), and Catalyst, *Missing Pieces Report* (20.2 percent) (July 7, 2016). Catalyst's statistics traditionally have been misleading, recording the number of directorships held by women as the number of women directors. The actual number of female bodies is actually less because of two factors. First is the trend toward males, especially male CEOs, not holding board seats at other corporations, or being limited by their companies to one seat. Second, by contrast, the number of "trophy directors" (individuals holding four, five, six, seven, or even eight board seats) has grown dramatically among women. Thus the number of women directors is smaller. *See, e.g.*, Branson, *No Seat at the Table*, at 97.

15. Jill Barad was the first, at least in the modern era, at Mattel in 1997. As late as 2002, after Hewlett-Packard's dismissal of Carleton Fiorina as CEO, the number had dropped to only two female CEOs: Andrea Young at Avon Products and Marion Sandler at Golden West Financial. Branson, *The Last Male Bastion*, at ix. The number began to accelerate with the late 2002 appointments as CEOs of Anne Mulcahy at Xerox and Patricia Russo at Lucent, accelerating to twenty-four today. Thus, as far as women as corporate CEOs are concerned, Ms. Sandberg was incorrect, at least given a slightly longer view.

16. The proportion of board seats held by women in Canada stands at approximately 20.8 percent. "One in Five Directors in Canada Are Women."

17. In Australia, the percentage of directors who are female increased from 8.5 percent in 2010 to 13.8 percent in March 2012, in part due to implementation of an inventive mentoring/sponsorship program by the Australian Institute of Company

Directors, as discussed in chapter 12. More recently, the figure has climbed to 20.8 percent. *See* www.companydirectors.com.au (visited August 26, 2015).

18. *See* Rosenblum, "Feminizing Capital," at 63.

19. Gabrielle Steinhauser, "EU Eyes Quotas for Women on Company Boards," Associated Press, March 5, 2012.

20. European Professional Women's Network, *EPWN Board Women Monitor* (2010), annex 4, "EU Countries: The Choice between Quota Legislation and Corporate Governance Codes: Are Codes and Legislation Impacting Numbers?" (table), www.europeanpwn.net; Steinhauser, "EU Eyes Quotas for Women."

21. Ley Orgánica 3/2007, de 22 Marzo, para la Igualdad Effectiva de Mujeres y Hombres.

22. Julie C. Suk, *Gender Parity and State Legitimacy: From Public Office to Corporate Boards*, SSRN Research Paper No. 1776263 (2011), *Int'l J. of Constitutional Law* (forthcoming); Rosenblum, "Feminizing Capital," at 71.

23. Loi no. 2011–103 du 27 Janvier 2011 relative à la représentation équilibrée des femmes et des homes au sein des conseils d'administration et de surveillance et à l'égalité professionnelle.

24. Report of Madame Brigitte Gresy to the Minister of Labor, June 2009. The 2008 level of women on boards in France was 7.6 percent.

25. *See, e.g.*, Suk, *Gender Parity and State Legitimacy*, at 14.

26. Steinhauser, "EU Eyes Quotas for Women." *Cf.* Liz Bolshaw, "Glass Ceilings Starting to Crack across Europe," *Financial Times*, December 12, 2011 (20.1 percent in France post quota law).

27. *See, e.g.*, Margaretta Neld, "Gender Quotas Would Benefit Sweden's Corporate Boards," The Local: Sweden's News in English, December 8, 2011, www.thelocal.se (last visited January 11, 2016); Niccola Clark, "Getting Women into Boardrooms, by Law," *New York Times*, January 27, 2010 (opposition of G. Rustad in Sweden).

28. *See, e.g.*, Claire Cain Miller, "Women on Boards: Where the U.S. Ranks," *New York Times*, March 10, 2015 ("Germany passed a law last week requiring public companies to give 30 percent of board seats to women").

29. Although the British government opposes a quota law, that opposition did not prevent a government-sponsored study group from releasing a lengthy report that set 25 percent as a goal for achievement by 2016. Julia Werdigier, "In Britain, a Big Push for More Women to Serve on Corporate Boards," *New York Times*, February 25, 2011, at B-6 (discussing report of the Davies Committee; *see generally* chapter 10 of this book).

30. Leonie Lamont, "Time Male Bosses Walked the Talk on Equality," *Sydney Morning Herald*, October 15, 2011. Impatient with their government's inactivity, in some cases dominant shareholders and executives have engaged in self-ordering. In Korea, for instance, "Samsung billionaire chairman Lee Kun-hee wants 10 percent of executive positions to be filled by women by 2020." *See also* Bolshaw, "Glass Ceilings Starting to Crack."

31. Joann Lublin, "Behind the Rush to Add Women to Norway's Boards," *Wall Street Journal*, December 10, 2007, at B-1 ("She spurned about 40 other offers"). By contrast, the new French quota law limits any individual, including a woman director, from service on more than four boards of directors. Darren Rosenblum, "Corporate Governance—Sex and Quotas: A Transnational Perspective, Perspectives on Gender and Business Ethics: Women in Corporate Governance," presentation, School of Law, University of Dayton, February 25, 2011 (notes on file with the author). In Norway, as an upshot of the scramble for talent that followed enactment of the quota law, an elite group of seventy women held three hundred board seats. They were dubbed the "golden skirts." Clark, "Getting Women into Boardrooms, by Law."

32. *See, e.g.,* Lublin, "Behind the Rush" ("rather than comply with the gender law, more than 30 affected companies [in Norway] are going private").

33. *See* Bolshaw, "Glass Ceilings Starting to Crack."

34. "Women on Corporate Boards: *La Vie en Rose*," *Economist*, May 6, 2010.

35. Branson, *No Seat at the Table*, at 93–94.

36. Lublin, "Behind the Rush"; Rosenblum, "Feminizing Capital."

37. Martin Johnston, "Report: Women Lose Boardroom Seats," *New Zealand Herald*, November 8, 2010.

38. Maria Slade, "Gender Quotas for NSX Panned," *New Zealand Herald*, March 21, 2010. By contrast, the Australian minister for the status of women has stated that the option of mandatory quotas in Australia is "still on the table." Ruth Williams, "Crunching the Gender Numbers," *Sydney Morning Herald*, October 15, 2011.

39. Werdigier, "In Britain, a Big Push for More Women."

40. *See* Goodhew, "Report to the United Nations Committee"; O'Brien, "Women in the Boardroom"; and Shambaugh, "Should U.S. Follow Europe's Lead?"

41. Ranked fourth by *Global Finance Magazine*, after Qatar, Luxembourg, and Singapore. *See* www.gfmag.com (visited August 14, 2015).

42. *See, e.g.,* www.data.worldbank.org, Norway data (visited August 14, 2015).

43. Transparency International CPI Index ranks Norway fifth, after Denmark, New Zealand, Finland, and Sweden, in these qualities. www.transparency.org (visited August 14, 2015).

44. *See, e.g.,* Shambaugh, "Should U.S. Follow Europe's Lead?"; and O'Brien, "Women in the Boardroom."

45. *See generally* Ezra Klein, "The Unpopular Mandate," *New Yorker*, June 25, 2012; Jarrad Saffren, "Why Americans Hate the Affordable Care Act: It's the Individual Mandate," Syracuse.com, November 18, 2014 ("Basically, Americans do not so much oppose the Affordable Care Act as the individual mandate"). *See also* Grace-Marie Turner, "For Many Americans, Opposition to Obama Care Has Become Personal," *Forbes*, March 23, 2015.

46. Branson, *No Seat at the Table*, at 97.

47. Chief operating officer, chief information officer, chief legal officer, chief compliance officer, chief marketing officer, and chief financial officer.

48. *See, e.g.,* Pareto, "On the Equilibrium of Social Systems," at 1288.

49. Rawls, *A Theory of Justice.*

50. *See, e.g.,* Rawls, *Justice as Fairness.*

51. *See generally* Joann Lublin, "How Many Board Seats Make Sense?," *Wall Street Journal,* January 21, 2016, at B-1. Seventy-seven percent of S&P 500 corporations now limit the number of board seats their directors are permitted to hold. Four is the most frequently encountered limit, but 20 percent of the corporations set the number at three seats. Just 5 percent of S&P 500 directors hold four or more seats. Only five directors occupy six or more seats, down from an amazing 308 directors in 2005.

52. Not all trophy directors are men. Patricia Russo, former CEO of Alcatel Lucent, sits on five boards and chairs one of them (Hewlett Packard Enterprises, Merck, Alcoa, General Motors, and Kravis Kolberg & Roberts). In fact, a troubling trend is that while the number of male trophy directors has been declining for some years, the number of female trophy directors has been rapidly increasing. *See, e.g.,* Branson, *No Seat at the Table,* at 100–101. One implication of the trend is a crowding out of younger equally qualified director aspirants.

Chapter 10. Certificate and Pledge Programs

1. *Principles of the Charter, Talent to the Top* (May 2008), www.biac.org (visited November 2016).

2. Monitoring Committee, *Talent to the Top, Summary Monitoring Report* (2010), www.scp.nl (visited December 2014).

3. Several of those, such as Royal Dutch Shell and Unilever, had dual domiciles (the Netherlands and the United Kingdom, for example) at that time but today no longer do.

4. European Professional Women's Network, *EPWN Board Monitor,* at 29 (4th ed. 2010) (bar chart), www.europeanpwn.net (visited December 2014).

5. Dorine Rouillon, "Where Are the Women: Quota Legislation to Increase the Percentage of Women on French Boards of Directors," at 14 (unpublished seminar paper, University of Washington, 2010) (on file with the author) (French boards of directors).

6. Rouillon, "Where Are the Women," at 12.

7. Yann Le Gales, "Quotas: 13 Leaders Judge the Law That Requires Women in Administrative Councils," *Le Figaro,* January 19, 2012. Laurence Parisot later became controlling shareholder and CEO of the Parisot Group, a large retailer of home furnishings. *See also* "Laurence Parisot: From Door-Making to Director," *Financial Times,* January 27, 2006.

8. Le Gales, "Quotas: 13 Leaders Judge the Law."

9. Steinhauser, "EU Eyes Quotas for Women." *See also* James Kanter, "Europe to Study Quotas for Women on Corporate Boards," *New York Times,* March 5, 2012, at B-3.

10. Steinhauser, "EU Eyes Quotas for Women."

11. *See generally* Damon Hack, "The HFL Spells Out New Hiring Guidelines," *New York Times*, December 9, 2003; David Anderson, "Minority Candidates Should Get a Fairer Shake," *New York Times*, December 16, 2003; and William C. Rhoden, "Working with the NFL on Diversity," *New York Times*, December 23, 2009 (extension of Rooney Rule to hiring of assistant football coaches).

12. Mike Freeman, "The Rooney Rule 10 Years Later: It's Worked . . . Usually," *Bleacher Report*, October 24, 2013.

13. The NFL recently extended the Rooney Rule to include a woman finalist for executive position vacancies at NFL franchises. Kevin Patra, "Roger Goodell: NFL Creating a Rooney Rule for Women," Around the NFL, February 6, 2016, www.nfl.com (visited February 13, 2017).

14. "Report of the Equality and Human Rights Commission," at 3 (UK 2011), www.equalityhumanrights.com (visited March 13, 2017).

15. Cranfield School of Management, "Female FTSE Report 2010," cited at Davies Report 11.

16. *Women on Boards*, at 2 (2011) (hereinafter cited as Davies Report).

17. Davies Report, at 18–20.

18. *See* Julia Kollewe & Shane Hickey, "A Third of Boardroom Positions Should Be Held by Women, UK Firms Are Told," *Guardian*, October 29, 2015.

19. Comments of Nora Senior, reported in Kollewe & Hickey, "A Third of Boardroom Positions."

20. Comments of Krystyna Nowak, of executive search firm Norman Broadbent, and Fiona Wolf, former Lord Mayor of London, reported in Kollewe & Hickey, "A Third of Boardroom Positions." The comparable figures for the United States are 25.1 percent but only 6.2 percent for the information technology industry.

21. Davies Committee, *Women on Boards—Davies Review: Five Year Summary*, October 29, 2015 (hereinafter cited as *Five Year Summary*), at 28 ("We recommend . . . increasing the voluntary target for women's representation on Boards of FTSE 350 companies to a minimum of 33% to be achieved in the next five years").

22. *See generally* Cadbury, *Corporate Governance and Leadership*.

23. Hamilton, *Corporations in a Nutshell*, 8.6 at 190, 11.1 at 269.

24. The U.S. answer is for public corporations to appoint a senior director as the "lead director," who under the bylaws would have the power to convene the board for certain tasks or in the event of inability of the formal designated board chair.

25. It is important to note that despite whatever media types may lead the public to believe, traditionally it is state law that governs most aspects of corporate governance, including these ones. Branson, *Corporate Governance*, at v. The traditional state law monopoly has been modified by congressional enactments, namely, the Sarbanes-Oxley Act (2002) and the Dodd-Frank Act (2010), but in ways not directly relevant here.

26. Branson, "Some Suggestions from a Comparison," 715 & n. 150.

27. Davies Committee, *Five Year Summary*.

28. Davies Committee, *Five Year Summary*, at 6.

29. Davies Committee, *Five Year Summary*, at 7.
30. Davies Committee, *Five Year Summary*, at 12.
31. Davies Committee, *Five Year Summary*, at 10, 11 (table).
32. Davies Committee, *Five Year Summary*, at 10 (graphic).
33. Davies Committee, *Five Year Summary*, at 11.

Chapter 11. Comply or Explain Regimes

1. Public Company Accounting and Investor Protection Act, Pub. L. 107–204 (2002).
2. Wall Street Reform and Investor Protection Act, Pub. L. 11–203 (2010).
3. *See, e.g.*, Pinto & Branson, *Understanding Corporate Law* §5.08(A), at 141–46 (Sarbanes-Oxley) & §5.08(B), at 146–47 (Dodd-Frank).
4. G20/OECD, *Corporate Governance Code* (most recent edition approved, OECD, Paris, September 4–5, 2015), www.oecd.org (visited April 30, 2016). The OECD currently has thirty-four member nations, including most but not all of the developed countries of the world. The OECD is known, *inter alia*, for its anti-corruption initiatives.
5. Swedish Corporate Governance Board, "Statement on Comply or Explain Approach," www.corporategovernanceboard.se (visited April 30, 2016).
6. Australian Stock Exchange (ASX), *Corporate Governance Principle and Recommendations*, at 3 (3rd ed. 2012) ("If the board of a listed company considers that a Council recommendation is not appropriate . . . it is entitled not to adopt it. If it does so . . . it must explain why it has not adopted the recommendation—the 'if not, why not' approach").
7. Dodd-Frank Act § 952.
8. *See* SEC Release No. 33-9330 (June 20, 2012) (directing exchanges to adopt comply or explain rules). The exchanges then did so. *See, e.g.*, SEC Release No. 34-68635 (January 2013) (NYSE); Release No. 34–640 (January 2013) (NASDAQ).
9. Rhode, *Women and Leadership*, at 125 & n. 160.
10. *See, e.g.*, Singapore Stock Exchange (SGX), Listing Rule 701; White Page, Ltd., *Hong Kong Corporate Governance—A Practical Guide*, at 14 (2014).
11. The leading piece is Skeel, "Shaming in Corporate Law."
12. "While substantive regulation is unusual in federal securities legislation, which in most other areas is based on the philosophy of full disclosure rather than substantive control, such regulation is not unknown." Hamilton, "Some Reflections on Cash Tender Offer Legislation," at 275.
13. *See, e.g.*, Douglas Branson, "Teaching Comparative Corporate Governance: The Importance of Soft Law and International Institutions," 34 *Georgia L. Rev.* 669, 671–72 (2000). Another exercise is to break soft law into "hard" soft law (stock exchange listing requirements, for example), on the one hand, and "soft" (or softer) soft law requirements (the purely aspirational elements of a corporate governance code, for instance), on the other.

14. Actually, Dean Christopher Langdell of the Harvard Law School began using the case method, presumably along with Socratic dialogue, in approximately 1870. Those are the bedrocks of modern legal education.

15. ICAEW, "When Is Comply or Explain the Right Approach?," www.icaew.com (visited April 30, 2016).

16. Jo Iwasaki, "Comply or Explain—Is It Sustainable?," www.financialdirector.co.uk (visited April 28, 2016).

17. Financial Reporting Council, *The UK Corporate Governance Code*, at 4 (2010), www.frc.org.uk (visited April 28, 2016).

18. Financial Reporting Council, *The UK Corporate Governance Code*, at 13 (emphasis added).

19. In Australia and New Zealand, I have also spoken widely on the subject, including at the University of Melbourne, to the Melbourne Bar, the University of Technology–Sydney, Bond University, the University of Adelaide, and the Australian Corporate Law Teachers Conference as well as at the University of Auckland School of Law and School of Business and the New Zealand Law Reform Commission.

20. Australian Stock Exchange, *ASX Corporate Governance Code*, at 11 (2d ed. 2010).

21. "Companies should disclose in each annual report the proportion of women employees in the whole organi[z]ation, women in senior management, and women on the board." Australian Stock Exchange, *ASX Corporate Governance Code*, at 11.

22. ASX, "Improving Gender Diversity," Listed @ ASX Newsletter, September 2012, www.asx.com.au (visited April 26, 2016).

23. Australian Stock Exchange, *ASX Corporate Governance Code*, at 11 (3rd ed. 2014) (Recommendation 1.5).

24. ASX, "Progress on Gender Diversity Continues," media release, April 10, 2014.

25. *See* NYSE Euronext, *Listed Company Manual*, Section 303 (2009).

26. Iwasaki, "Comply or Explain—Is It Sustainable?"

27. Jim Collins, *Good to Great: Why Some Companies Make the Leap While Others Don't*, at 165 (New York, Harper Business, 2001). The complete quotation is as follows:

> We expected good-to-great leaders would begin by setting a new vision and strategy. . . . We found instead that they *first* got the right people on the bus, got the wrong people off the bus, and the right people on the right seats—and *then* they figured out where to drive it.

Chapter 12. Mentoring and Sponsorship

1. *See, e.g.*, Wellington, *Be Your Own Mentor*; Clements, Lunding, & Perkins, "Everyone Who Makes It Has a 'Mentor,'" at 89; Ellen Sherberg, "The Art of Mentoring," *Pittsburgh Business Times*, April 1, 2016, at 8 ("Why Mentoring Makes All the Difference").

2. Sherberg, "The Art of Mentoring," at 9 (quoting Sabrina Houser, CEO, Big Brothers/Big Sisters, Albany, NY).

3. A recent piece is John T. Thompson & Karen R. West, "How Directors Can Mentor Potential CEOs," 38 *Directors & Boards*, No. 5, at 44 (2014).

4. *See, e.g.*, the books cited in chapter 8.

5. Bartol & Aspray, "The Transition from the Academic World to the Workplace," at 390–91.

6. Sherberg, "The Art of Mentoring," at 9 (quoting Carol Lowe, CFO, Sealed Air Corp., Charlotte, NC).

7. Wellington, *Be Your Own Mentor*, at 3 (at the time she wrote, Ms. Wellington was CEO of Catalyst, Inc.).

8. *See, e.g.*, Joann Lublin, "How to Cope When Your Mentor Moves On," *Wall Street Journal*, November 23, 2016, at B-5 (devoid of advice save to enlist the departing mentor in finding a replacement mentor).

9. Kanter, *Men and Women of the Corporation*, at 188.

10. *See, e.g.*, Branson, *No Seat at the Table*, at 83.

11. Kanter, *Men and Women of the Corporation*, at 182–83.

12. The author served as a consultant to Nike on the relationships between and among Nike Worldwide, its "Geographies," and its 139 (more or less) subsidiaries. Nike utilizes a matrix form of organization.

13. Mirembe Birigwa & Karen Sumberg, "Lack of Sponsorship Keeps Women from Breaking through the Glass Ceiling," *Harvard Bus. Review*, January 2011.

14. Karen L. Proudford, "Isn't He Delightful? Creating Relationships That Get Women to the Top," quoted in Rhode, *Women and Leadership*, at 64 & n. 92.

15. Kanter, *Men and Women of the Corporation*, at 184.

16. Quoted in Rivers & Barnett, *The New Soft War on Women*, at 22–23.

17. Rivers & Barnett, *The New Soft War on Women*, at 23–24.

18. Williams, "Crunching the Gender Numbers"; Teresa Oio, "Women Groomed in the Art of Smashing the Glass Ceiling," *Australian*, January 25, 2011.

19. ASX, "Chairmen's Mentoring Program 2011 Q & As," Australian Institute of Company Directors, March 7, 2011.

20. *See, e.g.*, Amanda Saunders, "AICD Program Aims to Get More Women on Boards," *Western Australian* (Perth), April 23, 2010.

21. Oio, "Women Groomed in the Art of Smashing the Glass Ceiling."

22. *See* www.companydirectors.com.au (visited August 26, 2015).

23. Carla Harris, vice-chair, global wealth management, Morgan Stanley, quoted in Hilary Burns, "You Can't Do It Alone," *Pittsburgh Business Times*, August 21, 2016, at 10.

24. Rhode, *Women and Leadership*, at 28.

25. Harris, quoted in Burns, "You Can't Do It Alone," at 10.

26. Harris, quoted in Burns, "You Can't Do It Alone," at 10.

27. Rivers & Barnett, *The New Soft War on Women*, at 21. *See also* Liz Rappaport, "Networking Isn't Easy for Women, but It's Crucial," *Wall Street Journal*, September 30, 2015, at R-8 (men are more likely than women to have sponsors).

28. Hewlett, *Forget a Mentor, Find a Sponsor*.

29. Rivers & Barnett, *The New Soft War on Women*, at 231.

30. The Catalyst website previews future programs. *See generally* www.catalyst.org (visited April 25, 2016).

31. Janice Ellig & Irene Lang, "Gender Balance on Boards: Five Steps to Achieve Success," 39 *Directors & Boards*, No. 2, 28, at 29 (2015) (Irene Lang is a former president of Catalyst).

32. *See generally* Boardroom Bound, www.boardroom-bound.com (visited March 30, 2015).

33. *See generally* DirectWomen, www.directwomen.org.

34. *See* WomenCorporateDirectors, www.womencorporatedirectors.com (visited March 30, 2015).

35. Joyce Gannon, "Women Still Not Sitting in Many of Region's Board Seats," *Pittsburgh Post-Gazette*, June 5, 2016, at G-1.

36. Ellig & Lang, "Gender Balance on Boards," at 29.

37. *See* Bosch, "The Changing Face of Corporate Governance," at 281 ("Not only has it become universal for the offices of chairman and CEO to be held by different people . . . but it is now accepted as good practice that the CEO of a company should not go on to become chairman of the company").

38. *See, e.g.*, Douglas M. Branson, "Initiatives to Place Women on Corporate Boards of Directors: A Global Snapshot," 37 *Journal of Corporation Law* 793, 809 & n. 124 (2012) (University of Iowa).

39. Catalyst, "Catalyst Taps Global Leaders to Champion Board-Ready Women, Gender Diversity on U.S. Corporate Boards," press release, May 12, 2016 (selection of class "in progress").

40. Ellig & Lang, "Gender Balance on Boards," at 29.

41. *See* Joann Lublin, "Group Vows to Advance More Women at Work," *Wall Street Journal*, December 7, 2016, at B-5.

Chapter 13. Mandatory Disclosure

1. Business Roundtable v. SEC, 905 F.2d 406 (D.C. Cir. 1990).

2. SEC Exchange Act Release No. 34–9052 (December 16, 2009) (announcing a February 28, 2010, effective date).

3. SEC Regulation S-K, 17 C.F.R. section 229.10 (2010).

4. SEC Regulation S-K, 17 C.F.R. section 229.407(c)(2)(vi) (2010).

5. Bryce Holzer, "Proxy Statement Diversity," University of Washington School of Law (Seattle), 2010 (on file with the author).

6. Proctor & Gamble, Inc., 2010 Definitive 14A (proxy statement).

7. Dhir, *Challenging Boardroom Homogeneity*, at 190.

8. Rhode, *Women and Leadership*, at 126.

9. *See, e.g.*, Black, "Stalled: Gender Diversity on Corporate Boards."

10. *See, e.g.*, Rhode, *Women and Leadership*, at 126: "In their proxy statement, Berkshire Hathaway and Warren Buffett disclose that, '[o]ur nominating committee does not seek diversity, no matter how defined.'"

Chapter 14. Proposals for STEM Education

1. Eleanor Chute, "Central Catholic Launches Major Capital Campaign," *Pittsburgh Post-Gazette*, December 3, 2014, at B-1 ("Central is working to raise $27 million, including $12 million for the STEM building").

2. *See, e.g.*, Chevron, Inc., advertisement, *Pittsburgh Post-Gazette*, December 7, 2014, at A-8 (half-page ad):

   Many energy jobs require science, technology, engineering and math (STEM). So we're helping students get those skills. Chevron has invested over a million dollars to support STEM-education programs at . . . middle schools and high schools in the tri-state area. Helping provide curricula, lab equipment and teacher-training. We want kids to know what science can do. And what they can do with it.

3. S. Kusic, "Chevron Spearheads 3-State STEM Initiative," *Pittsburgh Business Times*, October 24, 2014, at 14.

4. Alexandra Ossola, "Is the U.S. Focusing Too Much on STEM?," *Atlantic*, December 2014, www.theatlantic.com (visited November 15, 2016).

5. Gary Ford, "The Stem Focus," *Pittsburgh Post-Gazette*, November 15, 2013, at A-12.

6. *See* www.nsf.gov (visited May 8, 2016) ("Increasing the participation and advancement of women in academic science and engineering careers").

7. Natalie Sportelli, "Best Value STEM Colleges for Women," *Forbes*, March 29, 2013, www.forbes.com (visited May 6, 2016).

8. Sportelli, "Best Value STEM Colleges for Women."

9. By way of example, undergraduate fees at Case Western Reserve University are $62,387 per year (books and supplies not included); at Carnegie Mellon University, $67,980 per year; and at Stanford University, $62,801. *See* www.case.edu; www.cmu.edu; and www.tuition.startclass.com (Stanford University) (visited May 13, 2106).

10. At the University of California Davis, the costs to a resident is $34,232 per year and to nonresidents, $59,031 per year. *See* www.ucdavis.edu (visited May 13, 2016). At the University of Michigan, costs to residents are $24,401 per year and to nonresidents, $54,030 per year. *See* www.umich.edu (visited May 13, 2016).

11. "The 10 Best Colleges for Females in STEM Fields," *Fortune*, May 10, 2015, www.bestcollegesonline (visited May 6, 2016).

12. Bartol & Aspray, "The Transition from the Academic World to the Workplace," at 383.

13. Karen Chapple, "Foot in the Door, Mouse in Hand: Low Income Women, Short-Term Training Programs, and IT Careers," in Cohoon & Aspray, *Women and Information Technology*, 439, at 439.

14. Melissa Korn & Lauren Weber, "Coding Schools Tone Down Rosy Job Script," *Wall Street Journal*, May 21, 2014, at B-8.

15. *See* Korn & Weber, "Coding Schools Tone Down Rosy Job Script," table: Dev Bootcamp, 9 weeks, $12,200; Flatiron School, 12 weeks, $12,000; General As-

sembly, 12 weeks, $11.500; Hackbright Academy, 10 weeks, $15,000; and Software Guild, 12 weeks, $13,500. Despite the high costs, "the number of code-school graduates is doubling every year," accounting for 18,000 graduates from "91 full-time coding 'boot camps' in the US" (2016 statistics). Christopher Mims, "Code-School Boot Camps Offer Fast Track to Jobs," *Wall Street Journal*, February 2, 2017, at B-1. "Code schools aren't the place to go if you want to be a 'rock star' at Google or Facebook. These [program] are designed to turn out junior developers."

16. *See generally* Bartol & Aspray, "The Transition from the Academic World to the Workplace," at 383, Table 13.2.

17. It has been estimated that in 2013 there were forty-five or more single-sex colleges for women left in the United States. *See, e.g.,* Laurence Biemiller, "Armed with Data, a Women's College Tries a Transformation," *Chronicle of Higher Education*, February 4, 2013.

18. Full text of responses on file with the author.

19. *See* www.stem.stkate.edu (visited April 30, 2016).

20. The results are from a study the *Wall Street Journal* conducted. *See* Douglas Belkin, "Freshmen Are Picking Their Majors Earlier," *Wall Street Journal*, March 20, 2015, at A-3.

21. Cappelli, *Will College Pay Off?*

22. *See also* John Cassidy, "College Calculus: What Is the Real Value of College Education?," *New Yorker*, September 7, 2015, 80, at 83.

23. Daniel Gelernter, "Why I'm Not Looking for Computer Science Majors," *Wall Street Journal*, August 29, 2015, at A-9.

24. Lewis, *The Flash Boys*, at 133.

Chapter 15. The Industry's Answer

1. Bartol & Aspray, "The Transition from the Academic World to the Workplace," at 407.

2. June Kronholz, "Visa Window Opens: Scramble Is About to Begin," *Wall Street Journal*, March 28, 3007, www.rit.edu (visited March 13, 2017).

3. *See* King, "IBM CEO Offers Advice to Trump."

4. Jodi Kantor, "A Brand New World in Which Men Ruled: Instead of Narrowing Gender Gaps, the Technology Industry Created Vast New Ones," *New York Times*, December 23, 2014.

5. Laura Meckler & Laura Stevens, "H-1B's Future Causes Rift," *Wall Street Journal*, February 10, 2017, at B-4.

6. Meckler & Stevens, "H-1B's Future Causes Rift."

7. Peter Elstrom & Saritha Rai, "The Trump-Valley Fight Starts to Take Shape," *Bloomberg Business Week*, February 6, 2017, at 26.

8. Elstrom & Rai, "The Trump-Valley Fight Starts to Take Shape," at 27.

9. *See, e.g.,* U.S. Citizenship and Immigration Services, "Understanding H-1B Requirements," www.uscis.gov (visited May 12, 2016).

10. *See, e.g.*, Sarah K. Baruah, Joseph D. Roman, & Dennis Yablosky, "More H-1B Visas, Please," *Pittsburgh Post-Gazette*, April 28, 2016, at A-11.

11. Henry J. Chang, "Immigrant Intent and the Dual Intent Doctrine," *American Lawyer*, 2011, www.americanlawyer.com (visited December 1, 2017).

12. *See* www.travel.state.gov (2011 statistics).

13. *See* www.travel.state.gov/visa (2012).

14. *See, e.g.*, Meckler & Stevens, "H-1B's Future Causes Rift" ("The H-1B visa program . . . each year grants 65,000 visas for skilled workers and another 20,000 for people with advanced degrees").

15. *See, e.g.*, Newley Purnell, "Indian Workers Fear H-1B Curbs," *Wall Street Journal*, February 28, 2017, at B-1 ("Demand is so high for H-1B visas that for the last four years the number of applications has surpassed the entire fiscal year's 85,000 supply").

16. Paul Roberts, "It's High Time to End the Abuse of H-1B Visas," *Wall Street Journal*, May 11, 2016, at A-10.

17. Hearings on Immigration Reforms Needed to Protect Skilled American Workers, Senate Judiciary Committee, March 17, 2015 (prepared statement of Sen. Chuck Grassley).

18. Donald Trump, quoted in Lauren Collins, "The Model American," *New Yorker*, May 9, 2016, 22, at 23.

19. "Workers Betrayed by Visa Loopholes," editorial, *New York Times*, June 15, 2015.

20. Available at www.uscis.gov (visited March 10, 2017).

21. Thirty-one percent of the sample of applications tested misrepresented the bachelor's degree education level requirement. USCIS, "H-1B Fraud and Compliance Assessment," September 2008.

22. *See, e.g.*, David Alba, "Investigation Reveals Silicon Valley's Abuse of Immigrant Tech Workers," *Wired*, November 4, 2014.

23. Betty Lou Raskin, "A Woman's Place Is in the Home," *New York Times*, April 9, 1959, cited in Collins, *When Everything Changed*, at 6.

24. Bartol & Aspray, "The Transition from the Academic World to the Workplace," at 407.

25. Joseph Guzzardi, "U.S. Workers Are Displaced by Those with H-1B Visas," *Pittsburgh Post-Gazette*, May 4, 2016, at A-6.

26. Nick Wingfield & Mike Isaac, "Tech Industry Frets over Visa Program," *New York Times*, January 28, 2017, at A-10.

27. Christopher Mims, "U.S. Tech Faces Homegrown Threat," *Wall Street Journal*, February 3, 2017, at B-4.

28. Wingfield & Isaac, "Tech Industry Frets over Visa Program."

29. Wingfield & Isaac, "Tech Industry Frets over Visa Program."

30. Wingfield & Isaac, "Tech Industry Frets over Visa Program."

31. Mims, "U.S. Tech Faces Homegrown Threat."

32. Mims, "U.S. Tech Faces Homegrown Threat."

33. Len Lindenmeyer, Letter to the Editors, *Wall Street Journal*, February 9, 2017, at B-4.

34. James Phelan, Letter to the Editors, *Wall Street Journal*, February 9, 2017, at B-4.

Chapter 16. Leavening STEM Education

1. *See, e.g.*, Barker & Aspray, "The State of Research on Girls and IT," at 18.

2. *See, e.g.*, Goldin & Katz, *The Race between Education and Technology* (technological progress has greatly increased the demand for skilled workers, including in information technology, and the American educational establishment has failed to meet the challenge by supplying enough graduates who can carry out the tasks a high-tech economy requires).

3. Cassidy, "College Calculus," at 83.

4. *See generally* Cappelli, *Will College Pay Off?*

5. Branson, *The Last Male Bastion*.

6. The twenty-second, Ursula Burns, became CEO of Xerox while the book was in final stages of the editorial process.

7. One refrain advice books often repeat for women in business is to forgo having children or to limit yourself to a single child. A counterintuitive finding from studying the women who had reached the CEO position by 2010 was that nineteen of the twenty-one women CEOs *The Last Male Bastion* categorizes have children. *See* Branson, *The Last Male Bastion*, at 199. If Ursula Burns, who became CEO of Xerox while the book was in press, is factored in (she has two children) the total becomes forty-four children for twenty women CEOs (out of twenty-two total). Several of these women CEOs have three children. The late Brenda Barnes, then CEO of Sara Lee, spoke for many female CEOs when she stated that rather than her children needing her, she needed her children, to give her unconditional love and a sense of perspective at the same time.

8. They were Jill Barad at Mattel, Pat Russo at Lucent, Mary Sammons at Rite Aid, Laura Sen at BJ's Wholesale Club, and Anne Mulcahy at Xerox.

9. *See, e.g.*, Lindsay, *The MBA Slingshot for Women*.

10. Lindsay Gellman, "Why More People Want an MBA," *Wall Street Journal*, October 1, 2015, at B-5 (statistics from Graduate Management Admission Council).

11. Gellman, "Why More People Want an MBA."

12. Laurie Weingart, "Forging Stronger Connections for the Tepper School," *Pittsburgh Business Times*, December 11, 2015, at 15.

13. Indra Nooyi at PepsiCo, Irene Rosenfeld at Kraft (now at Mondelez), and Meg Whitman, now at Hewlett Packard Enterprises.

14. Ossola, "Is the U.S. Focusing Too Much on STEM?"

15. Thomas Friedman, "Trump Voters, Just Hear Me Out," *Pittsburgh Post-Gazette*, November 4, 2016, at A-17.

16. Evan Osnos, "Kaine Country," *New Yorker*, October 24, 2016, 40, at 47.

17. Ossola, "Is the U.S. Focusing Too Much on Stem?," quoting Drew, *STEM the Tide*.

18. Teitelbaum, *Falling Behind?*
19. *Cf.* Kim S. Nash, "Payouts, Risks Grow for Tech Leaders," *Wall Street Journal*, October 8, 2015, at B-7. A countertrend is that corporations are becoming extremely reliant upon and are promoting to officer status certain persons with deep tech backgrounds. Firms are increasing pay and status for chief information officers, or CIOs, as the position frequently is titled.
20. Larry Page, quoted in Vance, *Elon Musk*.

Chapter 17. Paying Close Attention to the Pool Problem

1. Branson, *No Seat at the Table*, at 90–92, 105.
2. *See, e.g.,* Branson, *No Seat at the Table*, at 105–6. That is not to gainsay experience in, say, the not-for-profit sector. Women and men managing health care organizations or United Way chapters may be managing organizations with budgets in the hundreds of millions of dollars.
3. Ron Lumbra & Victoria Reese, "Getting Board Diversity out of the Doldrums," 40 *Directors & Boards*, No. 4, 70, at 70 (October 2016).
4. The number of women trophy directors increased from thirty in 2001 to seventy-nine in 2005 and continued to increase thereafter. Branson, *No Seat at the Table*, at 96; *see also* 98–101 (example of leading women trophy directors).
5. *See* chapter 1. Studies vary. In another study, figures ranged from 15 percent (S&P 500) to 19 percent (Fortune 500). Rhode, *Women and Leadership*, at 112.
6. Spreadsheets prepared by Jacqueline Jones and Michael Wikoff, Law Fellows, University of Pittsburgh School of Law (on file with the author).
7. *Time*, May 18, 2013. The accompanying article was Belinda Luscombe, "Don't Hate Her Because She's Successful," *Time*, May 18, 2013.
8. *See, e.g.,* "Facebook COO Urges Graduates to Be Resilient," *Oakland News*, May 14, 2016 (degree from University of California–Berkeley); *Grindstone*, April 27, 2012 (Spelman College). *See also* "Sandberg Named Chief Marshal at Harvard Graduation," *Harvard Gazette*, April 20, 2016.
9. *See, e.g.,* Vinda Goel & Randal Archibald, "David Goldberg, Silicon Valley Executive, Died of Head Trauma, Mexican Official Says," *New York Times*, May 4, 2015; Marco della Cava, "Death the Result of Head Trauma While Exercising," *USA Today*, May 5, 2015.
10. Rolfe Winkler, "For Google CEO, a $70 Million Package," *Wall Street Journal*, March 27, 2015, at B-2.
11. *See, e.g.,* James Bandler, "HP Should Have Listened to Its CFO," *Fortune*, November 20, 2012.
12. *See* Iris Dorbian, "Oracle's CFO Safra Catz Is Highest-Paid Woman Exec," *CFO Magazine*, July 29, 2014, www.cfo.com.
13. Kanter, *Men and Women of the Corporation*.
14. *See, e.g.,* Branson, *No Seat at the Table*, chap. 5, "Bully Broads, Iron Maidens, Queen Bees and Ice Queens," at 65–74; Douglas M. Branson, "Pathways for

Women to Senior Management Positions and Board Seats: An A to Z List," 2012 *Michigan St. L. Rev.* 1555, 1562–63 (bully broad), 1570–71 (iron maiden/ice queen).

15. *See, e.g.,* Maggie Wilderotter, Lulu Wang, Eileen Kamerick, Bonnie Gwin, & Donna James, "The Power of Three," 35 *Director & Officer*, No. 5, at 22 (2011).

16. Vicki W. Kramer, Alison M. Konrad, & Sumru Erkut, "Critical Mass on Corporate Boards: Why Three or More Women Enhance Corporate Governance," 11 *Wellesley Center for Women Rep.* 3 (2006).

17. Lisa L. Broome, John M. Conley, & Kimberly D. Krawiec, "Does Critical Mass Matter? Views from the Boardroom," 34 *Seattle U. L. Rev.* 1049, 1050 (2011).

18. Broome et al., "Does Critical Mass Matter?," at 1080.

19. Other articles by the same three authors seem further intent on inflicting serious damage to enlarging the female role in corporate leadership. *See, e.g.,* Lisa Broome, John M. Conley, & Kimberly Krawiec, "Dangerous Categories: Narratives of Corporate Board Diversity," 89 *N.C. L. Rev.* 759 (2011).

20. The case may well be different if a newcomer was the nominee of an activist investor, or nominee of a potential takeover threat, but those hypotheticals are far removed from the situation under discussion.

21. Congresswoman Barbara Mikulski in 1978, quoted in Collins, *When Everything Changed*, at 241.

22. Charles Dickens, *Hard Times: For These Times* Enriched Classics ed. (1854; New York, Simon and Schuster, 2017).

23. *See, e.g.,* Boris Grayberg & Deborah Bell, "2012 Board of Directors Survey," cited in Rhode, *Women and Leadership*, at 118 & n. 85.

24. Christine Silva, Nancy M. Carter, & Anna Beninger, "Good Intentions? Imperfect Execution? Women Get Fewer of the 'Hot Jobs' Needed to Advance," at 5–7 (Catalyst, Inc., New York, 2012).

25. *See* Rhode, *Women and Leadership*, at 59.

26. Branson, *The Last Male Bastion*, at 134–39.

27. Rhode, *Women and Leadership*, at 115.

28. "Who's on Boards 2105," 40 *Director & Officer*, No. 4, 73 (October 2016).

29. Lumbra & Reese, "Getting Board Diversity out of the Doldrums," at 71.

30. *See also* cover issue, "Recruiting the Digital Director," 37 *Director & Officer*, No. 2, at 21 (2013).

31. University of Southern California president C. L. Max Nikias, quoted in Douglas Belkin, "How USC Became a Leader in Recruiting Minorities," *Wall Street Journal*, May 31, 2016, at R-7.

Chapter 18. Enlarging the Pool

1. *See, e.g.,* Branson, *No Seat at the Table*, at 51.

2. Hewlett, *Off-Ramps and On-Ramps. See also* Foster & Hewlett, *Off-Ramps and On-Ramps Revisited*.

3. Dhir, *Challenging Boardroom Homogeneity*, at 38–39.

4. Dhir, *Challenging Boardroom Homogeneity*, at 41.

5. *See, e.g.*, Branson, *The Last Male Bastion*, chap. 6, "Go Where They Aren't," at 65 (over the preceding twenty-five to thirty years, barriers to progress for women have disappeared almost entirely, surprising at industries once viewed as male-dominated, such as oil and gas, electric utilities, paint and chemicals, and the like).

6. An excellent exposition on the phenomenon is Belkin, "The Opt-Out Revolution," *New York Times Magazine*, October 23, 2003, at 42.

7. Dhir, *Challenging Boardroom Homogeneity*, at 45.

8. Dhir, *Challenging Boardroom Homogeneity*, at 46 (footnote omitted).

9. Branson, *No Seat at the Table*, at 90–92.

10. Slaughter, *Unfinished Business*, at 105.

11. *See generally* Belkin, "The Opt-Out Revolution," at 42.

12. Branson, *No Seat at the Table*, at 40.

13. Reported in Belkin, "The Opt-Out Revolution," at 44.

14. *See, e.g.*, Branson, *No Seat at the Table*, at 39.

15. Crittenden, *The Price of Motherhood*, at 13.

16. California Employment Development Department, "About Paid Family Leave," www.edd.ca.gov (visited January 26, 2017) (also termed California Temporary Disability Insurance, or CTDI).

17. Rachel Emma Silverman, "Deloitte Says It Will Offer Leave for a Range of Caregiving Needs," *Wall Street Journal*, September 9, 2016, at B-6.

18. California Employment Development Department, "About Paid Family Leave."

19. *See, e.g.*, Adrienne Lu, "Paid Family Leave Now the Law in New Jersey," *Philadelphia Inquirer*, May 3, 2008.

20. Danielle Paquette, "Family Leave Pushed by U.S. Labor Department," *Pittsburgh Post-Gazette*, August 5, 2016, at A-4.

21. Rachel Emma Silverman, "Family Leave Gaining Momentum in the Workplace," *Wall Street Journal*, January 6, 2016, at B-4.

22. Public Law 103–3, 29 U.S.C. § 2611 (1993).

23. Silverman, "Family Leave Gaining Momentum."

24. Lori M. Goler, Facebook Global Head of People, announcement, www.facebook.com (visited January 13, 2017).

25. "Retail: IKEA Becomes Paid-Leave Pioneer," *Week*, December 16, 2016, at 36.

26. Silverman, "Deloitte Says It Will Offer Leave."

27. "Retail: IKEA Becomes a Paid-Leave Pioneer."

28. Elissa Goodman & Catherine Saint Louis, "Maternity Leave? It's More Like a Pause," *New York Times*, July 22, 2012, Sunday Styles section, at 1.

29. Silverman, "Family Leave Gaining Momentum."

30. *See, e.g.*, Slaughter, *Unfinished Business*; Williams & Dempsey, *What Works for Women at Work*; Williams, *Reshaping the Work-Family Debate*; Crittenden, *The Price of Motherhood*. The classic is, of course, Williams, *Unbending Gender*.

31. Families and Work Institute, "Generations and Gender in the Workplace," New York, 2004.

32. Rhode, *Women and Leadership*, at 34.
33. Rhode, *Women and Leadership*, at 20.
34. Debra Cassens Weiss, "Jack Welch: Women Take Time Off for Kids at Their Peril," *American Bar Assoc. Journal*, July 16, 2009.
35. An example is IBM's alumni network. *See, e.g.,* Georgia Wells, "Tech Firms Help Get Women Back on Track," *Wall Street Journal*, April 11, 2016.
36. Belkin, "The Opt Out Revolution," at 55.
37. *See* Wells, "Tech Firms Help Get Women Back on Track."
38. Kanter, *Men and Women of the Corporation*, at 305.
39. Miller, "The Real Women's Issue: Time."
40. Slaughter, *Unfinished Business*, at 16.
41. Rhode, *Women and Leadership*, at 75.
42. Shipman & Kay, *Womenomics*, at 204.
43. Deloitte leads in many ways, including its implementation of a broad fully paid family leave program (Silverman, "Deloitte Says It Will Offer Leave") and in being the first to name a female CEO. *See* Lillian Cunningham, "Deloitte Is First of 'Big 4' Firms to Name a Female CEO," *Washington Post*, February 11, 2015.
44. Charlie Wells & Joann Lublin, "Flexibility Is Great But," *Wall Street Journal*, September 30, 2015, at R-6.
45. Rhode, *Women and Leadership*, at 72.

Chapter 19. Measuring What You Intend to Manage and Ways to Manage It

1. *See, e.g.,* Rick Wartzman, "How to Consult Like Peter Drucker," *Forbes*, September 11, 2012, www.forbes.com (visited December 1, 2017).
2. Daniel Johnson, "The Lessons of His Life," review of Peter F. Drucker, *The Last of All Possible Worlds and the Temptation to Do Good*, Wall Street Journal, July 21, 2016, at A-11.
3. Drucker, *The Ecological Vision*, at 75–76.
4. Drucker, *The Practice of Management*, at 12.
5. Quoted in Jeff Shore, "These Ten Peter Drucker Quotes May Change Your World," *Entrepreneur Magazine*, www.entrepreneur.com September 16, 2014.
6. Drucker, *Managing for Results*.
7. Rich Karlgaard, "Drucker on Leadership," *Forbes*, November 19, 2004, www.forbes.com (visited June 1, 2016).
8. Shone, "These Ten Peter Drucker Quotes."
9. Ellig & Lang, "Gender Balance on Corporate Boards," at 29.
10. Branson, in *No Seat at the Table*, at 32–33, recounts the Hopkins story.
11. Ann Hopkins v. Price Waterhouse, 920 F.2d 967, 970 (D.C. Cir., 1990), *quoting* 109 S. Ct. 1775, 1782 (1989).
12. Collins, *When Everything Changed*, at 315.
13. 920 F.2d 967, at 970-71 (italics in court of appeals opinion).
14. Susan Adams, "Making a Female-Friendly Workplace," *Forbes*, April 3, 2010.

15. Adams, "Making a Female-Friendly Workplace."
16. *See, e.g.*, Edmund Tadros & Agnes King, "Deloitte, KPMG Most Female-Friendly Accountants," *Financial Review*, November 10, 2015 (20 percent at KPMG) (Australia).
17. The 2006 rankings were: "Deloitte's percentage of women partners, principals and directors is currently 19.3 percent, surpassing that of KPMG (16.8 percent), Pricewaterhousecoopers (16.8 percent), and Ernst & Young (13.5 percent)." Deloitte & Touche, press release, December 20, 2006, www.prnewswire.com (visited June 3, 2016).
18. "2015 Best Public Accounting Firms for Women," June 2, 2015, www.afwa.org (visited June 3, 2016).
19. Peter J. Reilly, "How to Shatter the Public Accounting Glass Ceiling," *Forbes*, April 24, 2013.
20. Cunningham, "Deloitte Is First of 'Big 4' Firms to Name a Female CEO."
21. An early and influential work was Eisenberg, *The Structure of the Corporation*.
22. *See, e.g.*, SEC Schedule 14A, Item 7(d)(2) (requiring disclosures regarding the nominating committee, nominations, and elections).
23. Branson, *No Seat at the Table*, at 181.
24. *See, e.g.*, Branson, *No Seat at the Table*, at 66–67; Kanter, *Men and Women of the Corporation*, at 236; Hollands, *Same Game, Different Rules*, at xxvi.
25. Collins, *When Everything Changed*, at 294–95.
26. Collins, *When Everything Changed*, at 295 (internal quotation marks omitted).
27. Deloitte & Touche, press Release, December 20, 2006.
28. *See* Adams, "Making a Female-Friendly Workplace" (appointment of Antoinette Leatherberry to the position in consulting division).

Chapter 20. Adopting a Version of the Rooney Rule

1. The Steeler franchise has been in the Rooney family's hands continuously since the franchise was granted and the team formed in 1933.
2. *See, e.g.*, Rhode, *Women and Leadership*, at 127.
3. Ashley Fox, "How the Rooney Rule Succeeds and Where It Fails," *ESPN Magazine*, May 14, 2015, www.espn.go.com (visited June 28, 2016).
4. Travis Waldron, "The NFL Will Implement a 'Rooney Rule' for Women," *Huffington Post*, February 4, 2106. NFL front office positions, such as legal counsel and community relations director, are currently held 22 percent by women.
5. Tom Vanden Brook, "Pentagon Proposal on 'Rooney Rule' for Minority Officers Raising Internal Concerns," *USA Today*, April 1, 2016 (noting the "lack of minorities in key jobs such as aide-de-camp and military assistant to senior leaders, . . . slots often springboards to higher ranks").
6. Discussed in this chapter.
7. Rhode, *Women and Leadership*, at 122. Professor Rhode is a faculty member at Stanford University School of Law.
8. Fox, "How the Rooney Rule Succeeds," at 3.

9. Quoted in Warren Waren, "An Update on the Rooney Rule: The NFL, Facebook, and Universities," *Racism Review*, February 8, 2016, www.racismreview.com (visited June 30, 2016).

10. Fox, "How the Rooney Rule Succeeds," at 5.

11. Aaron Kasinitz, "NFL Rooney Rule Hasn't Fixed Black Coaching Issue Even as It Turns to Women," *Penn Live*, February 5, 2016, www.pennlive.com (visited June 30, 2016).

12. In 2013 the league considered and rejected such an expansion of the rule's applicability, albeit without permanently closing the door to such a modification. *See* Steve Wyche, "Rooney Rule Will Not Be Extended to Coordinators," NFL Network, March 20, 2013 (internal quotation marks omitted).

13. Fox, "How the Rooney Rule Succeeds," at 1.

14. Fox, "How the Rooney Rule Succeeds," at 5.

15. Quoted in Jessica Guynn, "Facebook Turns to NFL Playbook to Fix Diversity Problem," *USA Today*, June 18, 2015. *See* also Michelle Quinn, "Will Facebook Become More Diverse under the Rooney Rule?," Silicon Beat, June 18, 2015, www.siliconbeat.com (visited June 30, 2016).

16. *See* Jessica Guynn, "Diversity Takes Center Stage at Microsoft Annual Meeting," *USA Today*, December 3, 2014.

17. Laura Lorenzetti, "What Pinterest Is Learning from the Pittsburgh Steelers about Diversity," *Fortune*, July 30, 2015.

18. Courtney Seiter, "7 Lessons from Facebook, Pinterest, and Google on Building Diverse Teams," Fast Company, November 24, 2015, at 5, www.fastcompany.com (visited June 30, 2016).

19. Lorenzetti, "What Pinterest Is Learning from the Pittsburgh Steelers," at 2.

20. Emily Peck, "Pinterest Is Not Messing Around in Diversity," *Huffington Post*, January 7, 2016.

21. Seiter, "7 Lessons from Facebook," at 6.

22. Peck, "Pinterest Is Not Messing Around," at 2.

23. Losse, *The Boy Kings*, at 4–5.

24. Sarah Frier, "Facebook Starts Its Rooney Rule to Increase Diversity on Tech," *Bloomberg Business Insider*, June 17, 2015, www.bloomberg.com (visited June 30, 2016).

25. *See* Laura M. Holson & Nick Bitton, "Facebook's Royal Wedding," *New York Times*, May 25, 2012.

26. *See, e.g.*, Deepa Seetharaman, "Facebook Is to Test the Rooney Rule Approach to Hiring," *Wall Street Journal*, July 17, 2015.

27. Richard Feloni, "Facebook Is Using the Same Approach the NFL Took to Increase Diversity in the League," *Business Insider*, January 24, 2016, www.businessinsider.com (visited January 28, 2017).

28. Valentina Zarya, "Why Is the 'Rooney Rule' Suddenly Tech's Answer to Hiring More Women?," *Fortune*, August 10, 2015, www.fortune.com (visited June 20, 2016).

29. Seiter, "7 Lessons from Facebook," at 8.
30. Statement of Intel CEO Brian M. Krzanich, "Our Goal at Intel," www.intel.com (visited June 30, 2016).
31. *See generally* Intel, Inc., "A Brighter Future Requires Bolder Steps," 2016, www.intel.com (visited June 30, 2016).
32. Davey Alba, "Intel Isn't Diverse Enough and It Knows It," *Wired*, February 3, 2016.

Chapter 21. Theoretical Feminist Views

1. A partial list would include the following:
   - Susan Adams, *The New Rules of Success for Women* (2000).
   - Esther Wachs Book, *Why the Best Man for the Job Is a Woman* (2000).
   - Donna Brooks & Lynn Brooks, *Seven Secrets of Successful Women* (1999).
   - Catalyst, *Advancing Women in Business* (1998).
   - Nina DiSesa, *Seducing the Boys' Club* (2008).
   - Gail Evans, *Play Like a Man, Win Like a Woman* (2000).
   - Carol Gallagher, *Going to the Top* (2000).
   - Pamela Gilberd, *The Eleven Commandments of Wildly Successful Women* (1996).
   - Harvard Business Review Books, *Reach for the Top* (1994).
   - Pat Heim & Susan Golant, *Hardball for Women* (rev. ed. 2005).
   - Pat Heim & Susan Golant, *Smashing the Glass Ceiling* (1995).
   - Sylvia Ann Hewlett, *Off-Ramps and On-Ramps* (2007).
   - Linda Hirshman, *Get to Work* (2006).
   - Jean Hollands, *Same Game, Different Rules* (2000).
   - Kelly Johnson, *Skirt! Rules for the Workplace* (2008).
   - Anthony Stith, *Breaking the Glass Ceiling* (1998).
   - Sheila Wellington, *Be Your Own Mentor* (2001).
2. Mara H. Washburn & Susan G. Miller, "Still a Chilly Climate for Women in Technology: A Case Study," in Fox, Johnson, & Rosser, *Women, Gender and Technology*, 60, at 64.
3. Deborah G. Johnson, introduction to *Women, Gender and Technology*, 1, at 2.
4. Winner, *The Whale and the Reactor*.
5. Citizens United v. Federal Elections Commission, 558 U.S. 310 (2010) (corporations are persons for purposes of the First Amendment, guaranteeing them the same free speech rights and rights to donate to and participate in the political process as flesh-and-blood individuals have). *Cf.* Burwell v. Hobby Lobby Stores, Inc., 200 U.S. 321 (2014) (courts and legislators may look behind the corporate veil, treating corporations differently depending upon what lawmakers discern as differences in owners' religious views). The two decisions seem irreconcilable.
6. Sue V. Rosser, "Using the Lenses of Feminist Theories to Focus on Women and Technology," in Fox, Johnson, & Rosser, *Women, Gender and Technology*, at 14. Much of the material that follows draws heavily from Ms. Rosser's work.
7. *See* Heidi Hartmann, "The Unhappy Marriage of Marxism and Feminism," in Sargent, *Women and Revolution*, at 1.

8. Rosser, "Using the Lenses of Feminist Theories," at 19.

9. *See, e.g.*, Wester, *Sharing Women's Work*; Ynestra King, "The Ecology of Feminism and the Feminism of Ecology," in Plant & Kelly, *Healing the Wounds*, at 18–28.

10. *See* Rosser, "Using the Lenses of Feminist Theories," at 22.

11. Two relevant works are Easlea, *Fathering Masculinity*; and Merchant, *The Death of Nature*.

12. An adherent of this view is Tong, in *Feminist Thought*. An older work espousing such a view is Beauvoir, *The Second Sex*.

13. *See* K. Sorenson, "Toward a Feminized Technology? Gendered Values in the Construction of Technology," 22 (1) *Social Studies of Science* 5, at 10 (1992).

14. Rosser, "Using the Lenses of Feminist Theories," at 29.

15. MacKinnon, *Feminism Unmodified*.

16. Rosser, "Using the Lenses of Feminist Theories," at 29–30.

17. Cockburn, *Male Dominance and Technological Change*, at 132.

18. Rosser, "Using the Lenses of Feminist Theories," at 33.

19. *See, e.g.*, Rosser, "Using the Lenses of Feminist Theories," at 38–40.

20. Millar, *Cracking the Computer Code*, at 200.

21. Rosser, "Using the Lenses of Feminist Theories," at 38.

22. Hawthorne & Klein, *Cyber Feminism*.

23. Early works include Fuentes & Ehrenreich, *Women in the Global Factory*; and Mitter, *Common Fate, Common Bond*.

24. *See, e.g.*, Harding, *Is Science Multicultural?*; Williams & Chrisman, *Colonial Discourse and Post-Colonial Theory*, at 1–20.

25. Branson, *No Seat at the Table*, at 183–84.

26. Reported in Piper Fogg, "Female Professors Assail Remarks by Harvard's President, Who Says It's All a Misunderstanding," *Chronicle of Higher Education*, January 19, 2005, at 3.

27. *See, e.g.*, "Sexism at Harvard," *Business Week*, February 28, 2005, at 100 (provable differences between the sexes are at least three in number, including visuospatial skills, variability in intellectual skills, and interests in core subjects).

28. Dave Shiflett, "Penalizing the Palefaces," *Wall Street Journal*, April 10, 2016, reviewing King, *Redskins*.

Chapter 22. Reforming the Gaming Industry

1. Monica Anderson, "Views on Gaming Differ by Race, Ethnicity," Pew Research Center, December 17, 2015, www.pewresearch.org (visited June 30, 2016).

2. *Compare* Malathi Nayak & Liana Baker, "A Look at the $78 Billion Video Games Industry," Reuters Factbox—Technology News, June 1, 2012, www.reuters.com (visited March 5, 2013) *with* "IBIS World Industry Report Q8611: Global Movie Production and Distribution," at 4 (October 2012).

3. Ben Fritz, "Warner Bros.' Savior: Video Games," *Wall Street Journal*, October 12, 2015, at B-1.

4. *CBS Evening News*, December 7, 2014, notes on file with the author.

5. Jackie Wong, "Nintendo's Share Price Inflation Is No Pokemon Bubble," *Wall Street Journal*, July 25, 2016, at C-6.

6. Wong, "Nintendo's Share Price Inflation." *See also* Takashi Mochizuli & Sarah Needleman, "Pokemon Game Jolts Nintendo," *Wall Street Journal*, July 12, 2016, at B-1.

7. Jonathan Soble, "Pokemon Go, with Tie In, Makes It Home to Japan," *New York Times*, July 23, 2016, at B-3. As to the tie-in, Nintendo struck a deal with McDonald's Japanese affiliate to make its 2,900 stores in Japan special Pokemon game locations.

8. James Surowiecki, "One-Hit Wonders," *New Yorker*, March 17, 2015, at 23.

9. Miriam Gottfried, "'Grand Theft Auto' Doesn't Make Take-Two's Stock a Steal," *Wall Street Journal*, October 2, 2013, at C-16.

10. Dan Gallagher, "Activision's Game Still Isn't Over," *Wall Street Journal*, February 13, 2017, at B-10.

11. Robert Scherrer, "How to Raise a Scientist in the Xbox Age," *Wall Street Journal*, December 15, 2015, at A-15. Professor Scherrer is chair of the department of physics at Vanderbilt University.

12. *See generally* Kevin Kelly, "Getting Girls into the Game: Designing and Marketing Games for Female Players," Joy Stick, March 21, 2008, http://archives.org (visited December 2, 2017).

13. *See, e.g.*, Chris Kohler, "Opinion: Why Shovel Ware Is a Good Thing," *Wired*, March 5, 2008.

14. *See generally* Sarah E. Needleman, "Rovio CEO Will Leave after Just One Year," *Wall Street Journal*, December 10, 2015, at B-4.

15. Surowiecki, "One-Hit Wonders."

16. Bryant Harland, "What You Need to Know about Diversity in the U.S. Video Game Industry," October 23, 2014, www.mintel.com (visited January 30, 2017) (statistic from Women's Media Center, *The Status of Women in U.S. Media in 2013*).

17. Entertainment Software Association, "2014 Essential Facts about the Computer Game Industry," www.theesa.com (visited March 6, 2016).

18. *See* www.na.lolesports.com (visited April 10, 2016).

19. "Video Games Have a Diversity Problem That Runs Much Deeper Than Race or Gender," *Guardian*, June 30, 2016, www.theguardian.com (visited January 31, 2017).

20. "Video Games Have a Diversity Problem."

21. Colin Campbell, "How to Tackle Gaming's Lack of Racial Diversity," Polygon, September 16, 2013, www.polygon.com (visited January 20, 2107).

22. *See, e.g.*, Needleman, "Rovio CEO Will Leave."

23. Surowiecki, "One-Hit Wonders."

24. Surowiecki, "One-Hit Wonders."

25. Soble, "Pokemon Go, with Tie-In, Makes It Home."

26. GameStop Corp. (GME) profile, Yahoo! Finance, finance.yahoo.com (visited August 8, 2016).

27. Spencer Jakab, "Tough for GameStop to Level Up," *Wall Street Journal*, August 21, 2014, at C-1 (GameStop's annual earnings growth increased 19 percent per year, on average, over the 2004–2014 decade).

28. "GameStop's shops earn chunky margins by acting as a clearinghouse for used games. . . . Gross margins on pre-owned games are seen at 42% to 48% this year." Jakab, "Tough for GameStop to Level Up."

29. Harland, "What You Need to Know about Diversity in the U.S. Video Game Industry."

30. Harland, "What You Need to Know about Diversity in the U.S. Video Game Industry."

31. "Video Games Have a Diversity Problem."

32. *See, e.g.*, Don Gallagher, "EA Can Still Feel the Force of Star Wars," *Wall Street Journal*, December 14, 2015, at C-6.

33. "Video Games Have a Diversity Problem."

34. Jonathan Krim, "Will Tech Have Its Own NFL Moment?," *Wall Street Journal*, September 26, 2014, Upshot column, at B-1.

35. *See, e.g.*, Aaron Boulding, "Dead or Alive Xtreme Beach Volleyball Review," www.ign.com (visited April 8, 2016).

36. Krim, "Will Tech Have Its Own NFL Moment?"

37. *PC Magazine Dictionary*, www.pcmag.com (visited April 2, 2016).

38. *See generally* Shoshana Kessock, "When Sword and Shield Are Not Enough: Geek Girls and Trolling," www.tor.com (visited April 6, 2016).

39. *See* Jon Robinson, "Life of a Professional Gamer," *ESPN Magazine*, January 3, 2012, www.espn.go.com (visited April 6, 2015).

40. *See* Christopher Mims, "What Tech Firms Can Do to Stop Internet Trolling," *Wall Street Journal*, March 6, 2017, at B-1.

41. Mims, "What Tech Firms Can Do to Stop Internet Trolling."

42. "Bro Culture," Controversy of the Week, *Week*, April 1, 2016, at 6.

43. *See* Helen Lewis, "The Six Most Absurd Booth Babe Moments at CES," *New Statesman*, January 2013, www.newstatesman.com (visited April 7, 2016).

44. *See generally* www.ces.tec.com (visited April 7, 2017).

Chapter 23. Final Observations

1. *See* Hewlett, *Forget a Mentor, Find a Sponsor.*

2. With apologies to columnist George Will for borrowing his metaphors. *See* George Will, "Surging by Design," *Pittsburgh Post-Gazette*, April 8, 2016, at A-11.

3. Lewis Menard, "The Sex Amendment," *New Yorker*, July 21, 2014, 74, at 74.

4. Noted women's rights advocate Gloria Steinem came to prominence with her essay "After Black Power, Women's Liberation," which appeared in 1969.

5. Pew Research Center statistics, www.pewresearch.com (visited April 12, 2017).

6. Rhode, *Women and Leadership*, at 5, citing the Pew Research Center Report.

7. Sandberg, *Lean In.*
8. Belkin, "The Opt-Out Revolution," at 42.
9. Barbara Kellerman, "You've Come a Long Way, Baby—and You've Got Miles to Go," in Rhode, *The Differences "Difference" Makes,* at 55.
10. *See, e.g.,* Rhode, *Women and Leadership,* at 128–29.
11. Quoted in Kaplan, *The Singular Mark Twain,* at 512–13.

BIBLIOGRAPHY

Adams, Susan. *The New Rules of Success for Women.* New York, Celebrity Press, 2000.

American Association of University Women. *Tech Savvy: Educating Girls in the Information Age.* Washington, D.C., AAUP, 2003.

Barnard, Jayne W. "At the Top of the Pyramid: Lessons from the Alpha Woman and the Elite Eight." 65 *Md. L. Rev.* 315 (2006).

Beauvoir, Simone de. *The Second Sex.* New York, Vintage, 1947.

Beyer, Kurt W. *Grace Hopper and the Invention of the Information Age.* Cambridge, MIT Press, 2009.

Black, Barbara. "Stalled: Gender Diversity on Corporate Boards." 37 *University of Dayton L. Rev.* 7 (2011).

Black, Jeremy. *The Power of Knowledge: How Information and Technology Made the Modern World.* New Haven, Yale University Press, 2014.

Book, Esther Wachs. *Why the Best Man for the Job Is a Woman.* New York, Harper Business, 2000.

Bosch, Harry. "The Changing Face of Corporate Governance." 25 *University of New South Wales Law Rev.* 270 (2002).

Branson, Douglas M. *Corporate Governance.* Charlottesville, VA, Michie, 1993 (with annual supplements).

———. *Greatness in the Shadows: Larry Doby and the Integration of the American League.* Lincoln, University of Nebraska Press, 2016.

———. *The Last Male Bastion: Gender and the CEO Suite in America's Public Companies.* New York, Routledge, 2010.

———. *No Seat at the Table: How Governance and Law Keep Women Out of the Boardroom.* New York, New York University Press, 2007.

———. *Problems in Corporate Governance.* Pittsburgh, Cathedral Press, 1997.

———. "Some Suggestions from a Comparison of British and American Tender Offer Regulation." 56 *Cornell L. Rev.* 685 (1971).

Branson, Douglas M., Joan Heminway, et al. *Business Enterprises: Structure, Governance and Policy.* 3rd ed. Durham, NC, Carolina Academic Press, 2016.

Brooks, Donna, & Lynn Brooks. *Seven Secrets of Successful Women: Success Strategies of the Women Who Have Made It—And How You Can Follow Their Lead.* New York, McGraw-Hill, 1999.

Cadbury, Adrian. *Corporate Governance and Leadership: A Personal View.* London, Oxford University Press, 2002.

Cappelli, Peter. *Will College Pay Off? A Guide to the Most Important Financial Decision You'll Ever Make*. New York, Public Affairs, 2015.

Catalyst. *Advancing Women in Business: Best Practices from Corporate Leaders*. San Francisco, Jossey-Bass, 1998.

Clarke, Thomas, & Douglas M. Branson, eds. *The Sage Handbook of Corporate Governance*. New York, Sage, 2014.

Cockburn, Cynthia. *Male Dominance and Technological Change*. London, Pluto Press, 1983.

Cohoon, J. McGrath, & William Aspray, eds. *Women and Information Technology: Research on Underrepresentation*. Cambridge, MIT Press, 2008.

Collins, Gail. *When Everything Changed: The Amazing Journey of American Women from 1960 to the Present*. Cambridge, MIT Press, 2008; reprint ed., Boston, Back Bay Books, 2010.

Collins, Jim, & Jerry I. Porras. *Built to Last: Successful Habits of Visionary Companies*. New York, Harper Business, 1994.

Crittenden, Ann. *The Price of Motherhood: Why the Most Important Job in the World Is Still the Least Valued*. New York, Metropolitan Books, 2010.

Dhir, Aaron. *Challenging Boardroom Homogeneity: Corporate Law, Governance, and Diversity*. New York, Cambridge University Press, 2015.

DiSesa, Nina. *Seducing the Boys' Club: Uncensored Tactics from a Woman at the Top*. New York, Ballantine, 2008.

Drew, David. *STEM the Tide: Reforming Science, Technology, Engineering, and Math Education in America*. Baltimore, Johns Hopkins University Press, 2011.

Drucker, Peter F. *The Ecological Vision*. Piscataway, NJ, Transaction, 1993.

———. *The Last of All Possible Worlds and the Temptation to Do Good*. Philadelphia, Paul Dry Books, 2016.

———. *Managing for Results*. New York, Harper & Row, 1964.

———. *The Practice of Management*. New York, Harper, 1954.

Easlea, Brian. *Fathering Masculinity*. London, Pluto Press, 1983.

Eaton, Jeanette, & Bertha M. Stevens. *Commercial Work and Training for Girls*. New York, Macmillan, 1915.

Eisenberg, Melvin A. *The Structure of the Corporation*. New York, Aspen Business, 1976.

Evans, Gail. *Play Like a Man, Win Like a Woman*. New York, Broadway, 2000.

Fairfax, Lisa. "The Bottom Line on Boards: A Cost-Benefit Analysis of Rationale for Diversity on Corporate Boards." 2005 *Wisconsin L. Rev.* 795.

Fiorina, Carly. *Tough Choices: A Memoir*. New York, Penguin, 2007.

Foster, Diana, with Sylvia Ann Hewlett. *Off-Ramps and On-Ramps Revisited*. Seattle, WA, Rare Bird Books, 2013.

Fox, Mary Frank, Deborah G. Johnson, & Sue V. Rosser. *Women, Gender and Technology*. Champaign-Urbana, University of Illinois Press, 2006.

Friedan, Betty. *The Feminine Mystique*. New York, Norton, 1970.

Fuentes, Annette, & Barbara Ehrenreich. *Women in the Global Factory*. Boston, South End, 1983.

Gallagher, Carol. *Going to the Top: A Road Map for Success from America's Leading Women Executives*. New York, Penguin, 2000.

Gerstner, Louis V., Jr. *Who Says Elephants Can't Dance? Leading a Great Enterprise through Dramatic Change*. New York, Harper Business, 2003.

Gilberd, Pamela. *The Eleven Commandments of Wildly Successful Women*. New York, MacMillan Spectrum, 1996.

Goldin, Claudia, & Lawrence F. Katz. *The Race between Education and Technology*. Cambridge, Harvard University Press, 2008.

Greer, Germaine. *The Female Eunuch*. London, Paladin Press, 1970.

Griffin, Jill. *Earn Your Seat on a Corporate Board*. Austin, TX, Jill Griffin Books, 2016.

Hamilton, Robert. *Corporations in a Nutshell*. St. Paul, MN, West, 1997.

———. "Some Reflections on Cash Tender Offer Legislation." 15 *N.Y.L.F.* 269 (1969).

Harding, Sandra. *Is Science Multicultural? Postcolonialisms, Feminisms, and Epistemologies*. Bloomington, University of Indiana Press, 1998.

Harvard University. *Reach for the Top*. Cambridge, Harvard Business Review Books, 1994.

Haslam, Alexander, & Michelle K. Ryan. "The Glass Cliff: Evidence That Women Are Over-Represented in Precarious Leadership Positions." 16 *British J. of Management* 81 (2005).

Hawthorne, Susan, & Renate Klein, eds. *Cyberfeminism: Connectivity, Critique and Creativity*. Melbourne, Australia, Spinifex, 1999.

Heim, Pat, & Susan Golant. *Hardball for Women*. Rev. ed. New York, Plume, 2005.

———. *Smashing the Glass Ceiling*. New York, Simon & Schuster, 1995.

Heminway, Joan MacLeod. "The Last Male Bastion: In Search of a Trojan Horse." 37 *University of Dayton L. Rev.* 77 (2011).

Hewlett, Sylvia Ann. *Forget a Mentor, Find a Sponsor: The New Way to Fast-Track Your Career*. Cambridge, Harvard Business Review Press, 2013.

———. *Off-Ramps and On-Ramps: Keeping Talented Women on the Road to Success*. Cambridge, Harvard Business Review Press, 2007.

Hirshman, Linda. *Get to Work: A Manifesto for Women of the World*. New York, Penguin, 2006.

———. *Sisters in Law: How Sandra Day O'Connor and Ruth Bader Ginsburg Went to the Supreme Court and Changed the World*. New York, HarperCollins, 2015.

Hollands, Jean. *Same Game, Different Rules: How to Get Ahead without Being a Bully Broad, Ice Queen, or "Ms. Understood."* New York, McGraw-Hill, 2000.

Johnson, Kelly L. *Skirt! Rules for the Workplace*. Guildford, CT, Skirt Publishers, 2008.

Kanter, Rosabeth Moss. *Men and Women of the Corporation*. Rev. ed. New York, Basic Books, 1993. Originally published 1977.

Kaplan, Fred. *The Singular Mark Twain*. New York, Anchor, 2005.

Khurana, Rakesh. *Searching for the Corporate Savior: The Irrational Quest for Corporate CEOs*. Princeton, Princeton University Press, 2002.

Kiesler, Sara B., & Lee S. Sproull, eds. *Computing and Change on Campus*. New York, Cambridge University Press, 1987.

King, Richard. *Redskins: Insult and the Brand*. Lincoln, University of Nebraska Press, 2016.

Kristof, Nicholas D., & Sheryl WuDunn. *Half the Sky: Turning Oppression into Opportunity for Women Worldwide*. New York, Vintage, 2009.

Lewis, Michael. *The Flash Boys: A Wall Street Revolt*. New York, Norton, 2015.

Lin, Marcia, & Sherry Hiss. *Teachers and Peers: Computer Science Learning Partners*. New Brunswick, NJ, Erlbaum, 2000.

Lindsay, Nicole. *The MBA Slingshot for Women: Using Business School to Catapult Your Career*. Boston, Praeger, 2014.

Losse, Katherine. *The Boy Kings: A Journey into the Heart of the Social Network*. New York, Free Press, 2012.

Lublin, Joann. *Earning It: Hard-Won Lessons from Trailblazing Women at the Top of the Business World*. New York, Harper Business, 2016.

MacKinnon, Catharine A. *Feminism Unmodified: Discourses on Life and Law*. Cambridge, Harvard University Press, 1987.

Margolis, Jane, & Allan Fisher. *Unlocking the Clubhouse: Women in Computing*. Cambridge, MIT Press, 2003.

Marx, Christy. *Grace Hopper: The First Woman to Program the First Computer in the United States*. New York, Rosen, 2003.

McLaughlin, Debora J. *Running in High Heels: How to Lead with Influence, Impact and Ingenuity*. Carlsbad, CA, Balboa, 2014.

Merchant, Carolyn. *The Death of Nature*. New York, Harper & Row, 1979.

Millar, Melanie S. *Cracking the Computer Code: Who Rules the Wired World?* Toronto, Second Story Press, 1998.

Misa, Thomas, ed. *Gender Codes: Why Women Are Leaving Computing*. New York, Wiley, 2010.

Mitter, Swasti. *Common Fate, Common Bond: Women in the Global Economy*. London, Pluto Press, 1986.

O'Brien, Justin, ed. *Albert Camus: The Myth of Sisyphus and Other Essays*. New York, Vintage, 1991.

O'Connor, Marleen. "The Enron Board: The Perils of Groupthink." 71 *U. Cincinnati L. Rev.* 1323 (2003).

Packard, David. *The HP Way: How Bill Hewlett and I Built Our Company*. New York, Harper Business, 1996.

Pareto, Vilfredo. "On the Equilibrium of Social Systems." In *Theories of Society: Foundations of Modern Sociological Thought*, edited by Talcott Parsons. Vol. 2. Scotland, Free Press of Glencoe, 1961.

Pinto, Arthur, & Douglas M. Branson. *Understanding Corporate Law*. 4th ed. New York, LexisNexis, 2013.

Plant, Judith, & Petra Kelly. *Healing the Wounds: The Promise of Eco-Feminism*. Philadelphia, New Society Press, 1989.

Rawls, John. *Justice as Fairness*. Rev. ed. Cambridge, MA, Belknap, 2001.

———. *A Theory of Justice*. Cambridge, MA, Belknap, 1971.

Rhode, Deborah, ed. *The Differences "Difference" Makes*. Palo Alto, CA, Stanford University Law & Politics, 2003.

———. *What Women Want: An Agenda for the Women's Movement*. New York, Oxford University Press, 2014.

———. *Women and Leadership*. New York, Oxford University Press, 2016.

Rhode, Deborah, & Barbara Kellerman. *Women and Leadership: The State of Play and Strategies for Leadership*. San Francisco, Jossey-Bass, 2007.

Rhode, Deborah, & Amanda Packel. "Diversity on Corporate Boards: How Much Difference Does a 'Difference' Make." 39 *Del. J. Corp. L.* 377 (2014).

Rivers, Caryl, & Rosalind Barnett. *The New Soft War on Women: How the Myth of Female Ascendance Is Hurting Women, Men—and Our Economy*. New York, TarcherPerigee, 2015.

Rosenblum, Daren. "Feminizing Capital: A Corporate Imperative." 6 *Berkeley Business L. Rev.* 55 (2009).

Salmansohn, Karen. *How to Succeed in Business without a Penis: Secrets and Strategies for the Working Woman*. New York, Three Rivers, 1996.

Sandberg, Sheryl. *Lean In: Women, Work and the Will to Lead*. New York, Knopf, 2013.

Sandberg, Sheryl, with Adam Grant. *Option B: Facing Adversity, Building Resilience, and Finding Joy*. New York, Knopf, 2017.

Sargent, Lydia, ed. *Women and Revolution*. Boston, South End, 1981.

Schmidt, Eric, & Jonathan Rosenberg. *How Google Works*. New York, Grand Central, 2014.

Seymour, Elaine, & Nancy M. Hewitt. *Talking about Leaving: Why Undergraduates Leave the Sciences*. Boulder, Westview, 1997.

Shipman, Claire, & Katty Kay. *Womenomics: Work Less, Achieve More, and Live Better*. New York: Harper Business, 2010.

Skeel, David A., Jr. "Shaming in Corporate Law." 149 *U. Pa. L. Rev.* 1181 (2001). www. scholarship.law.upenn.edu. Visited April 30, 2016.

Slaughter, Anne-Marie. *Unfinished Business: Women, Men, Work, Family*. New York, Random House, 2015.

Solomon, Barbara. *In the Company of Educated Women: A History of Women and Higher Education in America*. New Haven, Yale University Press, 1982.

Stith, Anthony. *Breaking the Glass Ceiling: Sexism and Racism in Corporate America; The Myths, The Realities and the Solutions*. St. Charles, IL, Warwick, 1998.

Strom, Sharon Hartman. *Beyond the Typewriter: Gender, Class and the Origins of Modern Office Work*. Champaign-Urbana, University of Illinois Press, 1992.

Stross, Randall E. *eBoys: The First Inside Account of Venture Capitalists at Work*. New York, Crown Business, 2001.

Taylor, Frederick Winslow. *The Principles of Modern Scientific Management*. 1911. Rev. ed. New York, Norton, 1967.

Teitelbaum, Michael S. *Falling Behind? Boom, Bust, and the Global Race for Scientific Talent*. Princeton, Princeton University Press, 2015.

Tong, Rosemarie. *Feminist Thought: A Comprehensive Introduction.* Boulder, Westview, 1989.

Vance, Ashlee. *Elon Musk: Tesla, SpaceX, and the Quest for a Fantastic Future.* New York, Harper Business, 2015.

Watson, Thomas J., Jr., and Peter Petre. *Father, Son & Co.: My Life at IBM and Beyond.* New York, Bantam, 1990.

Wellington, Sheila. *Be Your Own Mentor.* New York, Random House, 2001.

Wester, Juliet. *Sharing Women's Work: Gender, Employment and Information Technology.* New York, Longman, 1995.

Whitman, Christy, & Rebecca Grado. *Taming Your Alpha Bitch: How to Be Fierce and Feminine (and Get Everything You Want).* Dallas, BenBella Books, 2012.

Williams, Joan C. *Reshaping the Work-Family Debate: Why Men and Class Matter.* Cambridge, Harvard University Press, 2012.

———. *Unbending Gender: Why Family and Work Conflict and What to Do about It.* New York, Oxford University Press, 1999.

Williams, Joan C., & Rachel Dempsey. *What Works for Women at Work: Four Patterns Working Women Need to Know.* New York, New York University Press, 2014.

Williams, Kathleen Broome. *Grace Hopper: Admiral of the Cyber Sea.* Annapolis, MD, Naval Institute, 2004.

Williams, Patrick, & Laura Chrisman. *Colonial Discourse and Post-Colonial Theory.* New York, Columbia University Press, 2007.

Winner, Langdon. *The Whale and the Reactor.* Chicago, University of Chicago Press, 1996.

INDEX

ACA. *See* Affordable Care Act

ACLU. *See* American Civil Liberties Union

admission policies, 61

"adult in the room" scenario, 20; Schmidt and, 21

advocacy, 93; critical mass, 176; pledge programs and, 105; pool problem and, 174; quota laws and, 101, 104; for scientific management, 69. *See also* Catalyst

Affordable Care Act (ACA), 98

AICD. *See* Australian Institute of Company Directors

airline industry, 5

Albright, Madeleine, 14

Alcatel. *See* Lucent

Alibaba, 24, 34

Allen, Paul, 147, 148

AltSchool, 74

alumni programs, as on-ramp initiative, 187

American Association of University Women, 57

American Bar Association, 128–29

American Civil Liberties Union (ACLU), 12

American Woman's Society of Certified Public Accountants (AWSCPA), 193–94

Angry Birds, 219, 220

Apotheker, Leo, 26–27

Ash, Carter, 199

Aspray, William, 60

ASX. *See* Australian Stock Exchange

Atkinson, Robert, 156

Australia: ASX and, 117–19, 126–27; boards in, 127, 197; comply or explain regime in, 114, 117–19; pledge program and, 111

Australian Institute of Company Directors (AICD), 119, 127, 129–30; results of, 126; sponsorship and, 126, 257n17

Australian Stock Exchange (ASX): KPMG testing compliance for, 117–19; mentorship and, 126–27

Autodesk: Bartz at, 28–29

Avon Products: Jung at, 49; McCoy and, 22; trickle-down effect at, 15, 49

AWSCPA. *See* American Woman's Society of Certified Public Accountants

Barad, Jill, 257n15

Barnes, Brenda, 21–22

Barra, Mary, 22–23

Bartol, Kathryn, 60

Bartz, Carol, 20, 165; at Autodesk, 28–29; on diversity, 29; on Facebook, 37; glass cliff theory for, 28–29, 249n30; poor performance of, 36–37; STEM and, 36–37

Belkin, Lisa, 228–29

Belser, Ann, 81

Be Your Own Mentor (Wellington), 84

Bill and Melinda Gates Foundation, 75

biological determinism, 208

blue software, 58

board chair: CEO in U.S. and, 108–9, 177, 197; management and measurements and, 196–97; United Kingdom and, 108–9, 196–97; U.S. mentorship and, 129–30

ABOUT THE AUTHOR

Douglas M. Branson is the W. Edward Sell Chair at the University of Pittsburgh. He has been a visiting professor at Cornell University, the Universities of Washington and Hong Kong, and Melbourne University, among others. He has been a State Department–sponsored corporate governance consultant to New Zealand, Indonesia, Ukraine, Slovakia, Serbia, and Bulgaria. He is the author of twenty-three books, including several on diversity in corporate settings.